EVERY SHITTY THING

One woman's journey through brothers, betrayals, and botox

Marcia Abboud

What Others Are Saying

Sometimes the biggest mistakes of our lives turn out to be the greatest miracles.

Marcia pulled herself from the brink of self-extinction for one good reason – she had a daughter. Funny thing is, she had never wanted to be a mother.

From the youngest age, she had borne the brunt of male brutality. Yet she survived her childhood and teenage years only to encounter further betrayals and losses. And just when she thought she couldn't go on, she did – with wicked humour and a will to outsurvive every shitty thing that had ever happened to her.

This is a tough and tender ode to a heart and spirit that refused to shatter. A gift of hope to anyone who has ever wanted to give up and then tries again.

~ JOANNE FEDLER
Internationally bestselling author

Many come to me to discuss writing a book and my response to each is typically glib. Imagining writing a book is easy, I tell them. But actually writing a book, taking that seemingly endless and often painful journey from first word to last, is far more difficult than you could ever imagine, I say. Then finding an agent, an editor, a publisher etc who will treat your work with respect… well, that's an entirely new mountain to climb. Only the very toughest make it. That's what I told Marcy.

Of course, at the time I didn't know her full story. Now I do. And now I understand how she developed the mental toughness to put together this hard-hitting, autobiographical masterpiece. This is hip-hop's literary equivalent, a stark, no-holds-barred story of courage, perseverance, tenacity and desperation that is as real as it gets. Of course she finished it. Nothing stops Marcy, as you'll discover amongst these pages.

Don't expect teddy bears or ponies, princesses or ballerinas. *Every Shitty Thing* is one woman's story of survival in what often amounts to suburban hell. It is a story to which we can all, in one way or another, relate. It is deeply and intensely personal and real, and contains lessons for every reader. Don't miss out.

~ CHRIS SHEEDY
Director, The Hard Word

I couldn't put it down. I read *Every Shitty Thing* in one sitting. I felt like I inhaled and didn't exhale until I'd consumed all of it. An engrossing and agonising read… just when I thought nothing worse could happen… it did… but at the same time the story is engaging, witty and warm. This is a book about courage and resilience, and what it means to keep showing up even when the odds are stacked against you. Marcia writes bravely and fearlessly. Thank you for sharing your story. Especially the difficult parts.

~ Kate Shand
Author

Every Shitty Thing is a heart-wrenching tale that peels back the cover of childhood trauma and its long-lasting effects. But it is so much more than that. It is a tale of family, of betrayal, of the things we do for love and what is done to us in love's name. Marcia's armour is dented in places, shattered in others, but with hope as her weapon, she fights for the life and love she deserves. Told with honesty and humour, this is a book I couldn't put down.

~ Amanda J Spedding
Two-time Australian Shadows Award winner

You would assume that being a part of someone's life for many years you would get to know them really well – what they stand for, how they plug into society, who they are and what makes them tick. But we hide in closets, behind our alter egos or simply wear a mask. *Every Shitty Thing* is a testament that until you know yourself, no one will ever get to know you. Our memories make us who we are today. It takes courage to relive those moments. A beautiful and thought-provoking journey where I, too, learnt many lessons. An inspiring read and one I am grateful Marcia chose to share.

~ Sean Ashby
aussieBum

Everyone has a story. These stories, positive or negative, affect the way we think, feel and act. Our stories mould us and make us who we are. Marcia's story is painful, raw and, in a strange way, beautiful for she writes in the light of truth. I was captured from the first word to the last, drawn in by the bravery and courage of her truth. Although it sounds like a cliché, this memoir is definitely a 'must read'!

~ John Scott
Founder & CEO, Platform Me

It's Marcia's ability to tell her truth and find the light in darkest of moments that makes her story so engaging. It's her strength, resilience and open heart that makes her story relatable to many women. It's her willingness to talk about the somewhat unspeakable and heartbreaking moments that so often as a society we shy away from that give others the opportunity to not feel alone. As a writer myself, I know it takes a lot to look within and deal with those hard emotions or experiences that have happened to us. And, to then tell the truth about these — it's a courageous act of itself. If you know heartbreak, if you know pain, if you feel alone in the challenges life has presented you, this book may just be the catalyst to helping you heal. It may just remind you that you are human and we each have a story and no matter what it looks like, you can learn, grow and live the life you want, despite what has happened to you along the way. You just have to listen to your heart and realise, you always have a choice.

~ MONICA KADE
Writer & Podcast Host

Marcia Abboud openly comes to terms with the betrayals, shame and self-loathing which took her to the edge of the darkest abyss. This compelling memoir is about family violence, addiction, sexual abuse, suicide, motherhood, secrets, loss, sorrow, resilience, honesty — and is written with the authentic voice and wry humour which only insight and hindsight can bring – a rare achievement.

~ CAROLYN LEIGH
Author and curator

Here is a ripping yarn. Marcia knows how to tell a good story and will have you living her world within the first few pages.

~ MONIQUE HOHNBERG
Founder of the worldwide phenomenon #RiseRegardless

Published in Australia by
Jubel Publishing
Postal: PO Box 23405, Docklands VIC 8012
Email: media@jubelpublishing.com
Web: www.marciaaboud.com

First published in Australia 2018
Copyright © Marcia Abboud 2018

All rights reserved. No part of this publication may be reproduced, stored in a retrieval system, or transmitted, in any form or by any means, electronic, mechanical, photocopying, recording or otherwise, without the prior written permission of the publisher, nor be otherwise circulated in any form of binding or cover other than that in which it is published and without a similar condition being imposed on the subsequent purchaser.

 A catalogue record for this book is available from the National Library of Australia

Creator:	Abboud, Marcia, author
Title:	EVERY SHITTY THING: One woman's journey through brothers, betrayals, and botox
ISBN:	978-0-6483058-0-4 (paperback)
	978-0-6483058-1-1 (ebook)

Cover design by Dimitar Stanchev
Typeset by Toni-Tomislav Dalmatin
Back Cover photography by Simon Taylor
Styling by Marina Saker Jewellery
Printed by IngramSpark

Disclaimer
The author has made every effort to ensure the accuracy of the information herein, including recollections of events and conversations to the best of the author's knowledge.

While the author and publisher have made every effort to ensure the accuracy of information in this book, the author and publisher take no responsibility for, and hereby disclaim, any and all liability to any party for any loss or damage caused, or alleged to be caused, by a party's misinterpretation of work, and no guarantee is expressed or implied and neither the author nor the publisher accept liability for any loss or damage that may arise from any errors or omissions.

I am a woman in process.
I'm just trying like everybody else.
I try to take every conflict, every experience, and learn from it.
Life is never dull.

Oprah Winfrey

This book is dedicated to every shitty experience I've ever had. Without them I'd have no material and this book wouldn't exist.

And for Tony... Thanks for giving me the blue pen and the thumbs up. You'll be famous yet, my brother.

For Mum... I still smell you when you're near...

For Dad... I'm so glad you won't read this book. Let's hope there's no Amazon on the other side of the pearly gates.

Contents

Preface ... 1

CHAPTER 1
Into the Abyss ... 5

CHAPTER 2
Not Like in the Movies ... 13

CHAPTER 3
In the Spotlight ... 19

CHAPTER 4
The Wedding Part 1 – She's Thinking of the Bad Times ... 27

CHAPTER 5
The Wedding Part 2 – Chim Chiminey ... 37

CHAPTER 6
The Trouble with Brothers ... 43

CHAPTER 7
Cruel, Cruel World ... 49

CHAPTER 8
A Gypsy Life ... 59

CHAPTER 9
A Lot Can Happen in a Minute ... 69

CHAPTER 10
A World Gone Mad ... 79

CHAPTER 11
Dogsville ... 89

CHAPTER 12
Three's a Crowd ... 99

CHAPTER 13
Signs and Bad Decisions ... 107

CHAPTER 14
Miracles in Disguise 119

CHAPTER 15
The Ring 149

CHAPTER 16
Flipping Out 157

CHAPTER 17
Once an Addict 167

CHAPTER 18
Back to the Future 179

CHAPTER 19
Twenty Days to Freedom 193

CHAPTER 20
Fix You 207

CHAPTER 21
It's About the Rent… 217

CHAPTER 22
Into the Abyss – Part 2 227

CHAPTER 23
Take Me Away 235

CHAPTER 24
In the Aftermath 241

CHAPTER 25
The End of Wars 249

CHAPTER 26
50 Shades 257

CHAPTER 27
Sundays 265

CHAPTER 28
Second Chance 273

Epilogue 277
Acknowledgements 283
About the author 285

Preface

Shitty things happen. It's a given in everyone's life. I'm sure most people could write a long list of all the challenges they've faced. But challenges are met differently by each one of us. Some of us are smashed, while others simply get on with it. Take fat days for example: a Victoria's Secret model having a fat day is a catastrophe. For the rest of us it's an irritation, and nothing a baggy t-shirt won't fix.

I had a lot of shitty days growing up, and I was jolted into my teens. I imagined things would improve, but they didn't. Shit kept coming – hard, fast, and intense. I'd experienced enough dysfunction and trauma to last me three lifetimes by the time I was 15. I often wondered if someone upstairs had made a huge mistake and was convinced I had been born into the wrong body. This wasn't supposed to be my life. My mind would run rampant at the 'what ifs' and the 'why mes'. I would try and rationalise – I must have been a real arsehole in a previous life, and this life was my punishment. Maybe I'd brought it all on myself, caused all the shit. For most girls – especially if you were a fat kid too – you'll understand the self-blame game we play, the self-loathing we instil in our psyches. At times I wasn't sure I could bear another moment. I would fantasise about all the ways I could kill myself. I would wish myself away. I just wanted the shit to stop.

If you know the darkness I speak of, then like me you know not to judge those who take their own life. It's no surprise that over 65,000 people attempt suicide each year, and that's just in Australia. Imagine all the others who turn to chemicals and alcohol instead, living in loneliness, often in isolation, depressed and feeling they've been marked or cursed.

I wrote this book to make sense of the events in my life. More often than not they have played out like a B-grade movie or bad soap opera. As I wrote, I revisited all the betrayals and heartaches of my past and I began to feel differently about them. I began to own my story, even though I have been the helpless victim for most of it. I have relived the pain as I returned to the scene of the crimes against my body and spirit, but somehow, by some miracle I have been able to meet my abusers with compassion, and – dare I say – even forgiveness.

Idealising suffering is not my intention. I hope when you read my story it will help in some way – small or profound – as you reflect on your own lives and look back at your own pain and trauma, and hopefully see, and know in your heart of hearts that your shit doesn't define you. Perhaps by reading my book you will also come to a place of forgiveness, for your abusers and for yourself, for the doubting beliefs you've carried through the chapters of your life. You may even be able to laugh at some of it. Trust me, you can only do that in hindsight.

I started writing my book long before the #metoo stories came to the surface. I, for one, am in awe of the courageous women who have raised their voices, stood tall and brave to tell their own stories of abuse and violence. Many of these women with so much to lose publicly, their reputations on the line, are fighting to dispel the attitudes and shame surrounding these issues. I hope the time is ripe for a massive social shift, that one day these stories will be a tragic time in our history and not an ongoing reality.

The trouble with writing a memoir is that it involves other people. Not just any people, your closest family and friends. And what happens if they are responsible for some of the shitty things that happened to you? All I wanted in writing this book was to tell the truth, but we all know that telling the truth is not a simple act. People can deny your truth and say you're lying, exaggerating the events. I struggled with the decision to change names and details to protect those who will recognise themselves in these pages and probably have a coronary at my raised voice. But I'm standing tall. I've survived, and I will be a warrior in the fight to protect myself as I tell my truth.

To this end, I haven't changed names or details in my story, and I've told the truth to the best of my knowledge and recollection. The beauty of a memoir is that it's an author's truthful perspective of events – as well as her memory serves her. And considering my fog brain – menopause is the root of all evil, just so you know – I'm astounded at the detail I do remember. And some I wish I didn't.

Every Shitty Thing is a journey through the dark (and light) places in my life. It's my celebration (not my wake) at overcoming all the shit I've endured. It's taken me decades to understand that everything I've been through was necessary to get me to where I needed to be. Like I said, you only figure it out looking back.

Many years ago a friend gave me the book *The Life You Were Born to Live* by Dan Millman. Using birth numbers, it sets out the path of our lives and describes our mindset in a nutshell. Under my number was this quote by Mahatma Gandhi 'My life is my teaching'. When I first read that I thought: Well I'm screwed! Now I get it.

If you, too, have stood at the edge of the abyss, turned to addictions or done things you're not proud of in the name of self-loathing and blame, if you've wished your life away, prayed for the end or simply hit the snooze button so you wouldn't have to face another day, I hope my story will be a beacon of light in your life, a reminder that your spirit is stronger than every shitty thing that could ever happen to you. And if I survived, so can you.

MARCIA ABBOUD

CHAPTER ONE

Into the Abyss

The car seat cradles me like a newborn baby strapped in a capsule, the safety of its birthplace gone in the wake of hospital doors closing, out in the big wide world for the first time with all its promises and dangers not yet understood. I wish I were a baby. I wish I were in my mother's arms listening to her heartbeat, the rhythmic melody of her voice, inhaling her smell, which I instinctively understood meant 'I am safe'. A clean slate, to start again from the very beginning, a second chance at life, to be someone else, someone better… Yes, that's what I want.

The darkness outside the car envelopes me, seals me in. I grip the steering wheel as if I'm still in control of the moving beast. I'm parked now, but I can't let go. I'm unsure how I got here, subliminally, intuitively, on autopilot – I don't know. I feel the sticky fake leather beneath my palms and it occurs to me it's been ages since I sanitised it. A million microscopic germs may be dancing on me right now, and suddenly I don't care. Let them dance. Let them penetrate my skin, swim in my bloodstream, find their way to my heart and make it stop. Like a horror movie, an alien invasion. If only it were possible.

My sobbing is the only audible sound, haunting, hollow, constant. That sound has become a part of me. For months it has taken hold, like a new behavioural pattern, an unwelcome habit that I can't control. I don't want to. I feel the heaving, the ebb and flow, the release, the unstoppable physical expression of everything that is broken inside me. I need to hear it. It validates my pain. I need to put sound to the shattered pieces that used to be whole. The things other people can't see. I look solid from the outside, but there is nothing solid about me. My psyche knows the truth, has always known deep down. On borrowed time as they say – at least that's how I see it in this madness. The sound of heartbreak can't be silenced.

I notice a single, red flashing light on the dashboard, a fake alarm to warn thieves 'don't even think about it, shithead'. I'd never seen it flash before. But then again, I've never sat in my car in the darkness in a moment so absolute, so present, to notice the warning beacon right there in front of me. What if my car thief works sensible hours? 9 to 5, daylight hours, then what? Come nightfall he'll know the owner of his new car was faking it, pretending to be something she's not. Just like my second-hand Nissan X-Trail SUV.

I remember the day we bought it, six months ago, November 2006. George, my husband, insisted it be in my name. We'd always done everything jointly – for 22 years since we met. I thought it was strange. The shock of it sucked me from my boredom. I would rather dust all day than visit car dealerships.

"No. It'll be in my wife's name only. Please print the paperwork accordingly."

CHAPTER ONE | INTO THE ABYSS

George rarely requested anything, let alone something so big. A brave first move in front of a salesman. He hadn't discussed it with me beforehand. Instead of being annoyed, I felt an overwhelming sense of pride. My husband was stepping up, finally taking the initiative after all these years. Maybe there was hope. Maybe boys do grow up. And maybe men can change. Looking back, I realise it was all premeditated. And I thought I was the fake. His love had never been in question before. His devotion was clear from the start. I was his Queen and he my loyal disciple, and everyone who knew us knew that.

As I signed my name on the papers – two solemn words, how foreign they looked without his name beside them – a rogue tear did its best to escape from the corner of my eye. I stopped it. As if I'd allow that in public. Never. Silly me, I assumed the emotional outburst waiting on the fringes of my being was more than just the effects of my husband's surprising gesture. A small gesture to some, but powerful to me. A car in my name, an asset that was mine alone, might be his way of giving back, paying forward, making up for past mistakes. Maybe, he may have thought, a car would be compensation for my long-lost independence, my free spirit that never quite got the chance to be free, cut short by our paths crossing. A car, the material symbol of freedom; perhaps my husband wanted me to feel free once more. Did he really think a car could do all that? His love had never managed it, try and try as he might. Still, I was sure – then – it was nonetheless a gesture made from love.

No. The fringes of my outburst weren't merely that my husband wanted to spoil me, to make me feel special with more than words, more than post-it love notes all over the house, more than cards filled with the most beautiful collection of verses threaded like magic on the page as if they were written especially for me, his words. He should've been a poet. Those cards could break the toughest heart, but the car was action, real action, spoken louder than any words. But most of all, my husband knew how sad I was at losing Mum three weeks earlier. Mum, my best friend, my first soulmate, my safe haven, gone from this earth without me. Her loss was great, greater than all the losses before. That's why he bought me the car. What a lovely, considerate kind thing to do.

What a fucking liar.

It doesn't matter now. Grief has won. Rage didn't stand a chance. Rage is superficial, fleeting, temporary, thinking it's strong, but side by side with grief it is nothing but a speck of dirt in the dense jungle of sorrow. Not sorrow for losing my mother; this anguish, this despair, this pit of darkness is the blackest I've ever seen, and God knows I've seen the blackest of black. But here, now, as I grip the steering wheel cocooned in my metal beast, I know I'll never see another sunrise. I have lost everything.

There is split second in your mind when this thought becomes real, whole, final, inevitable. The materialisation of an idea – it's floated there before, like a dream, like a wish, like an unanswered mathematical equation, a solution unthought-of until now. In that nanosecond it's like lightning, spark plugs igniting, an electric shock, a defibrillator probing some uncharted part of your brain – and something that was dormant comes to life. That split second is scary as hell, scarier than any hell you've already lived.

It was at this moment that I heard his voice, clear as if he were sitting next to me. I let out a gasp as I looked at the rear-view mirror, imagining I'd see him there. My head snapped around to double-check. Empty. My heart pounded, the thumping reached my ears, drowning out all external noise. It stopped. I held my breath expecting to hear more, to hear it again. Nothing. Is this how the end begins, I wondered?

I exhaled and slumped back into the seat. My hands finally dropped to my lap with a thud. A rush of blood reached my tingling fingertips. They relaxed, soaking up their precious food source that had been depleted: relief. I closed my eyes and let my chin fall towards my chest. In seconds she filled my mind: Morgan, my 16-year-old daughter. I imagined her at her sleepover, gossiping about boys maybe, anything to take her mind off her own dismal state of being. Getting up to mischief no doubt while

CHAPTER ONE | INTO THE ABYSS

Mum is none the wiser, she thinks. Sad, boring Mum, crying herself to sleep again, home in bed, the usual – where else would I be in her mind?

Memories exploded behind the windows of my closed eyelids. I saw it all, like a movie trailer. Her first heartfelt giggle at three months old, the moment I fell deeply in love with her. We called her Flip-top after that. George and I agreed she looked like a cartoon character on the toothpaste ad on TV. Unable to brush his back teeth properly, he flips open his head to reach every nook and cranny. It was a funny ad after that. Morgan's smile, her giggle, could light up a room, melt hearts, and it did.

She was 10 years old when we took her to a cocktail party. Our parents were away, and we had no babysitter. It was a party not to be missed. Our host said, "absolutely you can bring Morgan, that girl is the life of any party", and she was – she would be again, eventually. Ten going on twenty, mature beyond her years, a social butterfly – she loved the limelight almost as much as her mother back then.

"Mum, I'll just be over there mingling, those people look interesting," she said within minutes of entering the room.

Seriously, what child speaks like that? What child has that much confidence? She didn't inherit it from me. I was a different child. My daughter was special, an old soul, intuitive, clever. She was born for great things. Unlike her mother. I knew it the minute she became Flip-top all those years ago.

A thousand other memories welled up in me and burst into silent tears flowing down my cheeks. They fell when my eyes were closed, as I'd discovered when the world had turned black months before, and when I was asleep, too. Where all that water came from, I couldn't fathom.

More memories rushed at me as if they were in the past not the future. Memories not yet made, but I saw them anyway: her wedding day, the birth of her children, and all the milestones I would miss if I opened my car door right now. I thought about Mum then, actual memories made. Trying to imagine them without her made no sense, and yet there I was about to leave my daughter behind. How would that make sense to her or anyone? I remembered her face that day, that night, when George told her the truth. It changed in an instant. Gone her happy-go-lucky smile, the beauty and warmth sucked from her like a splash of acid. Scarred for life. How could a father do that to a daughter? Our beautiful, carefree, exceptional daughter who didn't deserve any of it – not like her mother. I would take her pain tenfold, twentyfold, to save her from the torture of life if only I could. I didn't stand a chance.

It was then my thoughts shifted gear: images of her hearing the news, the aftermath, her devastation and the mess left behind. How would she cope, losing me on top of what she'd already lost? I felt shame: heavy, consuming, deep – hers not mine. I'd carried mine for a lifetime, like hidden armour. It was part of me. But Morgan didn't have any shame and now I would pass it on, sure as if it were in my DNA.

Regret filled me like carbon monoxide, choking my lungs, and I recoiled with the pain of it, the disgusting taste of it. As if it were already too late to turn back. As if it were already done.

Then it came. A dead calm washed over me. I sat up and put my hands on the steering wheel again, gently, without tension, and looked out of the car window. Houses across the road shone with lit-up verandas, warning intruders to keep their distance. Happy families slept safe and sound, oblivious to the madness beyond their front fences. I noticed trees and flowers, manicured gardens. House-proud people lived in those homes. A yellow neon light illuminated a bus stop not far down the road as if it were daytime, not dead of night. Life was all around me, yet I hadn't seen any of it before. It hit me like a tsunami, the thing I had almost done if not for those words I'd heard or imagined.

"Sis, don't do it… don't take your life… it's not your time… think of Morgan… don't do what I did to my girls… You are going to make it."

Back home, I crawled into bed, my body a dead weight as if I'd returned with all the lost souls left there at The Gap, that famous clifftop where so many had stood and then jumped to their escape, their self-made destiny, their abyss.

CHAPTER ONE | INTO THE ABYSS

I dreamt of him, Tony, my dead brother. I was in his arms and he was so grateful I wasn't with him.

CHAPTER TWO

Not Like in the Movies

I had to identify his body.

Tony had hanged himself with a green bedsheet in a cell in Parramatta Gaol. Mum and Dad couldn't make the journey to Westmead Morgue. They were parents, and parents aren't meant to see their dead children lying on a cold, stainless-steel gurney. How would they ever un-see that? How would I?

Maybe Mum and Dad thought it would be easier for the sister.

"You have to go, Marce, I can't do it. We can't do it. And Greg can't go, it's too far for him and besides, you're the strong one, love. It has to be you."

I wanted to yell at Mum over the phone, object to her assumptions. I wasn't an alcoholic or a drug addict, so I guess that made me the strong one. It was laughable. Me, the strong one. If only she knew the truth. But no one did.

"It's okay, Mum, I'll go. George will come with me."

It was dark as George drove us along Parramatta Road towards the Western Suburbs. The balmy autumn night lingered with traces of summer, refusing to give in just yet even though March would soon be over.

We sat in silence most of the way. I was glad my husband knew me well. After 16 years of marriage he didn't have to second-guess what my silence meant. If I spoke I might burst into tears and wouldn't be able to stop. This was no time to cry. That was for lucky people who didn't have to be strong.

As I stared out of the window and watched the nightlife whoosh past, I wondered if it were real. Was it possible Tony had finally done it, pranked us all with the world's best practical joke? If anyone could pull it off, Tony could.

My fingers reached for the window. When it opened, the warm air blew in and tousled my long blonde hair. I didn't care if it was messed up and stuck to my lip gloss. I'm pretty sure my shoes didn't match my outfit either. Being fabulous didn't cross my mind after that phone call. My idiosyncrasies seemed trivial in that moment. There was something very freeing about that – not caring. I took a deep breath and wished it were cold air, winter air. The pain of icy cold air filling my lungs, seeping into my bones, making me shiver would have been more appropriate for a tragedy of this magnitude. It would be physical, and I couldn't deny it.

My eyes closed willingly, and I let my body sink into the sticky fabric seat. My thoughts went back as I tried to remember the last time I had seen Tony. It was in my kitchen. I was peeling vegetables at the sink. He'd come for dinner. He wasn't his usual muck-about self and I wondered what was wrong. Did I miss the signs then? Should I have paid more attention?

CHAPTER TWO | NOT LIKE IN THE MOVIES

He'd left his country life, his wife and three daughters, to move to Sydney for his art. Tony was an aspiring actor, convinced he'd be a star one day — the next Mel Gibson, Russell Crowe or Hugh Jackman. He'd recite lines from famous plays in his best Shakespearian voice. I'd have to hold back my laughter, he sounded so ridiculous. Like Steve Irwin playing Hamlet.

"To be or not to be: crikey, is that the question?"

Tony was more suited to comedy, but he loved the melodramatic and tragic.

I counted on my fingers. Six. How was that possible? How had six years passed without seeing my brother?

George and I arrived at the morgue and walked hand-in-hand towards the drab, dilapidated building that looked as if 50 years of housing the dead had seeped through to its outer walls. It was late. The morgue was closed, but they were expecting us. As the door opened I hadn't thought about what I would say, and a sudden surge of adrenaline made my heart beat faster.

"Can I help you?"

The voice was polite. The man was short and stocky and looked like a detective. Like a clean-cut, modern Columbo.

"I'm here to see my brother," I heard myself say. As if I were just passing and thought I'd drop in.

"Ah yes, Tony. Come in. This way please."

My heart pounded faster as the detective led us to an office at the end of a bright corridor. Fluorescent lights flickered as we walked past partitioned workspaces. There were pockets of dimness where the flickering had given up completely, casting creepy shadows here and there. It was eerily quiet; no one was around. It was messy too, as if everyone had left in a hurry to escape some imminent doom. It couldn't have been more clichéd.

"A warning if I may," the detective said as we sat down in the office. "I don't want you to be shocked. Your brother came directly from the incident. We have to leave him like this until the autopsy tomorrow morning. Nothing can be done tonight. I'm sorry."

My mind went blank as I processed his words. I hated the word sorry when it carried no weight, no substance – just filler for people who didn't really care. As we stood to follow him out of the room towards another corridor, a familiar numbness crept in and took hold. I'd often wondered if the part I didn't feel was actually the strong part of me, as if my mind knew to brace myself for the impact about to occur.

"Wait here. I'll get someone to bring him out and you just indicate when you're done, okay?"

The detective disappeared before I could answer, but I nodded anyway. He even shuffled like Columbo. All he needed was a crossed eye and a cigar and I would've snapped that for Instagram. Tony would've laughed at my brazenness.

We'd stopped along a corridor outside a big room with a glass wall. Like a nursery in a hospital where you peer at the newborn babies. If only it had been.

It wasn't like in the movies. I expected to walk into a cold room with evenly-spaced handles lining the walls. A man in a white laboratory coat would open one of the vaults and there would be Tony. And I would touch his face and kiss his forehead and say "Yes, that's my brother."

George was in my peripheral vision, a step behind as always. Ready to catch me should I fall.

Then he appeared from nowhere it seemed, the man in the white coat, pushing the gurney towards us. He stopped close to the glass just like they do in the nursery. I wanted to reach out and pull back the sheet myself, just to be sure it wasn't a trick. I longed to feel my brother's skin; then I'd know without doubt it was real.

That fucking glass barrier. I wanted to smash it. There would be no last kiss, no last touch of my brother.

In slow motion the sheet came back, and as it did I took a step closer and put the palms of my hands on the glass. My nose almost pushed up

CHAPTER TWO | NOT LIKE IN THE MOVIES

against it. As if getting closer would help me feel him telepathically.

George let out a whimpering sound and I knew he'd quickly looked away. I had a feeling he'd be the one who would fall, but I couldn't catch him. I was glued to the glass.

I looked down at Tony. I knew then I'd been holding my breath. I sucked in air, filled my lungs and let out a long slow sigh as I took in the details. I was mesmerised by his stillness. He could have been sleeping. He looked so human, but there was nothing peaceful about it.

A plastic tube protruded from his wide-open mouth like an unconscious patient about to have surgery. Deep purple patches dotted his face from the neck up, pooled blood from the pressure, I imagined. The mark on his neck from the makeshift rope was mockingly visible, and I noticed then his body, arms, torso, legs were covered in tattoos.

Since when had he become a criminal?

"Oh my God, Tony, what have you done? You bloody stupid idiot," I whispered to myself.

"Talk about a dramatic exit, Tony. This one deserves a standing ovation. You've really done it this time."

I looked up at the man in the white coat. He was waiting for my answer. I gave him a single nod, which was all I could manage. And in one quick dash they were gone.

Mum filled my thoughts. I was grateful then it was me. She couldn't have witnessed it. That sight might just have ended her for good.

Twelve months later I held the coroner's report in my hands. Each page revealed a piece of the story in the lead-up to Tony's death. But instead of giving me answers, it only provoked more questions.

Apparently as the guards had cut him down from the window in his gaol cell they had noticed Tony's television was on. Dr Phil was showing. As I read the report I wondered what episode it had been, and if it had played a part in his final decision.

I closed my eyes to envision it. I imagined him sitting in his cell. I saw the solemn, sad look on his face as if I'd seen it just yesterday. He tied the noose – his years of deep sea fishing, all those knots, had paid off. And he slowly placed it around his neck – the knot to the left, the report stated. Did it matter? Was it Tony's strategic thinking or just a curious detail? And as he stood on the chair under the window, did he take one last look at Dr Phil? As he kicked it away from under his feet and the bedsheet fulfilled its purpose, did he pause? In that last moment did he wonder if he'd made a huge mistake and realise it was too late?

Was it peace or fear he felt as he took his last breath? Did he see angels in the white light or black things coming up from the floor, like in the movie *Ghost*?

When I eventually stopped crying I wondered if Tony was with me, the way people talk about the dead and the dearly departed. And if he was, could he see the truth after all these years? Did he finally know what he had really done to me? And now that he was gone, our secret was mine alone.

CHAPTER THREE

In the Spotlight

Tony was like a kid on Christmas morning. The buzz at school that day was explosive as hundreds of small feet made their way into the assembly hall. It was the most exciting thing that had ever happened at Forest Lodge Primary School.

A troupe of upcoming actors was visiting the school to cast parts for a new play, *The Swagman*. They wanted real kids for the parts, not professionals. Two shows a day would be performed for two weeks at Newtown Theatre. Schools from all over the state would come to see it. And there'd be sessions for the general public, too, an actual audience. That could mean a ticket to stardom for the chosen few.

It was Michael Caton who led the troupe up onto the stage, long before he starred in *The Castle* in 1997.

The room went silent as the headmistress introduced him and his colleagues, but not before a stern warning about good behaviour.

We hung on Mr Caton's every word as he explained the process. The chosen ones would need a certain amount of confidence, but the rest they would teach us.

"Okay then, who'd like to give it a go?"

And he scanned the room of starry-eyed faces for volunteers.

Tony's hand shot up and his torso stretched skyward like a meerkat surveying the landscape.

"Pick me, Mister, I'm ya man," Tony yelled in his usual over-the-top voice.

The laughter was like a Mexican wave rolling over the sea of kids. Even the teachers joined in. Except the headmistress. Like whiplash, she snapped her head in Tony's direction with a look that would terrify any one of us. But not Tony. I knew he'd get the cane for that one later. Subtlety wasn't his forte, and neither was following instructions.

I was scared for him. He just never knew when to keep his mouth shut. He either had the memory of a gold fish or the fearlessness of a warrior. A caning wouldn't deter him when there was an opportunity for the spotlight. And anyway, compared to Dad's fists, a caning was like fly swatting.

"Well you seem like a good start, young man, come on then. Show us what you've got."

Mr Caton motioned Tony to the stage.

The audience was mesmerised as Tony put on a show. I wondered how, at age 11, he knew how to improvise. Tony couldn't remember his five-times tables, yet he could make up dialogue as if he were born with it embedded in his cells. I was in awe of my big brother. I envied his ability to be noticed. He had the self-assurance of a lion. I had the meekness of a sloth.

CHAPTER THREE | IN THE SPOTLIGHT

I am sure, looking back, that this was his light bulb moment. Perhaps all his practical jokes had prepared him for that performance. The room erupted in applause. Even the headmistress couldn't hide her approval. She would happily take credit for the star of the show being recruited from her school. She let the caning slide that day. It didn't surprise me. It wasn't the first time Tony had charmed his way out of trouble. His charisma and good looks worked wonders when he wasn't at home. His luck would run out a year later when he got to Cleveland Street Boys High where the principal and most teachers were male and weren't easily sweet-talked. His fly-swatting days would soon be over.

Tony got the lead part right there on the spot. All the kids cheered and clapped, excited for their leader.

"Sir, could my sista Marcy be in the play too? She's down there, see." And Tony eagerly pointed in my direction.

A fiery heat engulfed me. Every face in the room turned to stare. I wanted to disappear, melt into the floor never to be seen again. And I wanted lightening to strike Tony dead. How could he do that to me? He knew I was afraid of my own shadow. I'd spent the entire nine years of my life trying to be invisible, and there he was materialising me to the world.

"Come on then, sister, let's see what you've got. Can you outshine your brother?" Mr Caton's warm smile invited me to the stage.

Tony sat cross-legged, hands on knees like a proper student. It was my turn for the limelight, but my body wasn't listening. It preferred the cold anonymity of the assembly floor.

"Come on, sis, get up 'ere. You can do it," Tony yelled. His followers cheered in unison.

He was clueless to my overwhelming dread, as if my paralysis were nothing more than a little bit of shyness. Tony had the insight of a dung beetle. He wouldn't have time for wisdom. He'd be dead before we got home from school. I was going to kill him.

My legs finally obeyed, somehow. And there I was, centre stage, in the middle of my nightmare. A million expectant faces looked up at me.

Where did all those kids come from?

Everything stopped. Queen Elizabeth mocked me from her vantage point on the back wall of the assembly hall. I glared at her, willing her to give me the courage to do something, anything.

Please, Your Majesty, help me.

The memory of my Year 4 concert popped into my mind. I'd stood on that very stage, surrounded by my classmates. But that didn't seem nearly as confronting as the hellish moment I was currently in.

My teacher had coached me for the part of girl in the bath. We all had to have a part. There was no shying away from it, she'd said. And I was perfect for the role, which my classmates renamed fatty in the tub.

As I popped up out of my cupboard box bath, like Marilyn Monroe from a giant birthday cake, dressed in nothing but a bath towel and a shower cap, I sang my debut rendition of 'Rubber Ducky'.

"Rubber ducky, you're the one. You make bath time so much fun. Rubber ducky, you're my very best friend its true… bo bo bo de do."

The laughter of my classmates spurred me on. And I wriggled my bum like a duck shaking off water. I was the funny one then. Me, funny? How was that possible? But I realised why they were really laughing. I'd lost one side of my towel. It had come untucked from its position under my armpit. I had a full-piece cossie on underneath, shoulder straps pulled down so I appeared naked. My puppy fat oozed out in every direction in an effort to break free of its confines. My rolls did that a lot. They really hated clothes.

I quickly put the towel back in place and kept going. I pretended it was part of my act. I don't know how I knew to do that. Their laughter got louder. I could tell by their faces how much fun they were having. Making my friends laugh lit me up in ways I'd never imagined possible, and that feeling was better than any pain on the inside.

And so, I did it again for Mr Caton and his entourage and the entire school, including Queen Elizabeth. I wasn't wearing my cossie or shower cap, but it didn't matter, everyone laughed at my performance. Tony clapped wildly. He smiled at me as if I were the star, and gave me his wink of approval.

I was cast alongside Tony as his sister. We didn't really look alike. We were more like Laurel & Hardy. I wasn't convinced I got the part on my own merits. I wondered if Mr Caton had taken pity on me and did it for Tony. He was the favourite. Tony was everyone's favourite, except at home.

He was a much better actor than me. I'd forget my line cues on stage in front of the live audience. One of the other kids would jump in and save me. It never happened when we were rehearsing. I knew everyone's lines then. But when I was on stage I'd daydream. The bright lights would mask the audience and I was grateful for that. If I focused on the full house or even imagined them there, I might accidently wet my pants, and then I would die on the spot.

Tony came alive on stage, even more so if that were possible. I'd watch him practise his lines. He loved that make-believe world. I guess it was better than the real world. He was somebody on stage – funny, clever, and talented. He was appreciated when he wasn't at home.

Dad accepted our project as part of the school curriculum. Mum lied and said it was compulsory. Mum lied a lot when it came to Dad. She had a lifetime of secrets from him. I wondered how she didn't stuff up, considering how much she drank. Her drinking never seemed to cloud her judgement or cause any slip-ups. I couldn't decide if Mum was very clever or really stupid. She was definitely very brave.

"Love, whatever you do, don't tell ya father, he'll hit the roof."

She'd say this about anything, the cost of the grocery shopping, a broken vase, the time we really got home from the movies. A million little things like that were planted in my brain. Even as a young child I sensed it was wrong. Eventually I'd understand the reason for Mum's conditioning. Still, it didn't seem to make her life easier. What was the point of all that dishonesty if it didn't change anything?

"Love, trust me, it's just easier to lie. The last thing I need is more bloody drama."

Mum knew how much we wanted to be in the play. If Dad had known it wasn't compulsory school education, we'd never have been allowed to participate. Had I not been cast with Tony, he wouldn't have been allowed anyway. I might have been two years younger, but Mum always put me in charge. As if she knew even then I was the mature one.

I wondered if that was why Tony got me up on stage in the first place. He knew he wouldn't be allowed if I weren't with him. Maybe he wasn't so clueless after all. I know he came to resent being chaperoned by his little sister, even though he made out it was the other way around. I know I came to resent the responsibility.

Greg, our older brother, was in charge when Mum wasn't around. We'd spend Sundays riding our bikes with the other street kids. We learnt a lot on the streets, unlike my Sunday School friends. Those friends didn't last long.

But Greg did his own thing once we closed the front door behind us. He couldn't be bothered with siblings.

"Greg, you're supposed to stay with us. Mum and Dad said so," I'd bark as he rode away on his bike.

"Where are ya goin'?" I'd yell louder.

"None of ya business. Meet yous back 'ere before dark." Greg's voice faded as he turned the corner, out of sight.

"That's not fair, I'm goin' with him." Tony would always try and follow.

"You better not or I'm dobbin'. Dad'll kill you when he finds out ya left me."

And Tony would back pedal reluctantly. He'd rather put up with me than Dad's wrath.

"You're such a brat," he'd spit at me, but I didn't care.

I had to keep order, be responsible. I was the one who made sure we all came back together and got home on time. I'd threaten Greg in the same way I'd threaten Tony. The balance of power was in my favour. He'd return on time, just as I expected. Greg especially didn't want to feel Dad's wrath. He was the eldest. He should have known better. It was the standard response if anything went wrong.

I know my brothers thought I was a pain in the arse. They probably hated me for my privileged birthright. I was the girl, and mothers take care of girls. By Dad's standards, I was not important. Fathers take care of sons, unluckily for my brothers.

All I really wanted was peace, not power. I would have done anything to avoid them getting hurt. It was okay for me to hurt them. We were siblings, fighting was normal. Still, I knew I had the advantage, so they could never get too rough. I would always win. But being their witness was no easier. I felt every blow that came down on them. I wore the same scars, but mine were invisible.

If Dad had known *The Swagman* would set in motion Tony's hunger, he would have bellowed a loud 'no' to anything that resembled Laurel & Hardy, compulsory or not.

"An actor? Don' be ridiculous woman! Dat's airy-fairy bullshit, not a job. No son of mine be a raving poofter."

That was Dad's take on Tony's ambitions. Mum's opinions didn't stand a chance. She tried for Tony's sake; she knew her son better than anyone. He'd never win awards for academia, that was clear. Even though Mum thought acting was reserved for the lucky and the privileged, it might've been something he had a chance at. It didn't matter. Dad's word was law and God help anyone who objected.

Creativity wasn't a word used in our house. Dad had proper expectations for his sons. Greg would be a doctor; he was smart. Tony would follow in Dad's footsteps, in construction, and become what Dad couldn't – a mogul property developer.

I doubt Dad had any expectations for me. I was just a girl, a stupid girl at that.

Unfortunately for Dad, he had two dropout sons. Greg was a musician at heart. Bass guitar and Jimmy Hendrix were his obsessions. Those and heroin. He joined the high school band – at least that way Dad had to accept it. It was another compulsory, Mum told him.

Greg performed at the Opera House in a Battle of the Bands competition. They won. He seemed to come alive, too, with a guitar in his hand, as if he weren't an introvert at all. My brothers were opposites. Their common ground was their circumstance, not their creativity. They were brothers-in-arms, fighting a war when they weren't in the spotlight. And to them, what could their baby sister know about wars? Girls don't know anything – everyone knows that.

CHAPTER FOUR

The Wedding Part 1 She's Thinking of the Bad Times

The young girl who shunned the spotlight all those years ago was unwittingly thrust into its epicentre on her wedding day. Tony would be there again, only this time he would steal the attention for all the wrong reasons. High on speed and alcohol, he gave the gossiping Greeks plenty to talk about. His performance at the wedding reception was the culmination of a long day that was more like a scene from *Four Weddings and a Funeral*.

I wish I could say it was the happiest day of my life, like a normal bride might, but that would be a lie. The signs were there, at least a dozen of them. I was oblivious. I had the wisdom of gravel and the foresight of a shovel.

I wish I were making it up, but I'm not.

It started with my hair.

"Marcy, it looks fine. You're stressing when you should be enjoying the day. You need a drink," Sam, my Maid of Honour, said as she handed me a glass of something effervescent.

Sam's real name is Santina – I've called her Sam since we were kids, I'm not sure why, it sounded better than San I suppose – was once married to Greg. They'd been childhood sweethearts. Six weeks after they married she found out about Greg's secret. We all found out then. And as much as Greg loved her, his first love was heroin. Sam wasn't the type of woman to put up with that. It was the shortest marriage I'd ever heard of – before Brittany or the Kardashians.

"Oh, thank God. Someone give the girl a Valium or something for the sake of Holy Mary! I can't work like this," my hairdresser piped up.

"Marcy, I've never seen this side of you. What is it with women and weddings that turns them into psychotic bitches? Straight men are crazy, I tell you!"

I'd hardly eaten in six weeks. A few sips of the metallic-tasting bubbles and I felt instantly tipsy. I never drank wine, especially if it had bubbles. My badgering bridesmaids made me finish it. I'd deal with them later.

We were late, thanks to my hairdresser, not tradition. Fine wasn't good enough. I made him start over, twice, and I never went back.

As I stood with Dad, arms linked behind the closed church doors, any remnant of alcohol in my blood stream was gone. I was sober. I wasn't sure if that was better or worse.

The touch of my father's arm felt so foreign I might as well have been standing there with a stranger. Never before had our bodies touched in

CHAPTER FOUR | THE WEDDING PART 1 SHE'S THINKING OF THE BAD TIMES

such a way – in any way really. I'd kissed the side of Dad's head, as a greeting or a goodnight. He had never kissed me back. The only hug Dad ever gave was more of a pat on the back, like patting the top of a dog's head. Dad's hands were the size of dinner plates – gentle wasn't his strong point.

I'd felt the force of those hands only a few times. It wasn't a big deal, not compared to my brothers. Dad once slapped me when I was a teenager, unaware he was behind me as I gave Mum a mouthful of insults. I landed in the next room, stunned. Mum went ballistic. He wasn't allowed to touch her daughter. She couldn't protect her sons, but she would do her damnedest to protect her daughter. He never slapped me again. I was the lucky one.

The heat from Dad's arm felt like a hot-water bottle against the ivory lace of my dress. It was March, but autumn was nowhere in sight. Dad hated wearing formal clothes. On a day like that it would've been torture. He looked uncomfortable, like Conan the Barbarian in a suit. Dad would've worn his stubbies and singlet if he could have.

We didn't speak as we stood there waiting. At 24 I still found it hard to communicate with him. I was probably 16 before I could look him in the eye, let alone speak in sentences. Until then it was "Good morning, Dad." "Good night, Dad." "May I pleased be excused from the table, Dad?" "Yes, Dad." "No, Dad." "Sorry, Dad."

I learned from an early age, the less I spoke the better off I'd be. I just had to remember the cues, and Mum would remind me if I forgot. A slight tap of her hand, a gentle kick under the dinner table, a look in her eye, and a million other signs I became very good at reading.

What the hell was I thinking, saying yes to a wedding? Clearly, I hadn't thought it through properly. I should have listened to Mum and eloped, bypassed all the drama and expense, and the awkwardness of that moment. It felt more like my funeral than my wedding.

George proposed in the summer of 1986, a year after we started dating. We were in my car, parked at Glebe Point, looking out towards the Harbour Bridge. The giant coat hanger glowed orange in the setting sun, but George's words captured my attention.

"Marcy, I love you with all my heart. I want to be with you forever. Will you marry me?"

I thought he was joking. George was a lot like Tony when it came to jokes, but that was where the similarity ended.

He was 19 when we first met, still a boy really. He didn't even have body hair. It would grow eventually. An only child of strict Greek Orthodox parents, he still had a curfew by which he happily abided. He'd never rebelled, never done the usual teenage things. He was too respectful to dishonour his parents. I hadn't had a curfew since I was 13. That kind of freedom can be dangerous for a girl, and it was. Dad was a night worker – lucky me. He had no idea about my freedom. Mum couldn't say no to me, and she could whip out those white lies in an instant if need be.

George's world was rainbows and sparkles. Mine was devoid of any real colour. Streetwise wasn't anything he knew. I was attracted at first to his innocence and his humour. He was a rare species I'd never seen before. Boys like him didn't exist in my world. I had a feeling that if I tossed him aside I'd regret it. What were the chances of two Georges roaming the earth? More importantly, what were my chances of anyone else ever loving me?

"You're joking, right?"

"I'm not joking, sweetheart. Please say yes and make me the happiest man alive."

Visions of my life danced in front of me. As if he were Thelma and I was Louise and he'd just asked me to jump. That wasn't supposed to happen. I had plans, and none involved marriage or children. I wanted to travel and see the world. I would be a free-spirited gypsy with nothing but my backpack and an endless supply of money for all my adventures.

I wasn't sure where the money would come from or how I'd pull it off. My make-up and cosmetics would take up one backpack alone! And how would I carry all my shoes?

It never occurred to me to say we don't have to get married to commit to each other. We could still be happy without a certificate. The truth was, I wasn't sure I believed it. Why would someone stay with me if he didn't have to? As if a marriage certificate meant by law we'd have to stay together forever. To be honest, in that moment I wanted to marry George. I loved him. I'd never loved anyone before.

My inner gypsy wasn't happy. I was about to dump her for a marriage proposal. I ignored the twisting knot in my gut, and pushed it aside under the virtual carpet with all my other bits and pieces. It was getting crowded under there.

"Yes, I'll marry you. But I mean it, George, no kids. If you want kids, you should marry someone else. I'll never change my mind about that."

It was not that I hated children. Having a child meant there was a 50 per cent chance it would be a boy. I couldn't risk a boy with my DNA. It would be doomed from the start.

Mum's words echoed in my mind whenever children came into a conversation.

"Don't do it, love. Don't ruin ya life by having kids. You only get one, be selfish. Don't do what I did. Ya bloody brothers will be the death of me, little shits. Why couldn't they be more like you, my Chicken Licken?"

For as long as I could remember, the seeds of Mum's wisdom were sown in me. I got the message all right. Boys are good for nothing. I loved being Mum's favourite, but sometimes I felt sorry for my brothers. Then I grew up. Mum was right. What the world didn't need was more sets of balls attached to little shits.

"I don't care about kids, Marce. As long as I have you that's all I'll ever need."

And so it was settled. George and I would live for us. Do what we wanted, when we wanted, without the burden of children. And if anyone judged us for it, they could fuck off!

We made a pact with each other. We'd always be honest, loyal, and never have secrets between us. George was nothing like Dad or my brothers. There wouldn't be a need for secrets. He promised he'd never leave me and we would never divorce. And I believed his promises with the faith of a five year old. I figured if Mum and Dad could stay married anyone could.

Still, I doubted my decision as I stood waiting for those doors to open. My urge to run was strong. Imagine that, Dad standing alone, his daughter the runaway bride. He'd kill me.

I heard laughter coming from inside the church. *Oh Lord, the comic duo is at it.* George and the priest must have started their routine. Great. Dad would be wondering what the hell we're doing at the circus. I knew that priest would be trouble from the moment we first met!

"I understand you're Greek Orthodox, George?" Father David had said as we sat in his office for our first interview six months earlier.

"Yes, but don't hold that against me. I am Greek, but I'm not that Greek." George winked at him, implying of course that he was no homosexual.

My head snapped in George's direction. Oh my God, did he really just say that? I kicked him under the table. I was mortified at his blatant disrespect in front of a Catholic priest.

Father David did a double take and then let out a heartfelt chuckle. "Well, we're not so rigid these days and you seem like a good lad. We won't tell the Pope you're Orthodox, it'll be our little secret." And Father David winked back.

I wasn't sure which disturbed me more, my fiancé's disrespect or a funny priest. I wondered how Dad would react to a joke-cracking priest. He only had one opinion about religion. A comic priest might be a whole new ball game.

"It's a bloody scam to suck people in an' make da Pope rich. It'sa loda bullshit."

Dad was Roman Catholic, but not a very good one. Mum wasn't Catholic. She was never baptised. Dad loved taunting her about being a heathen.

"Well, I may be a heathen but at least I'm not a hypocrite, you fool,"

CHAPTER FOUR | THE WEDDING PART 1 SHE'S THINKING OF THE BAD TIMES

Mum would fire back.

She was so brave. I cringed every time she lost her temper and answered him back. Dad would either laugh at her or explode. And you didn't want to be in close proximity when he exploded. I always kept my distance for that reason.

Dad insisted we be baptised and have the sacraments, so we weren't heathens like Mum. Yet Mum was the one who encouraged us; she was there in the Church watching. Dad was always working so he was never there, and he didn't like churches. But what he really didn't like were Jehovah's.

"Get off my property, ya bloody scheming leeches, before I kick ya arses from here to kingdom come. Jehovah won't be able to save ya den, ya bastards!" Dad would bellow in his thick Italian accent. The poor door-knocking Jehovah's would run for their lives. Every time there was a knock on the door I'd almost wet my pants. I was sure one day someone would stand up to him, and that would be a very bad day.

The music started. The doors finally opened. Dad and I slowly walked the plank. I was grateful then for his arm of steel. I latched on tighter as it held me upright, sure I would fall if I let go. Dad hated crowds and attention more than I did, so I could only imagine his discomfort. But at that moment I didn't care about Dad's issues.

When I saw George's smiling face the tension left me, momentarily. He lifted my veil and his eyes saw something wrong. I tried to smile but my lips were quivering so much it was impossible. With each passing minute I felt a boa constrictor sliding up under my dress and slowly wrapping itself around me. I'd never fainted before, but I thought this was my moment.

"And, Marcy, do you take George to be your lawfully wedded husband? Will you love and cherish him, in sickness and in health, in good times and in bad, blah blah blah?"

The dull echo of Father David's voice bounced inside my eardrums like a caged bird flapping wildly. George's touch on my clammy hand brought me back into the present.

I heard a dog bark in the distance, the hum of a car engine as it slowed to a stop at the traffic lights out on Johnston Street. Someone cleared their throat and coughed, I had a feeling it was Tony. A few loud sniffs later and I knew for sure. It didn't take much to guess what he'd been up to while I'd been torturing bridesmaids. I was a Bridezilla long before the reality TV show.

I opened my mouth, but no words came out. I'd lost the power of speech.

"Marcy? Well do you?" Father David leaned closer to my ear as if I had a hearing problem. He was mystified. He hadn't experienced a bride hesitating for that long in his church before.

My eyes burned, and my body trembled. I looked to George in desperation, willing him to continue his comedy routine, anything to make it stop. If Tony had sashayed up the aisle reciting a scene from *King Lear* I wouldn't have cared, in fact I wished he would. Of all the attention-seeking moments he could steal, he chose to let that one slide.

Then it happened: deep, heaving, uncontrollable sobs, coming from me. Me. How was that possible? Never in my life had I ever displayed such pathetic girly emotion in public.

Just as I was about to fake my own collapse, Father David lifted his hand to my face and moved a chunk of hair out of my eyes.

"Is that what's bothering you, child? Let me just fix that," he said with genuine pity.

He actually said that. I wasn't thinking about my hair, and there he was bringing it back to my attention. It was a deal breaker. My hairdresser was dead to me.

I felt George take my other hand. He moved closer and whispered in my ear.

"It's okay, darling, it'll be over soon. Everything's going to be all right. You look so beautiful."

CHAPTER FOUR | THE WEDDING PART 1 SHE'S THINKING OF THE BAD TIMES

And with those words my trance was broken. Father David sensed it too.

"I think she's focusing on the bad times," he said loudly to the stunned crowd.

The church erupted in relieved laughter. Even Dad would have been grateful for that one.

When it was finally over we practically ran down that aisle, hand-in-hand as husband and wife, through the open church doors and into the bright, promising sunshine of our future. As I stood on the steps smiling at everyone, accepting their kisses and congratulations, I was so grateful the embarrassment was over. My relief, however, was premature. Things were about to get a whole lot worse.

CHAPTER FIVE

The Wedding Part 2 Chim Chiminey

I was certain my out of body experience in the church would be the topic of conversation for the rest of the day, and probably for a long time after. If that entire spectacle wasn't a sign, I'm not sure what was. I can say that now. It wouldn't have mattered then if there'd been actual warning signs flashing on Father David's head or above the statue of Jesus himself. I would've ignored them. Love is blind like that.

But there was no way I could ignore the signs at the reception. By the end of the day all we needed was a hailstorm and some lightning strikes for the place to go up in flames and it would've been a perfect wedding day for *The Addams Family*.

As George and I sat in the back of the limo on our way to the reception, debriefing about the debacle we'd just escaped, I cringed at the thought that his family would think I was fragile, meek, unstable. I'd already assumed their disappointment. George had married outside tradition, to an Italian of all nationalities. That feud had been raging for centuries. Someone forgot to tell the Greeks and Italians that The Battle of Greece was over.

Dad always said, "Never trust a Greek. Look what dey did at Troy with da horse. Shifty bastards, da lot of 'em."

But Dad trusted George. George was the type of son he wished he had: respectful, obedient and intelligent. Instead he ended up with two drongos, as he called my brothers.

And so it wasn't surprising that Dad didn't object to me marrying a Greek. If George's parents verbalised their objections, he never said.

"Oh sweetheart, stop worrying. They all love you. How could they not? And anyway, do you really care what anyone thinks? I don't," George said as he reached for my hand.

Of course I cared, but I wasn't about to confess that out loud. I cared more than I'd admit, especially to myself.

"No, I don't care. If anyone wants to judge me they can fuck off."

"That's the spirit, darling. Tell it how it is. And that's why I love you."

I wondered if I was George's rebellion. Had he married me just to piss his family off? If so, I'd bet he couldn't wait to introduce them to his new favourite brother-in-law, Steve Irwin II. And what an introduction it would be. If the Greeks thought I was unstable, they would probably think Tony needed gaffer tape and restraints.

When we arrived at our reception we were greeted by someone I'd never met before. The venue manager had called in sick. Looking back, this was the first sign. I'd spent hours with him going over every last detail in the months leading up to that moment. I wanted everything to be perfect. It was clear he hadn't done a handover with his fill-in protégé. The new guy didn't have a clue what was going on.

CHAPTER FIVE | THE WEDDING PART 2 CHIM CHIMINEY

The Master of Ceremonies was also a stranger. Sign number two. Our original MC was missing in action. His understudy couldn't pronounce our surname and he kept calling me Marsha, as in *The Brady Bunch*. I really don't like my name pronounced incorrectly. I made him stop. He called me Mrs M after that. He had the personality of an auditor. A politician would've been more entertaining.

I needn't have bothered with the painstaking decisions of the menu either. The meat was over-cooked and stringy. The chicken was dry and tasteless. And the vegetables were an inedible mush on the plate. What had happened to the glorious tasting menu I'd sampled only months before? I could only conclude the chef was MIA too. Someone from *Hell's Kitchen* cooked that meal. Had I had my usual appetite I would've gone into the kitchen and slapped everyone in there. As it was, the meal was the least of my problems.

As the guests pushed food around their plates, the background music suddenly stopped. I had a feeling something bad was imminent. The entrance door flung open and in danced a guy dressed like something out of *Oliver Twist*. His ill-fitting suit was filthy, so was his face. He had a top hat on and was carrying a witch's broomstick. When he came in a new kind of music blared and I wondered if it was a raid of some kind. With Greg and Tony in the room, anything was possible.

When the gate-crasher started miming the words to Chim-Chiminey, from the movie *Mary Poppins*, I realised he was supposed to be a chimney sweep. I just didn't know why he was dancing around my wedding reception as if he were in his lounge at home. He went from table to table, singing and pirouetting as he danced his way closer to the bridal table.

I wondered for a moment if we were all at the wrong venue. That would explain everything.

"Okay, what's happening now? What's going on, George? Did you do this?" I asked out of the corner of my mouth, leaning towards his ear. Not taking my eyes off the dirty guy.

If this were one of George's jokes, I would kill him later.

"No idea, darling. It wasn't me." George looked genuinely amused.

As the singing derelict approached our table I knew instinctively what was about to happen. He was going to kiss me. He was about to lean over my expensive ivory wedding dress and kiss me with his soot-covered lips.

At the thought of this new humiliation, something inside me snapped. I'm sure my poker face turned into an all-out death stare. My eyes spoke what my mouth couldn't.

Don't even think about it, buddy. I will stab you with my steak knife if you come anywhere near me or my dress!

The look on his face said it all. No kiss was worth his life. He skipped away out of sight. It was over. The nightmare was over. It was temporary.

I didn't dare look at the guests, especially the Greek half of the room. They would've been mystified at the strange cultures of this Italian/bogan wedding they had somehow ended up at.

The venue, we learned later, had organised the chimney sweep as a gift. It's a medieval English tradition that is supposed to be good luck for the new bride and groom. I'd never seen this at a wedding before or even heard of it. Why someone thought a Greek groom and an Italian bride would appreciate an old English tradition, I'm not sure. If I'd known beforehand, a firm no would have been my response to any surprises. The guy was lucky Dad didn't get hold of him. Had he dirtied any part of me I knew what Dad would've done with the broomstick.

Drinks were spilt on my dress. Someone almost burnt a hole in it with their cigarette. In those days people still smoked in aeroplanes, so smoking at a wedding – or anywhere else – was standard. There were fashion disasters, breakages, chairs falling backwards and people slipping on polished floors. The icing on our wedding cake was so hard the knife could barely penetrate the surface. One tier fell on the ground in our effort to cut it. By the time we got to the speeches I just wanted my wedding from hell to end.

CHAPTER FIVE | THE WEDDING PART 2 CHIM CHIMINEY

It wasn't over yet.

Out of all the mishaps that day, all the signs I would ignore – until years later – it was Tony's performance that we'd all remember. He decided the MC had bored us long enough, and so he took it upon himself to demote him. Tony snatched his mic and shooed him away like a stray dog. And there he was, front and centre in the glow of his beloved spotlight.

A sudden surge of adrenaline coursed through me as if I'd just taken a hit of cocaine. I anticipated what was coming. I'd seen it a hundred times before. Tony's alter ego was like watching 3-D animation in IMAX, in Dolby Surround Sound. For the average person it's way too big to absorb. If he were high on his usual concoction of speed and alcohol, multiply that by a hundred. The outcome wasn't going to be pretty.

"G'day, folks, how's it goin'? Yous havin' a good time…?"

I wasn't sure if it was just me or if Tony had the same effect on everyone. When he spoke, it was like fingernails down a chalkboard, or eating lemons. I tried to mask the shiver as my blood ran cold, and did my best to hide the sour taste in my mouth. If only I had some supersonic earmuffs to drown out the sound, just until the scary part was over… Tony's speech.

It was the worst scripted monologue of his life. He hadn't acted in years. He'd been busy working on his addictions. It was like a scene from *Dude, Where's My Car*. And, like a car crash, you couldn't look away even if you wanted to.

Every humiliation I'd felt that day was mild compared to that moment.

"George, for God's sake, can you please do something? Or just kill me now, either way."

George was giggling. He was clearly enjoying the scene before him.

"It's okay, darling, don't worry, it's just Tony being Tony," he said as he rose from his chair and made his way towards his new brother-in-law. Only George could've managed to get the mic away from Tony with such heroic ease.

I sometimes wondered how I could be related to my brothers. If it weren't for the subtle resemblances, I'd swear I was adopted. It probably would have made me feel better, knowing I didn't really come from that much dysfunction.

But they were my brothers, and Tony, despite all his eccentricities and his obnoxiousness, was the one I was closest to. We were more like twins growing up. And although I hated him sometimes, I loved him. I'd always loved him. That was the problem. Even after what he'd done to me all those years ago.

CHAPTER SIX

The Trouble with Brothers

Growing up, Tony was the only one I could trust. By the time I was 15 our love/hate relationship had been tightly woven into the threads of our psyche. We had each other, bound by the secrets of our family's hidden dysfunction. Greg was long gone by then. He was 14 when his destiny was set in motion. One shot of heroin was all it took. He wasn't the kind of older brother we could depend on, especially me.

Greg couldn't be trusted. I knew that for certain by the time I was 10 years old. He'd discovered a stash of *Penthouse* magazines hidden in a drawer under Dad's side of the bed. The thought of my father looking at porn disturbed me for years. A daughter doesn't want to know things like that about her father, ever. One night, Greg took it upon himself to attempt to teach me about the adult joys of our anatomy.

We were alone in the house. Dad would have been at work. Mum and Tony were probably at the hospital. He was always sick.

Greg called out to me from somewhere upstairs. As I entered Mum and Dad's bedroom all the hairs on my body stood on end. My skin prickled as if the temperature in the room had suddenly dropped. He was lying on their bed, magazines strewn everywhere. I caught glimpses of naked bodies, big boobs and hairy private parts. Greg had a look in his eyes I'd never seen before. My tummy surged like I'd just eaten some of Dad's homemade chilli mix. I only ever made that mistake once.

My heart pounded so loud I thought he could hear it. The room took on a feeling of ominous danger, as if a wild animal had been stalking me and it was just about to get its reward.

"Come 'ere, Marce, I wanna show ya somethin'," Greg held out his hand and beckoned me over to the bed.

I'm not sure how or why I did what I did. I imagine it was some sort of primal instinct – fight or flight. I only had a chance of surviving one of those options.

"I'm dobbin' on you."

My hands flew to my hips like an angry schoolmistress. My face pushed forward for emphasis as I yelled with an authority I wasn't feeling. My voice would have barrelled through the open windows down into the street three stories below, a voice usually reserved for Tony, not Greg.

"You're so dead. Dad's gunna kill you when he finds out what ya doin' with his books." As if I knew all about Dad's books, as if I wasn't in shock to see them scattered before me like it was an everyday occurrence. I didn't know exactly what Greg was doing, or what he wanted to show me, but whatever it was held no curiosity for me.

I fled from the room at warp speed. I didn't know I could move that

CHAPTER SIX | THE TROUBLE WITH BROTHERS

fast. I almost fell down the narrow stairs of that old terrace. I'd cut myself before on the razor-sharp metal strips that lined the edge of each step. My bare feet felt nothing that night. I had to reach the front door. My escape to freedom depended on reflexes. That didn't give me much hope. At any moment I might feel his grip on my ponytail, ripping me back to an unchangeable fate. I didn't dare turn around to face the commotion behind me.

"Marcy, stop! Stop, it's okay," he yelled as he ran down after me.

It wasn't over when I'd flung the front door open. At least 30 feet were between me and the front gate. I could see sanctuary, our street, through the steel latticework fence.

My grasshopper legs didn't let me down. I made it to the footpath – out in the open – safe. Neighbours had their front doors open, flickering TV screens beamed light into the early evening. Soft voices drifted on the warm breeze, normal families doing normal things, oblivious to the unnatural crime-in-progress in number 28.

When Greg reached me, I pretended I was busy playing, all else forgotten. I'd found a stick and was dragging it along the bars of the fence, pacing back and forth, praying for Mum to get home. I knew he'd try and bribe me with chocolate to keep my mouth shut. My brothers knew chocolate was my currency. And so I was the keeper of secrets, and rich in an abundance of chocolate.

Greg ran away not long after that. I never told anyone about the magazines, so I couldn't be blamed for him leaving. He went to Nan's house. Mum's mother lived in the country, a long train ride away. My brothers loved Nan and the bush. I wasn't keen on either. Even as a child I sensed she didn't like me. She thought I was a spoilt brat, I'm sure. Nan was the kind of woman who preferred boys to girls. All mothers have their favourites, Mum would say. I think Nan wanted Greg and Tony to live with her. She was the keeper of strays: dogs, cats, kids, the unwanted.

"Yvonne, ya better keep an eye on Greg. The eldest is always the most affected, ya know. Poor little bugger. It's not right what he goes through.

Bloody disgrace if ya ask me," Nan would sneer.

"Well, I didn't ask your opinion, now did I, Vera? So why don't ya mind your own business, you silly old woman!" Mum would fire back.

I found it disconcerting how Mum and her siblings would often call Nan by her first name. We would never be allowed to do that with our own parents. It was a sign of disrespect, Mum said. Tony did it once and Mum broke her wooden spoon on the back of his head. She broke a lot of utensils, and various other objects, on Tony.

Tony eventually ran away to Nan's house too. She would often hide my brothers for weeks before telling Mum and Dad. She'd lie and say she didn't know where they were. It would infuriate Mum when she found out the truth. There were weeks, months, even years when they wouldn't speak to each other.

Greg and Tony would suffer for running away. I never understood their recklessness, knowing what the outcome would be. They were either daredevils or idiots, I couldn't decide which.

Then one day Greg reached his breaking point.

He would've been 16. I was 12. He'd somehow slipped out of Dad's grip, saved from the next blow. It was a lucky break for Greg, but not so lucky for Dad. It enraged him even more. Greg bolted down the backyard into the shed where Dad kept his gun collection. Everything happened so fast after that. The commotion was dreadful.

"Greg, stop! Don't do it. Don't do it!" Mum yelled hysterically. She knew what was now inevitable. At the same time, she was hanging onto Dad's arm in an effort to pull him back. She might as well have been an annoying insect on the arm of The Hulk. Mum's stocky frame seemed weightless on Dad. As if anyone, especially Mum, could stop the force of The Hulk.

Tony was screaming in all directions. Like a mouse going wild on his wheel, racing but getting nowhere. He didn't stand a chance at being heard. That was unusual for Tony.

There I was in the background, cowering against the wall of the house. I went unnoticed. I was nothing in the scheme of things. I wanted to scream, to make them stop, but no words came out.

Greg had all the power then. He was the main attraction.

Our yard wasn't big. Greg stood outside the shed door and, even though he was holding the rifle, he looked like the prey not the hunter. All that stood between him and Dad was the old Hills Hoist clothes line. Escape would be a tricky manoeuvre.

Greg's eyes blazed as he held the rifle, his finger on the trigger ready to kill his attacker. For a moment, for one brief heart-stopping moment, Greg became the hunter and Dad became his prey.

"I hate you! I fucking hate you!"

As Greg yelled those words, his finger pulled the trigger.

Dad lunged for the barrel of the gun head-on. As if he were bullet-proof, untouchable. Mum let out a blood-curdling scream, like the kind in horror movies. Tony finally spun right off that wheel, out of control, screaming like a madman. I don't recall making any sound. I was paralysed, glued to that wall like paint.

A nanosecond was all Greg had to make his next move.

The gun was empty. Dad would never keep a loaded gun in the house or the shed. It was a lesson we all learned that day. Dad ripped the gun from Greg's grip with the strength of a dozen men. Unbelievably, Greg didn't fall.

"You wanna kill me ya little bas-tard. You think ya can fucking kill me do ya? I'll show you, you son-of-a-bitch!"

Greg wasn't a runner, but you wouldn't have known it. He took off up the side of the house and out the front gate, gone before we even realised. He was the luckiest bastard alive that day. He'd got away. We didn't see him for a long time after that.

He'd come and visit Mum while Dad was at work. She'd give him money. He'd tell her it was for food or rent. We knew it was for heroin. I'm sure Mum knew too. Dad would have killed her if he'd found out.

It seemed to me Mum played a dangerous game. I didn't think it was worth the sacrifice. She was risking her own life while aiding her son to ruin his. I doubt Mum would have done the same for Tony. But then again, he wouldn't have asked. He was the opposite of Greg.

Mum's soft spot for Greg became more obvious as each year passed. I wondered if Dad knew it too, and perhaps that was the reason he was even harder on him. In Dad's eyes weakness of any kind was unacceptable. Maybe he thought Mum's mothering would make him feeble. That maybe beatings would toughen him up. The more lessons Greg copped from Dad, the more Mum empathised with him. It was a lose-lose situation for everyone, but Greg was the biggest loser. Looking back, I wonder if Mum should have been firmer with him, though I doubt it would have made a difference. How could Mum's kindness have made the tragedy any worse?

"It's hard to explain, love. A mother knows the weakest of her brood, the one that needs the most help. What else can I do, turn him away? Ya bloody brothers are the thorns in my side, God help me. Not like you, my strong chicken. I thank the Lord every day for you."

For a supposed heathen, Mum spoke about God a lot. I never understood why she kept saying I was strong. I felt like a dandelion in a storm most of the time. It confused me more than her willingness to supply Greg's drugs.

But there'd be shitty times ahead and I'd have to be very strong, whether I thought I was or not. It was either that or die – which I would have gladly chosen a few times.

CHAPTER SEVEN

Cruel, Cruel World

Mum never learnt to drive for reasons that only made sense when I was much older. I'm sure some people are alive today because Mum wasn't behind the wheel. She was a back-seat driver though, and often – stupidly – took it upon herself to nag Dad in the car.

"Gary, will you slow down, ya friggin' lead foot? You're gunna kill us all."

"Shud up, woman, for Godsake. You wanna get out an' walk?"

Gary wasn't my father's real name. I doubt many Italians have such an Aussie name. It was a nickname that somehow stuck when Mum and Dad first met. I think Dad played a trick on Mum and pretended he had a twin brother to confuse her. At least that's what she told me.

The thunder in Dad's voice could stop traffic. Their yelling almost got us killed more than once. If it wasn't Mum, it was the knuckle-heads on the road. I grew up believing Dad was the only person in the world who could drive properly, and everyone else had found their driver's licence inside a Corn Flakes packet.

Mum couldn't have driven even if her fears had allowed her. Every morning she'd start her day with a whisky-laced coffee.

By the age of seven I knew that unmistakable stench. Mum was delirious if she thought we couldn't smell it.

"Mummy, what's that smelly stuff in your coffee?" I'd ask.

"It's Mummy's medicine, love. I need it to start my day. God knows I need a lot of medicine to cope with ya silly brothers. And ya bloody father."

And she did. She needed her medicine morning, noon and night, and in between if it was a particularly bad day. She also needed Bex Powders regularly, to ward off headaches and help her cope.

It was the 1960s. Google tells me Bex Powder was a strong compound analgesic, a powerful nervous system stimulant containing the addictive pain killer phenacetin. It came in the form of APC (aspirin–phenacetin–caffeine) and, in combination with aspirin, could give greater pain relief than aspirin alone. It was banned in 1983 due to increased risks of certain cancers and kidney damage. That would explain a lot later.

I assumed all mothers hid their Bex Powder in drawers throughout the house and drank Irish coffee as if it were water. It was a wonder Mum could walk, let alone drive.

As young kids, we had to walk everywhere. All the other mothers drove. It wasn't fair.

"Mum, why can't we take the bus?" Greg would whine.

"Because the bus costs money and money doesn't grow on trees, that's why. Walking is good for you. Now stop complaining or I'll tell ya father ya being naughty."

That would shut Greg up. That would shut all of us up.

CHAPTER SEVEN | CRUEL, CRUEL WORLD

Some Saturday mornings we'd walk two and a half kilometres from our house in Junction Street to King Street, Newtown. Mum liked the delis and fruit markets there. The delicious salamis and cheeses were a special treat when we could afford it. It was a long way for little legs, but worth the effort.

Mum's portable trolley would overflow with groceries, and she'd struggle to pull it behind her. Greg and Tony would be laden down with carrier bags. The walk home was always twice as long with all the stopping and resting. We'd cut through the grounds of Sydney University to shorten the trip. It was a good shortcut back in the years before gates were bolted or even closed. I would help Mum pull the trolley along. My tiny hand would grip the handle next to hers. I'm sure my help made it harder to steer, but Mum never complained. Her patience was all for me, everything else was for my brothers.

We lived around the corner from the Sydney Children's Hospital long before it moved out west to Westmead. Lucky we did. We must have walked there a hundred times or more. Three kids close in age were a health hazard, especially when two were boys.

Tony was always breaking a bone, which needed to be plastered, splinted, or bandaged. He was sickly too. He had every childhood aliment that seemed to bypass Greg and me, even shingles and meningitis, which almost killed him.

Mum used to say it was because he was so skinny. Tony would do anything rather than eat. He had no meat on his bones to protect him or fight off infection, she'd say. Not like Greg and me. We didn't have to worry about broken bones. We had plenty of protection.

Greg's bones weren't the problem. He had other things to worry about. Mum told me when he was little she had had to rush him to the hospital. He was complaining about sore ears. When she examined them, she knew they were blocked with something.

The doctor kept pulling with his long pair of tweezers. Greg squirmed and whimpered, trying to get away from him. Mum said she didn't think the doctor was ever going to stop. It just kept on coming out of his ears. Even the doctor was stumped.

"What on Earth is it?" Mum asked.

"Well, it's definitely newspaper. He must have shoved a whole page in each ear. Trying to learn to read the quick way, hey son?" the doctor joked.

Mum said she felt her face burn red with the embarrassment of it. Her worry quickly turned to impatience.

"Why would you do that, Greg? That's very naughty and dangerous, you silly boy. Go on, tell the doctor why."

I imagined Mum's tone to Greg would've been tame compared to what she would've unleashed on Tony if he'd done the same thing.

Mum wasn't prepared for Greg's response, and instantly regretted her question.

"I had to, Mummy. The voices made me do it. They were too loud, and I wanted them to stop."

Mum almost died on the spot when he spoke those words. The doctor gave her the strangest look as if she were responsible. It was the quickest exit she'd ever made from the hospital, once Greg's ears were clear of the wretched stuff. She hoped that doctor would get a transfer to another hospital, so she'd never have to see him again. It was likely though, with Tony's track record.

Years later Mum said it was a sign. She never understood it at the time and brushed it aside as childhood shenanigans, a funny story to tell at social gatherings. Mum was a great storyteller. Tony starred in most of them. It was only natural seeing as he was the mischievous one. He was always causing some kind of ruckus. Mum used to call him a delinquent, just one of her many terms of endearment for him. Tony was a walking cliché of the middle child, and everything that stood for.

"I should have named you Trouble, you little shit. Why can't you be more like ya sister? She knows how to behave," Mum would say at least once a day, for as long as I could remember.

The butcher, the pharmacist, the greengrocer and anyone else who

CHAPTER SEVEN | CRUEL, CRUEL WORLD

crossed our path would size the three of us up. They'd look from one to the other and rest their eyes on Tony.

"You sure this one belongs to you, love?" they'd say.

"I wonder about that myself," Mum would roll her eyes in response.

"Always causing me strife, this one. I think they swapped babies on me at the hospital." And she'd laugh jokingly. They'd all laugh.

We knew she wasn't joking.

Tony probably had Attention Deficient Disorder before anyone knew what that was. Either that or he was born with a death wish, or some other missing chromosome.

Some of his pranks were so elaborate in the planning, and executed with such brilliant strategy, he could probably have robbed a bank and got away with it. Mum used to say if only he'd applied that kind of dedication to his schoolwork, he might have amounted to something worthwhile. I imagined his larking about was the real reason he spent so much time at the hospital.

Tony was about 12 years old when he devised one of his greatest pranks of all time. It would be one of Mum's favourite stories eventually.

He and I were alone in the kitchen, my favourite room. I was sitting at the kitchen table eating something as usual, when I noticed Tony busying himself. I was mildly curious.

"Whatta ya doin'?" I asked without taking my eyes off my plate.

"Shhhh, keep ya voice down." That was rich coming from him. "I'm gunna trick Mum. Don't say anythin', just play along."

I ignored him and kept eating.

Mum was upstairs, cleaning. She was always doing something domestic.

Tony was like a kid in a lolly shop with only two minutes to devour everything he could get his hands on for free.

He wrote something on a piece of paper. He grabbed Mum's big carving knife from the second drawer and got the tomato sauce bottle from the pantry. He took off his shirt, tossed it aside then lay down on the kitchen floor. Tomato sauce went everywhere as he squirted it all over his body. He threw the bottle out of sight and placed the note next to him. He put the knife in his hand, assumed the star position and played dead.

"You're gunna cop it making all that mess! Mum's gunna kill you."

The black and white chequered vinyl floor was covered in red sauce. I knew Mum would go ballistic when she saw it. She used to clean that floor on her hands and knees, one square at a time. We could eat off the floor it was so clean. Just as well. Mum might make him lick it clean.

"Shhhh, she's coming! Quick, act scared," he said as he lifted his head in one last attempt to involve me. He gave up when I ignored him again, put his head back down and resumed the position.

I pretended I wasn't interested, but on the inside I was laughing.

Mum's scream was loud enough to break glass. Everyone at the hospital would have heard it. Then came the moment of realisation.

"You friggin' little idiot, I'm gunna throttle you!" Mum yelled at the top of her voice as Tony jumped up, doubling over in laughter.

I couldn't help it, I laughed too. That was a good one. He really had her fooled for a second.

"Marce, why didn't you stop him? Look at all that mess?" she said as she reached down to pick up the piece of paper. Tony was still laughing, hardly able to breathe.

"Don't blame me, Mum, he did it. How could I stop him?" I protested through a mouthful of food.

As she read the note she started giggling, which only made Tony worse. He was in hysterics.

'Goodbye, cruel world, it was nice knowing you' the note said.

"I'll give you cruel world! You'll know cruel when I flog ya arse!" Mum's stony face returned, and she lunged at him.

Tony bolted, and sauce flew everywhere. I didn't budge from my chair. I was grateful I wasn't Tony.

Mum didn't have many stories about me, but I didn't mind. That could only mean one thing. I was a good girl.

CHAPTER SEVEN | CRUEL, CRUEL WORLD

She'd tuck me into bed each night, tell me stories and read to me. Her voice was like a melody. It would float around me like a snug blanket as I drifted off to sleep. I doubt my brothers would've agreed. She had different voices for them.

Mum didn't leave my bedside until she was sure I was sound asleep. She knew I was afraid of the dark. Dad wouldn't allow lights to be left on. That cost money. The house would be bathed in utter blackness on moonless nights. I couldn't tell if my eyes were open or closed. When I'd wake during the night – I wet the bed until I was 11 years old, so I always woke up – the dark terror would paralyse me. I'd long for the full moon. On those nights I'd pull my curtains back so its bright light could drench my room and bathe me in its luminescence. Those were peaceful nights.

I still can't sleep without a nightlight.

Mum had a few stories of when I was a toddler. I found a pearl necklace in her jewellery box. I broke it and shoved all the loose pearls up my nose. She rushed me to hospital and the doctors tweezed them out one by one while I screamed the place down. I'm grateful I have no memory of that. Mum wasn't the kind of woman who wore pearls, and later I assumed that was the reason.

The only other naughty thing I did as toddler was finding Mum's contraceptive pills and eating the whole packet. Another desperate rush to the hospital, where they pumped my stomach. I'm really glad I don't remember that. But one day in the future I'd be reminded subconsciously, and there'd be no forgetting it then.

Mum thought I'd be damaged reproductively. The doctors assured her I wouldn't, but she didn't believe them. Her guilt subsided as the years passed and as her sons grew older. I was sure she wouldn't mind at all if I never gave her grandchildren, just in case they were boys.

"When you were born, my chicken, I was so happy. Finally, I had a little girl. That's all I ever wanted really. If only you'd come along first, I would've stopped right there. That's for bloody sure."

I often wondered if Mum voiced every thought in her head all the time, or just when I was around. With her strong sexist opinions, I was certain she wouldn't win any Mother of the Year Awards. The Silent Generation sure had a lot to say about things. Mum rarely held back.

"Oh love, it's only natural you'd be fat, you were born at lunchtime. Ya came out hungry and haven't stopped eating since. You're my big, fat, beautiful pork chop. My Chicken Licken."

Only Mum could make an insult sound like a compliment and deliver it so lovingly.

"And besides, love, you take after me. Nothin' you can do about genetics. Don't worry, chicken, you'll get used to it. There are worse things in life you could be."

I didn't know about genetics, but I was sure it was something to worry about. I didn't believe Mum. I knew I'd never get used to it.

Tony wasn't born at lunchtime, clearly. I never asked about Greg, but I assumed it must have been dinner time when he came into the world.

Tony was so different from us. Maybe Mum was right. Maybe the nurses did accidently switch babies when he was born. It was Christmas Day after all; maybe they were drunk. In the early 1960s it was more than likely.

"I should have called him Dennis. Dennis the bloody Menace he is."

Mum was right about that too. The years proved being example number two was no easier than being example number one.

Greg had replaced the newspaper with heroin in an effort to stop the voices, I assumed. It would be much later in life before his habits were gone for good. Tony never got that chance, even though he'd been sober for 11 years in his late twenties and thirties. It didn't last. A beer commercial he starred in would be the catalyst to his downfall. He forgot to spit. He gulped and swallowed for the camera. That was all it took to ignite the demons again. At 42 they finally caught up with him.

It was clear to me having kids was a risky business, no matter what I gave birth to. Boys meant a lifetime of struggle, if statistics in our family proved right. A daughter would probably take after me, like I did Mum. She'd be fat and miserable and I'd have to pretend, convince her she'd get used to it.

I prayed those doctors were wrong about my reproductive system.

CHAPTER EIGHT

A Gypsy Life

Dreams of a gypsy life were put on hold after I met George. That would turn out to be a decision I'd battle with for years.

Before George, my best friend was Cathy. She was blonde, petite, and lovely with a free spirit that matched my own, and the soul of an angel. We'd met the year before I met George, on South Molle Island in the heart of the Whitsundays in Far North Queensland. Surrounded by the Great Barrier Reef, it was the closest thing to paradise I'd ever dreamed of.

That was to be the first leg of my adventure, and from the moment I met Cathy I had a travel buddy, a partner in crime.

Cathy was four years older than I, and she'd travelled a lot already.

I loved listening to her stories. She knew more than I'd ever learned in geography and she was everything I wanted to be, inside and out.

I hadn't realised that to tour I'd need money, and plenty of it. I'd left school at the end of Year 10, and needed to get some quickly. Mum was all for my life of adventure but the worrywart in her told me not to be reckless.

"Love, you can't just roam around the world with a backpack on and think you'll be right. You have to have a backup plan, a career to fall back on. You'll need skills no matter what, so you should knuckle under for a few years and then think about travelling. You're only 16. You have all the time in the world."

Mum was married at 16. She had never travelled, except interstate on the back of Dad's motorbike before we were born. I still find that hard to believe. She hated motorbikes, as far as I knew. I just couldn't visualise Mum riding tandem with Dad, speeding along the great open road, crossing rivers and gorges with nothing but bush ahead of them, throwing caution to the wind and taking life one day at a time.

"Gary, slow down you freakin' lunatic, you're going to kill us! Jesus Christ Almighty!"

That was Mum every five minutes on every car trip of our lives. Mum was a nerve case and the worst back-seat driver!

"Shud up, woman, I'm doing the speed limit, but if you like I can double it!'

In reality, a gypsy life was probably Mum's worst nightmare, but she was grateful I was different to her at the same age.

"Don't make the same mistakes I made, love. There's more to life than marriage and children. You get one life to live. Be selfish and live it on your own terms. But work hard, so you can support yourself and never have to depend on a man for anything. Or, better still, marry a rich man so you never have to worry about money or working. That'd be the life!"

That was another one plucked from Mum's book of wisdom, which I'd also heard a million times for as long as I could remember; Mum had good intentions, but her delivery needed work. I came to realise much later that Mum was pretty much a walking contradiction.

I couldn't decide. I changed my mind about career paths almost as often as I changed moods.

School was like a continual visit to the dentist, each lesson like a drawn-out tooth extraction without gas or anaesthetic. The only things I excelled at were cooking class and English. I couldn't get my head around grammar, punctuation or spelling, so I'm not sure how I aced that one in my school certificate. I put it down to Ms Francis, my English teacher in Year 10. I think she felt sorry for me. I'm pretty sure she was psychic, and maybe saw something in me that no one else could. She must have had an inkling I'd need those skills more than I realised.

The social aspect of school was what helped me get up in the morning. Without my friends, life would have been dismal. It took a while to settle into high school, and Year 7 was pretty torturous. I was one of the fattest girls in my all-girls high school. Obesity wasn't as common then as it is today. Kids are cruel, but girls can be real bitches and I copped a lot that year. Petersham Girls High School was tough – not a school for sissies, that's for sure. I might as well have had the words 'I'm your target' stencilled on my back in the centre of a blazing red circle.

I learned quickly and retaliated with humour. Taking the piss out of myself became my weapon, and girls started to laugh along with me instead of at me. They also came to realise I had a hot older brother, Tony, and he could charm the pants off any impressionable girl, literally. He was my ticket to popularity, my currency, and all the girls were willing to pay it to get a date with Tony. He was the eternal heartbreaker, but it didn't seem to faze them. They all knew what he was like, but they didn't care – they'd still line up for Tony.

"You've got such a pretty face, Marcie, shame you're so fat. How come you're not like Tony? Are you sure he's your brother? You should go on a diet."

Yeah, I didn't think of that. Thanks, bitches. I'd heard it a million times. Was it supposed to be a compliment? I'd been dieting since I was 10 years old, a Weight Watchers veteran by the time I left school. That's when I discovered Duromine, and life as I knew it changed.

Diet pills were my new addiction. Food became irrelevant. Once I didn't eat for 18 days – just a dry piece of toast when I felt like collapsing. Insomnia became the enemy. Duromine was basically speed. Sixty milligrams a day of that kind of amphetamine will make you go a little crazy eventually. As much as I loved the rapid weight loss, I couldn't stand the side effects. I couldn't sustain it for long periods, but Duromine became my little helper to fall back on if I needed to fit into a party dress in a hurry.

I had to give them up for good when our family doctor committed suicide, and no other doctor would give them to me. He'd overdosed on prescription drugs; occupational habit clearly.

It was just as well – not about the poor doctor, but giving up little helpers. I needed all of my brain to concentrate, as studying never came easy. Career choices were limited for girls with my grades. I had three choices: a nurse, a secretary, or a beauty therapist.

I would've loved to work in crime or forensics, but that was a field for smart people. I had a morbid fascination for dead bodies, probably from all those years of watching movies that I was way too young to see. Mum didn't filter much when it came to me. I was the youngest and the girl and the least of her problems.

My aunty was a nurse and her stories were enough to turn me off. Cleaning vomit and sponging down old people who apparently wore nappies was not my idea of a good time. I did a year of secretarial school and six months of beauty school, just to be sure. Even though I was the fastest typist in the class and loved all things beautiful, anything that could change appearances, I still couldn't decide.

"Mum, I want to be a make-up artist… no, a photographer… maybe both… that way I can travel and work my way around the world if I have more choices."

CHAPTER EIGHT | A GYPSY LIFE

"Love, you have to make up your mind. You can't keep changing. Money doesn't grow on trees, you know, and all these courses of yours are costing us an arm and a leg. Your father's gunna hit the roof if you keep this up. Just bloody pick one, for God's sake, and stick to it!"

I did a bar course and learned remedial massage. I figured I could work in pubs and clubs on my travels, and massage could make a nice little side business. I'd heard you could save lots of money working the islands in Far North Queensland. That could be a good start for my travels. In the winter months, people headed from the islands to the snowfields in Perisher Valley and Thredbo. They'd work the ski season and make big bucks, then go overseas to Whistler in Canada or any number of the snowfields in Europe. It sounded like the perfect solution to me: getting paid to have fun – my kind of job.

I got a lot of acceptances to my applications. I lied about my experience of working in bars. How hard could it be, I thought, it's not forensics. And although South Molle wasn't one of the more popular islands, I chose it for no other reason than gut feeling.

Mum bought me a one-way ticket the next day. I was scared, but excited. I'd never been on a plane before.

"Love, you'll be fine. Go, be free, have adventures and then one day come back and tell me all about them. But not too soon. Give yourself time."

I think Mum had had a gutful of me by then. I'd been back and forth from home, one drama after another. My indecisiveness and erratic moods got on her nerves, I think. I had secrets that I never could bring myself to tell her, although Mum and I shared a lot of secrets. She was the most open-minded mother of all my friends, and they would envy our relationship. But some things I could never tell her no matter how open her mind was. Much later I'd wonder if Mum had known my secrets would it have changed things? Maybe her patience wouldn't have run out by the time I was 16. But she seemed glad to get rid of me once and for all when the time came.

63

I arrived on the island in 50-degree heat. I didn't know people could live in that kind of temperature without self-combusting. The shock of the air strangled my lungs and I could hardly breathe. The humidity was unbearable, and most days I felt like a stuffed sausage with fluid retention. My swollen feet hurt so much I thought my skin would rip. My back ached from standing all day serving icy cold, colourful drinks that I wasn't allowed to taste. The rule was no drinking during shifts except water, and even that out of sight of the customers. Customers were always around. It was a holiday resort. A paradise for them, but for the workers it was a paradise made in hell. And when I wasn't working, all I could do was put my feet up, rest them and try to get them back to a normal size before my next shift. There was no *Dirty Dancing* that's for sure.

I hated everything about it.

I called Mum. I didn't have enough money to buy a plane ticket home.

"But, love, it's only been a week. You haven't given it a chance."

"Mum, I don't want to be here. It's not what I expected. I've made a mistake," I sulked into the payphone.

"Well, we all make mistakes, love, and nothing is ever what we expect. No, you're not coming home. You stay and give this a good go. Trust me, you'll thank me for it one day."

I was about to protest, but I was speechless, temporarily dazed by probable heatstroke, and I wasn't used to Mum saying no to me.

"Now go and have fun, work hard and save money. I'm sure you'll make some new friends soon and that'll make you feel better."

And with that the phone line was cut. I wasn't sure if she'd hung up on me or my coins had run out.

I was livid. How dare she make me stay when I clearly didn't want to? I'd give her a mouthful next time I called! I had no choice but to stay.

The very next day I met Cathy and we became inseparable.

"Oh, what's wrong? Are you okay?" Cathy asked as she entered our dorm.

I shared a room with several girls, including Cathy, none of whom

I'd formally met. I'd said hi to a few in passing, but I hadn't seen Cathy before. I didn't hear the door open when she walked in. I was alone and crying into a towel, trying to muffle the sound.

"No," I said.

The softness in her voice just made me worse. I was suddenly so homesick that I wanted Mum to take me in her arms and calm me down like she did when I was little.

"There, there, it can't be that bad. Can I do something for you? I'm Cathy by the way."

Cathy sat down beside me and put her hand on mine. She was like an angel sent from heaven to save me. She looked like an angel and had the kindest eyes I'd ever seen. I lurched forward and wrapped my arms around her hugging her tight. She must have thought I was a complete head case, and a big wimp.

I let go, realising how it must have seemed.

"I'm so sorry, I'm just… I don't know anyone and I'm feeling a bit homesick… my feet are so sore… I can't believe this heat… I'm Marcie…" I said without taking a breath.

"It's okay, Marcie, you'll get used to it. I felt the same way when I first arrived, three months ago. Would you like me to rub your feet? I'm a massage therapist in my spare time. I bet it'll make you feel better."

She really was an angel sent from heaven. Cathy's beautiful warm smile instantly relaxed me. I had a good reason to stay after that.

Cathy had already done the ski season. She was at the end of her year of saving money. She was going to backpack around Europe and Asia, and she planned on being gone for at least 14 months.

"Come with me," Cathy said three weeks later. She could hardly contain her excitement.

I could hardly contain mine, either, but mine had a huge dampener. I was just starting – she was finishing and it was almost time for her to go home. She planned on spending some time with her family before heading off again.

"I'll tell you what," Cathy said. "Come back to Sydney with me and I'll wait for you. We can always make heaps of money there, and more travel money is better than less, right?" I think I fell in love with her on the spot.

Cathy lived 15 minutes from me. So close, yet we'd never crossed paths before. I was worried Mum would be angry if I went home after just a month, but I had a good reason. I was sure she'd be okay with it, knowing she'd get rid of me for a whole year, possibly a lot more.

Cathy's car was parked at Airlie Beach, back on the mainland. We decided to take it slow on the drive home and have some fun along the way. And boy, did we have fun in those few weeks on the road! I never wanted them to end. I wasn't ready to go back and face what might be waiting. After such a sweet taste of real freedom, I was scared I wouldn't go the distance back in reality. I never wanted to let Cathy down after the sacrifice she'd made for me. She was the closest thing to a sister I'd ever known.

I got an office job. It paid well. Cathy did her beauty therapy and massage. She was never demanding or impatient at my pace of saving money. It wasn't one of my greatest fortes. We had so much fun together anyway, it didn't really matter. Our dream was there waiting for us, ready when we were ready.

About six months later Cathy met a guy and they fell in love. Alan was a gypsy too, like us. He was four years older than Cathy and he'd already travelled a lot, but he wanted more. Travelling only made you want more, I came to realise. Alan was really cool and funny. He'd make us laugh with his silly jokes, and he had the best adventure stories. We were going to make a great team travelling together, backpacking around the world. I knew I was the third wheel in their relationship, but they never made me feel like that. I was always included in their plans. Well, I was there first after all. It was me and Cathy from the start. Alan could take his place behind us. I thought, girls first.

Two months later I met George and we became an awesome foursome, at least in the beginning. The age difference wasn't really the biggest divide. Alan was more than 12 years older than George, and they were complete opposites. They found common ground in their humour, but the similarities stopped there. George wasn't a gypsy. He was more of a white-picket-fence-type guy. His good Greek upbringing taught him education was the key to happiness. Do well at school, get a degree and land a good job, preferably in government, before settling down with a mortgage and family. George was a gypsy's worst nightmare.

"You should go, darling. Fulfil your dream. I would never take that away from you. You'll have a ball with Cathy and Alan. I'll stay here, start my new job, and I'll be waiting when you get back," George said within a few months.

Of course I didn't believe it. I couldn't possibly trust his word. Some good Greek girl would snatch him up in a heartbeat and I was sure he wouldn't give me a second thought. She'd be so much better and smarter than me, a bank teller more than likely. She'd flirt ever so subtly, and he'd be unable to refuse her once she went in for the kill.

"It's okay, George, I'll stay. I won't leave you. I'm sure we'll travel one day…"

And so I stayed, did my best to conform. I tried not to blame George for my choices. Mostly my fight was internal. But if I were down and feeling depressed I'd take it out on him. I'd remind him of my sacrifice and he would feel bad, as if he'd forced me to stay and given me no choice at all. I couldn't control my meanness when I was feeling regretful.

Cathy and Alan were gone for 15 months or more. Their adventures would fill dozens of dinner parties for years to come. And every time they told a story, I'd think damn, that could've been me.

Cathy and Alan are still married. Our relationship is long distance now, and contact is much less frequent. It doesn't matter though. When we do speak it's as if no time has passed at all. I knew I picked that island for a good reason! If only my gut had spoken to me as clearly a year later.

When they first left, I really missed them. I wondered where George and I would go when we finally got started – Greece, Italy, Spain, Africa,

America. I couldn't wait to see where our travels would take us.

We went to Bali for our honeymoon, and that was it apart from a trip to the tourist theme parks on the Gold Coast years later. I like theme parks about as much as I like salt in an open wound. George got Bali belly on the honeymoon and spent most of it on the toilet. I got drunk in the pool and talked to strangers. I would listen intently to their travel stories and marvel at their free-spirited bravery. How I longed to be one of them, telling my own stories to people hanging on my every word, awestruck by my courage! As it turned out I would come to realise how courageous I really was, but it would have nothing to do with travelling.

CHAPTER NINE

A Lot Can Happen in a Minute

I sat on the closed toilet seat and glared at the white stick resting on the vanity as if the damned thing were a snake about to strike. I would have preferred that. The alternative had far worse consequences. Pink lines were scarier than any reptile bite.

Our little house in Leichhardt was our sanctuary. George and I had bought the cosy two-bedroom cottage a year after we married in the depths of a property slump and the highest interest rates in history. We didn't care. We were a career couple with well-paid jobs. We planned on a childless marriage, so we could afford to be extravagant.

I'd grown up in the leafy suburbs of Sydney's Inner West. Of all the suburbs I've lived in, the Inner West felt more like home than any other. The house was long and narrow, with a small living area and tiny kitchen. Provincial French doors opened out from the lounge into a courtyard hardly big enough for a small dog, let alone a German Shepherd.

Tara was our child. Her eyes masked a human soul. She was everything a dog stood for: loyal, devoted, and fiercely protective. The dogs of my past, if they could talk, would tell different stories of their upbringing. Lucky for Tara I was her master, not Dad. They were all ingrained in my psyche, but none as permanently as Tara.

She was a perfect substitute child, without the upheaval or sleepless nights. George and I loved our threesome life. It was the kind of contentment I'd longed for as a child. Our little family was the family I'd dreamed of.

Mum and Dad lived in the next suburb. Being close to Mum reassured me. Our relationship was strong again after my volatile teenage years. I'm sure Mum regretted even a daughter then. Little shits without balls — who would have thought it! When I was 16, probably thinking I was possessed by a demon, Mum kicked me out. I went up the road to a friend's house. We'd been friends since early childhood. Her mum was Mum's best friend. I think Mum knew I'd go there. I stayed for a week until things cooled down. Then I went back home, but I didn't want to. I had no choice. I was still at school. It was home or homeless, and the thought of sleeping on a park bench appealed to me a lot less than dealing with my frustrated mother. It wasn't Mum's fault. She had no idea why her daughter was full of rage, acting like a crazed bitch. How could she know? I never told her where the rage came from. I never would.

Mum worried that we'd overcommitted with the mortgage repayments. I assured her there was nothing to worry about, but Mum worried about most things: cancer, strokes, paralysis, drug side effects, car crashes, flying, aliens invading, and that a meteorite might crash into the Earth while we were sleeping. But mostly she worried about money.

CHAPTER NINE | A LOT CAN HAPPEN IN A MINUTE

"It's cute, love, but such a lot of money for something so small. What if you get pregnant and can't work? How will you pay the mortgage? Not to mention fitting a baby into this space. You can't swing a cat in here."

I almost spat my coffee in her face. She was serious.

"What? Pregnant? Mum, don't be ridiculous. No way. I'd cut my own arm off and feed it to Tara before I'd let that happen."

"Well, let's hope so, love. A baby's the last thing ya need."

Mum had that look in her eyes again, as if her soul carried the burden of ten lifetimes. Her dark brown pupils concealed a trove of secrets, the load undeniably heavy on her prematurely-aging face.

I'd often wondered if it was Uncle Jacko she was thinking about. Uncle Jacko was her youngest brother, or so we were always led to believe. When I was 12, Mum told me the truth. He was her son, our half-brother.

My reaction wasn't as dramatic as Greg and Tony's.

"Really, Mum? Ya kidding. That's so weird. Uncle Jacko is our brother? Boy, he's lucky he doesn't live with us."

Mum was 15 when she fell pregnant the first time she had sex. She told me she didn't really know what was happening. Her mother had never spoken about sex or anything like that. When Mum first got her period, she thought she was dying. It was her grandmother, not her mother, she went to for help. Her grandmother gave her a pile of old rags and told her "You'll need these now, Yvonne, every month of your life forevermore. No kissing boys now. You'll have a baby and that'll be good for none of us, understand?"

When the blood stopped Mum knew something was wrong. The boy who got her pregnant was gone. That's all she told me about him. Three months later she met Dad and they fell in love. He had a plan. They would marry in six months' time when he returned from his job – cutting sugarcane in far North Queensland. He gave her money for an abortion. Abortions were risky in the 1950s, but they decided it was best. Dad didn't want to raise another man's child, and Mum accepted that.

When Dad returned Uncle Jacko had just been born. My nan was furious when she'd found out what Dad had suggested. She hated him from that moment on. My grandfather took the money and drank it at the pub before Nan had a chance to buy food or pay bills.

So, a new plan was made. Nan would raise the baby, and everyone would think he was her youngest. Mum's baby sister was seven at the time, so it was possible. Nan and Grandfather separated. She'd had enough of his drinking. With another mouth to feed they couldn't afford to bankroll Grandfather's addiction any longer.

I swear Mum's childhood was straight from the pages of *Angela's Ashes*, without the religion.

Dad had strict conditions for the agreement, and for Nan. He would support Uncle Jacko financially, and contribute towards Mum's three younger siblings now that Grandfather was gone. He couldn't be trusted. In return for Dad's commitment, Nan had to keep the secret; everyone had to. Any children Mum and Dad had were not to know the truth ever, or the financial support would end.

Nan loved money too much to risk that. It was an offer she couldn't refuse. She still hated Dad regardless. He had shamed her daughter, and in turn her daughter had shamed her. I'm sure Nan was glad to get Mum off her hands, even if it meant she married a 'dago'.

Nan kept her promise, but she forgot to tell her best friend, June Campbell, to keep her big mouth shut. She blurted it out one day when Greg was at Nan's house. Greg and Tony loved Nan's house in the country. Nan's house was quiet and peaceful with no rules or beatings. It's no wonder Greg and Tony got so angry at the news. Uncle Jacko was the lucky one. I'll bet they wished they were half-brothers so they could live with Nan. All those years they had a big brother, an awesome big brother whom they idolised and looked up to as Uncle Jacko. Maybe they thought if Uncle Jacko had lived with us things might have been different for them. Things would have been different for Uncle Jacko, that's for sure.

Dad wasn't cruel to Uncle Jacko. In fact, he'd always spoken highly of him and his achievements. In their minds the unfairness of it all must have been catastrophic.

By the time the secret was revealed, it no longer mattered financially. Uncle Jacko was working by then, and the other siblings were grown and gone. Still, both Mum and Dad wanted to kill Nan for telling June Campbell in the first place. That kind of shocking news should have come from Mum.

"That bloody nosy bitch, June Campbell. She should mind her own business. Ya nanna's no friggin' better — like girls in a schoolyard when they get together. I could kill the bloody pair of 'em."

Mum didn't speak to Nan for a long time after that. Greg and Tony got over it eventually. I'd wonder if Dad ever regretted his decision. Uncle Jacko would've been a perfect son, unlike his own two. I'm not sure Dad ever considered how our upbringing might have affected us. Even when I watched him take his last breath many years later, I was still wondering.

I never asked Mum if that boy had raped her. My instincts told me not to.

Mum didn't want me to make the same mistake. She put me on the pill when I was 13. It was our little secret.

"Better to be safe than sorry, love. We don't want history repeating itself."

Mum made sure she didn't make the same mistakes as her mother. Mum taught me a lot about boys and sex and discretion.

"Reputation is everything, love. Ya don't wanna get a name for yourself. Sex is a natural part of growing up. You'll want to experiment. Don't be a floozy. No one likes a slut. Discretion is key."

My friends were envious of my open-minded mother letting me take the pill. I thought so too. I've come to realise it probably wasn't one of her better decisions.

Mum's words echoed from somewhere deep in the past as I sat there watching the stick change colour. Lives were about to be ruined.

Tara howled as sirens in the distance got louder. It was such a haunting sound. I jumped, and almost fell on the bathroom floor. It had to be a sign. Did Tara know everything was about to change too?

There they were, those solid pink lines. My heart sank as if I'd been pushed out of a plane without a parachute.

Oh fuck. Fuck. Fuck!

Like a scene from a porn movie, I knew when the mistake was made. It was unprotected sex in a moment of passion a month before. I'd stopped taking the pill a year earlier. I thought after 12 years I should give my body a break, and I'd heard the pill makes you fat. Stopping it might make me skinny. I decided to test the theory. What a fucking idiot.

It still didn't make complete sense. I was a 28-day girl. My cycle had never been a problem. I was at the end of a period that day, when passion interrupted the ironing. The advantages of a childless marriage are many: sex when and where the urge takes you was at the top of my list. The honeymoon can last for years without children stealing the peace.

How the hell did a rogue egg find its way into my uterus while I was still bleeding? I didn't know that was even possible!

I was three days late. That had never happened before, but an unfamiliar feeling in my gut unnerved me. I didn't want to believe I could be pregnant. I only bought the stick to satisfy the niggling. At worst I would have wasted some money.

The next thing I remember, I was in the courtyard, sitting on the ground leaning against the French doors. Tara lay next to me with her head in my lap. I stroked her head to comfort myself. Her sad, brown, human eyes looked up at me. I was pretty sure she was frowning. I had a feeling she was reading my mind.

"Oh, Tara girl, what am I going to do? This is bad, very bad news."

By the time George got home I'd made my decision. I knew he'd agree like he always did. The bad news spilled from my mouth before he'd even closed the front door. My mental checklist was already in order:

Call Mum now that I've told George
Call doctor first thing in the morning
Book abortion as soon as possible.

CHAPTER NINE | A LOT CAN HAPPEN IN A MINUTE

What I didn't expect was the look on George's face. And then what he did next.

He lunged at me with the strength of a bear and hugged me so tight I could hardly breathe. He kissed me, lips, cheeks, forehead, as he cupped my face in both hands. His eyes were full of love, as if he were Romeo and I were Juliet and we weren't dead after all. We were having a baby.

Oh my God, he wants it!

I pushed back, breaking his embrace. Sensing my distress, his face returned to an acceptable look in response to the bad news I'd just delivered.

"I'm sorry, darling. I just thought, well, I just can't believe it. What do you want to do?" His voice was gentle, but it didn't soothe me.

"What do you think I want to do? Why are you even asking me that? I don't want a baby. We agreed. We can't have a baby." My voice rose to new decibels with each word.

"Don't be upset, darling. Whatever you want I'll support you. Either way, we'll get through this."

He came to hug me again, but I pushed him away.

"Either way?" My voice was nearing fever pitch. "There is no either way. There's one way. Tara is the only baby we need, and the only kind I want."

The next day I booked the abortion.

When I told Mum, I really wasn't expecting her response.

"Love, all I'm saying is, things happen for a reason. I know you never wanted it, but abortion is a big decision. There's no goin' back after that. I'm not judging you, love. God knows, I'd do the same, but… Are ya sure that's what George really wants?"

Had the world gone mad? Had Mum? Was this some new kind of wisdom? If it was, I didn't like it. There was something in her undertone that unhinged me. Shouldn't it be about what I really want? Wasn't this my decision? It was my body, my life, my future, and now I had to consider George's feelings? What the hell was going on?

I felt like I'd been kicked in the guts. Was it all a huge conspiracy? Had Mum and George been waiting all along for this moment just to see if I'd crack? Had I been fooled into thinking we were all on the same page about having children?

"Don't be upset, love. I'm just trying to help you make the right decision, that's all. You know I'll support you either way."

There were those bloody words again.

I cut the conversation short. I couldn't stand another minute of the madness. Misery was unfurling in my mind, thanks to Mum. The next 24 hours were like a scene from *The Terminator*. Something big and scary was chasing me. My senses felt like a broken GPS. Instinct pulled at my core while my brain went in another direction. My gut and head weren't in sync. I'd never felt so indecisive about which way to go.

By morning I'd made my decision. I had to go with my heart. Deep down it knew instinctively the right thing to do. Any other decision would eventually tear at it. With so much scar tissue already, my heart might not cope. And besides, I couldn't bear looking into George's eyes for the rest of our lives seeing the truth behind them. The wonder of what could have been, and the deep well of untapped love that never had a chance. I couldn't do that to him. If I deprived him of his one true gift of life, I imagined his eyes would eventually cloud over and that's when he would leave me.

I loved him. It was a baby conceived in passion, not rape. So I made the right decision – for George, for his baby, and for my heart.

George beamed like a floodlight in the darkness. He had a new purpose, a new role. And Mum, even though she was already a grandmother to Tony's two girls, took the news as if it were a lottery win. A daughter having a baby was different to a son, she told me. Mothers and daughters were connected in ways boys will never know.

"Let's hope to God it's a girl. That's all I pray."

Mum wasn't the only one praying.

When I was alone in the house I'd sit with Tara and mope. She was

CHAPTER NINE | A LOT CAN HAPPEN IN A MINUTE

the silent witness to my prayers.

"Please God, make me have a miscarriage. Give this baby to someone else. Someone who really wants it. Someone who knows how to be a mother. Someone better than me."

Then I'd pray for forgiveness for my unthinkable prayers.

When my window of opportunity to terminate closed, I took on a new persona. I'd be brave and strong and capable. I was having a baby. I was going to be a mother whether I liked it or not. I had to shut the fuck up and get on with it. But as my unborn baby grew, so too did my shadow. It had always been there, birthed long ago in childhood. In the darkest times I would feel it, like a living, breathing entity. And it had come to life once again.

CHAPTER TEN

A World Gone Mad

I stared down at the two swollen puffy things resting on the coffee table. They looked like they belonged on a Telly Tubby, not on a human.

Four months pregnant, and I'd already gained 20 kilos. The remaining five months held no excitement. I was going to be one of those women so big that people won't know if I'm pregnant or obese.

My gynaecologist would scold me at every visit, warning me of the probable dangers of being so overweight. She'd struggle with the blood pressure cuff around my chubby arm.

"Marcy, if your blood pressure gets any higher you won't have a choice. A caesarean will be your only option. And we have to try and avoid that now, don't we?"

Do we? I assumed it was rhetorical. I was counting on a caesarean. Who in their right mind looks forward to a supersized vagina? I'd seen the videos in prenatal class. An episiotomy was like a scene from *Game of Thrones*. I didn't want to star in that show. Women should see the videos before they get pregnant. There'd be a lot less people in the world.

I didn't care how fat I got. It was the only time in my life I could eat without guilt. I had an excuse, a real excuse. Eating for two meant I could eat often and plenty. By the time I was full term I'd gained 46 kilos and weighed 138 kilos. I would've felt at home in the ocean with my orca relatives!

Pregnancy was a form of torture, I decided. Women who glowed in pregnant glory were liars. My stretched skin was the only thing glowing! I could've seen my reflection in my feet had I been able to get close enough.

The women in my class were nesters and gatherers – they were real mothers-to-be. I faked it. I waited for my maternal instincts. Maybe if I clocked up enough pregnant hours they'd seep into my psyche, magically enlightening me. I organised the prep work, cot, bassinet, changing table – everything – long before my due date. Just in case I got brownie points for efficiency.

What I lacked maternally I made up for domestically. I could never be found guilty of not having things in order.

The spare room blossomed into a nursery. Every new addition was a pale shade of peach, lime or yellow. I had subconsciously (or consciously) created a girl's room before I knew the sex of the baby.

"What if it's a boy?" George would ask with each new girly addition.

"It's not a boy. I know it's not. I can feel it."

If I kept saying it out loud it would be true.

"But what if it's not? Then we're in trouble."

"If it's not, I'm sending it back. I'll want a refund on that delivery!"

And we'd joke about it.

Deep down I'd feel the twinge. If I were wrong, I'd be shattered. How would I fake it? I wasn't sure I could pull it off. I didn't have Tony's

CHAPTER TEN | A WORLD GONE MAD

courage, or his acting skills.

I'd push the thought aside as quickly as it occurred. I didn't want to jinx myself. The thought alone might turn that embryo into the wrong sex.

At 20 weeks my instincts did a virtual high five. I was having a girl. Had it been possible I would have jumped up from that bed and done a fairy dance around the nurse. It wasn't. My growing body was relentless in its effort to create a human. It seemed to get bigger by the day. I'd vent to George and Mum, but to everyone else I faked it. I couldn't wait to get that baby out of me so I could feel normal again.

"Careful what ya wish for, love. Trust me, you'll be wishing it was back in there soon enough!"

Sometimes I was certain Mum's wisdom came from a packet of Weet-Bix. As if I'd ever wish that. Women who do it more than once have rocks in their heads. That was my conclusion about pregnancy.

The only time I felt comfort, not so surprisingly, was submerged in the ocean. George would take me to secluded beaches where fewer people were likely to see me. Public pools were out of the question. I didn't want young children to stare and point at the circus freak waddling into the water.

My last trimester was the summer of 1990/91, the hottest summer in decades unluckily for me. We didn't have air-con. I spent my last three months trying to keep dry. Sweaty rolls of flesh are not a fun time. I swore that I would lose all that weight before her first birthday. That didn't happen.

I'd stay in the water for hours, floating weightlessly, no pain. I'd gaze up at the summer sky, cloud guessing the shapes as they materialised then dissolved as quickly as they appeared, like we did when we were kids.

I could've stayed in the cool, delicious, blue forever. If a shark came I wouldn't scream or struggle – I'd let it eat me. What a feast, lucky shark. At least then I'd never have to feel gravity again. I'd be free of all burdens, past, present, and future.

When my waters broke at 1am they woke me up. I didn't know if I'd wet the bed or I was sweating profusely. I felt no pain. I wasn't in labour. But then I realised, and my mind went into action. I wasn't prepared for my mental breakdown. Mum's words echoed. I should have been more strategic about my wishes. I didn't want it out now. I wanted it to stay there forever. I didn't even mind being a circus freak for the rest of my life. I wasn't ready for reality.

Oh, dear God, help me.

As it turned out, my doctor was on leave – probably holidaying in the Bahamas on our hefty fees! The audacity; why couldn't she take a break after my due date? All that money for private privileges and I end up in the public health system anyway!

The emergency doctor on duty was very sorry, but I would need a caesarean. I pretended to be disappointed. I thought it was the right reaction. The sisterhood from prenatal class would be mortified if they knew my truth – I couldn't wait for that jab in my spine.

Fill 'er up, doc, as many drugs as possible. Feel free to give me a full paralysis. Thanks for your assistance. I didn't dare say it out loud in case one of the sisterhood were in the next room.

"I'm sorry, Marcia, but the epidural isn't working," a bewildered anaesthetist said. "It's quite a… dense area. It can be difficult when we can't feel the spine. I'm really sorry. It happens. You'll have to have a general, I'm afraid."

My translation: Lady, you are way too fat for this needle. It's never going to happen. What the hell have you been eating anyway – a village of small children?

I was disoriented in my anaesthetic haze. I was back at the beach, in the water, rising and falling with the momentum of each wave. And then it happened. The shark came from nowhere and bit my body in half. Was I dead? I mustn't be dead. Surely there's no pain in the afterlife, not like this excruciating bullshit? That bloody shark was supposed to eat all of me, not leave me there limbless.

CHAPTER TEN | A WORLD GONE MAD

I tried to reach down to feel what was missing. The simple motion of moving my arms caused my stomach to flip. I was going to vomit.

"Help, please help me," I heard myself whisper.

The sharp stab in my leg ripped me back into the present. The nausea subsided in an instant. Disaster averted, thank God. I wasn't sure how I'd vomit with half a body.

I drifted in and out of the ruckus, and then I saw George through the slits of my eyes. It was quiet then. He was looking down at something and didn't notice I'd woken up. I followed his line of sight.

"Why is that baby here?" My voice was groggy.

My temporary amnesia was back. Shouldn't I be in the shark bite ward, or somewhere more appropriate than amongst babies?

George's head jerked in my direction and his face lit up, beaming at me. He stood to kiss me, and his hand gently caressed my face. "It's our daughter, darling. Isn't she beautiful?"

I'd never heard that tone in George's voice before. I wondered what the hell was happening.

Then someone slapped me on the face.

"Oh my God, I had a baby. That's our baby? But she's so tiny – how did that come out of me?"

As I tried to sit up, a sledgehammer came down on me. I let out a sound like I'd just been shot. Moving wasn't an option, I realised. I looked down at my belly. Still the same size. How was that possible? Shouldn't I be miraculously skinny? Disappointment wrapped its ugly arms around me. All that pain for nothing, except a baby.

Morgan was 6 pounds 14 ounces, a tiny wrinkly thing that looked more like the runt of a litter. Beautiful wasn't the first word to mind. Not so for George. His face looked celestial, like he could hear all the angels in heaven singing. I heard nothing. But worse than the pain and my deafness was what I couldn't feel.

George, as if he knew what I was thinking, reached down to pick her up and give her to me. The first touch would make the maternal connection for sure.

"Here, darling, hold her?"

"No," I said in terror. "Don't touch her. You'll wake her up and then what'll we do?"

Mum walked into the room. Seeing her made my eyes fill with tears, and they silently rolled down my cheeks.

"Oh love, don't cry. It's just those bloody hormones runnin' wild. It'll be okay. You'll be fine in time."

Mum smiled lovingly and rested her arm near my pillow. She leaned towards me, stroked my hair and kissed the top of my head like she did when I was a little girl. And I wished then we could swap places. Mum could be the new mother. She'd know what to do. I could be old and wise, with the scars of my history behind me.

Hospital stays were long in those days, especially after a caesarean. Mum and George rarely left my side, except at night when the nurses took the babies to the nursery. The other mothers didn't like that time of day, when their babies would leave their side. I wished the nurses would take my baby all day and night so I could sleep away the pain, and not face the bleakness of my failures.

Not like the other mothers, who shone even brighter than before. They were naturals, born to it. They went about their duties effortlessly. I wondered if I were the only female without motherly instincts. I couldn't even breastfeed. It hurt like razor blades cutting at my nipples. I hated it. I imagine that's how dairy cows feel every day of their lives. I felt humiliation and shame, not joy. It wasn't just the breastfeeding. My belly hurt with the weight of the baby, small as she was. She felt more like a bowling ball than the runt of the litter. An episiotomy took on a new appreciation then. I'd definitely wished for the wrong things. I hadn't planned for bottle-feeding. It seemed like a lot of extra work. But there was an upside.

"Just think, love, me and George can help if she's bottle-fed. We can all take turns. Take the pressure off. I can even take the little munchkin on weekends to give you a break. Wouldn't that be nice, love?"

CHAPTER TEN | A WORLD GONE MAD

Yes, it would, Mum. That would be very nice.

It was date night in hospital. It was customary back then. The nurses would babysit while the parents went out to dinner, a kind of last night of freedom before going home. Imagine that. Decades later, new millennial mothers wouldn't believe us. They'd be lucky to have one night in hospital, and they'd be happy about it.

I couldn't comprehend the thought of going out in public. I'd been in a bubble for two weeks and it felt like two months. I wasn't the same person as when I'd arrived. And the world wasn't either. It had gone mad while I'd been in that other realm. I decided we'd go to Mum and Dad's instead of a real date. It was all I could manage.

As we walked through the doors of King George's Hospital, nothing looked familiar. I'd walked Missenden Road a hundred times or more. I thought of all those Saturday mornings when we were kids, dragging Mum's trolley up and down that road from Forest Lodge to Newtown and back again as Greg and Tony whinged the entire way home. It seemed like someone else's memory, surely not mine.

The late daylight-saving sun cast dull shadows over the urban backdrop. A muggy, warm breeze caressed me as if I'd just stepped out the doors of winter. I stopped to feel the thawing, unaware I'd been frozen inside the cool air-conditioned ward. George felt the tug on his arm and slowed to a stop with me. I turned my head skyward and closed my eyes to take it in, the unmistakeable heat of a January night in Sydney. The air was thick with the sweat of three million bodies. The stratosphere held it down, unable to release it through the invisible layers of smog.

It was seconds or minutes – I don't remember how long we stood there, but then we continued the shuffle. My body felt like a great green turtle pushing upwards on a sandy beach, carrying a load of a hundred eggs ready to be laid. The physical struggle seemed irrelevant. My mind was the real problem.

Peak hour traffic crawled alongside us; another normal day in reality. A packed 412 bus stopped at the pedestrian crossing to let us go. I looked at all the poker faces on their way home after a hard day at work. I wondered what they were going home to. Did they have babies waiting, or were they power couples living in childfree zones, where I used to live?

An overwhelming sense of doom filtered through me, as if every cell in my body were absorbing the pollution and choking me with poison fumes.

I didn't want to go back to the hospital. I wanted to leave the baby there with the kind babysitting nurses. Maybe one of them could take her home, give her a life she deserved. They'd know what to do; they had maternal instincts. At least then the baby would have a chance. What chance would she have with an imposter mother like me?

The voice in my head was screaming as it looped in circles repeating the chant. I held back my tears somehow. I wasn't sure George would know what to do with them. But when I saw Mum standing at the stove stirring spaghetti, and the familiar aroma filled my nostrils and every pore of my body with nostalgia, that was my breaking point.

"Oh love, come on now, don't cry, my chicken."

I was in Mum's embrace then. Her body was a wall of comfort. The smell of her hair against my cheek was like a field of wild flowers right there in the kitchen. I didn't want to let go. I was safe in Mum's arms. She would protect me. Only Mum knew how.

"It's normal to feel this way. All new mums feel it, they just don't let on. Trust me, love, I know all about post-natal depression. God knows I do."

Post-natal depression hadn't been a thought and now Mum put it there, all out in the open. It couldn't be true. Hormones had nothing to do with what I was feeling. It was me. It was just who I was, who I'd always been, except now I had a baby on top of it.

"Ah bullshit, woman," Dad piped up, overhearing us from the next room as he sat on his throne at the head of the dining table.

"It's all in ya head. Ya think too much. It's a babe. People have dem every day. Stop ya worryin'. Nothin' to worry about."

CHAPTER TEN | A WORLD GONE MAD

End of topic. And that was the extent of Dad's wisdom.

If we'd had a proper father/daughter relationship I would have punched him in the arm. I would have been comfortable enough to do that. And I would have said something like

"Oh, shut up, Dad, what the hell would you know anyway? You're just a stupid man."

But I wasn't ready to die, not at the hands of my father. I ignored him instead. I was brave enough to do that at least by then. I wasn't a little girl any more.

CHAPTER ELEVEN

Dogsville

Wikipedia says the dog is a propitious symbol, standing for faithfulness, companionship, protectiveness, loyalty, watchfulness, courage, and skill in the hunt. A powerful totem, dogs display blind love and obedience. They symbolise the sun, wind, and fire and are believed to share the afterlife with humans…

Dad would've called Wikipedia a load of bullshit. He didn't believe in the afterlife or trust the printed word, most of it anyway. It was false information to brainwash idiots (i.e. the general population). To Dad, dogs had to serve a purpose. The only way a dog could be a totem would be to tie it to a pole and beat it into them. Not unlike wayward sons.

Naughty things needed to be disciplined. Words were secondary to my father. Still, when he used words they were harsh, and the harsher they were the better they'd stick. I could never decide which was worse, the physical or the mental anguish. My brothers could answer that better than me. I knew one thing for sure. The dogs couldn't tell me. But their eyes held the grief of their circumstance. That was easy to see.

Dad would bring stray dogs home and Mum would always complain.

"Gary, for God's sake do ya have to bring every mongrel home that ya find on the street? They could be vicious. They'll bite the kids."

"Ah shud up, woman. Vicious me arse. I'll train dem quick smart."

That could only mean one thing, and it didn't involve doggy treats for paying attention.

The unfortunate strays had crossed the wrong street on those days. Dumped and forgotten, probably gifts no longer wanted by stupid people who hadn't realised puppies grew up. I wondered how they could do it. Their heartless actions had most likely condemned the poor dogs to a horrible fate. They could starve to death or be mistreated if the wrong hands got hold of them.

Dogs weren't pets in Dad's eyes. He'd train them as work companions for his security guard business, and to rid the yard of stray cats.

One of my earliest memories involves cats rather than dogs. Pregnant cats would wander into our yard, before any dogs were there, looking for a safe place to have their kittens. We'd hear them meowing in the rubble in the back shed. Dad was a hoarder. He collected old window frames, steel gates, kitchen sinks, bricks and timber from demolished building sites, and an accumulation of other useless things just in case he'd need them one day. Mum would vent her frustration at every new addition.

"It's like bloody Steptoe an' Son out there, friggin' fool, as if there isn't enough shit in the yard already."

It was a perfect environment for cats to hide from predators.

"Those bus-tard cats an' their kittens."

CHAPTER ELEVEN | DOGSVILLE

Dad slammed the back door as he raced down the yard into the shed, a tornado of debris being hurled in every direction in his search for the culprits.

"Can I keep one of the kittens, Mummy?"

I stood next to Mum at the kitchen sink while she washed vegetables. I rarely left her side, especially when Dad was around. I would hide behind her skirt if he looked at me, thinking it made me invisible.

"No, love, you can't. Ya father won't let you do that. And besides, you're allergic to cats. Now go to ya room please."

Mum wiped her hands on her apron and hugged me to her side. I wrapped my arms around her legs to return the hug. She bent down and kissed the top of my head, like she always did.

"But Mummy, I want to see the kittens. I'm not 'ergic."

I didn't know what allergic was, but I was sure I didn't have it. I'd never seen newborn kittens before and I didn't want to miss that event.

"I said go. Now off."

Mum gently pushed me in the direction of the door. I turned around to protest again, but I saw that look on her face. I didn't know what it was, but I knew it wasn't happy. She saw me hesitate.

"Trust me, love, you don't wanna see the kittens. Now off you go please."

I didn't understand why Mum said that. I just told her I wanted to see them. I sensed it was better to do what she said. I wanted to be a good girl, not like my brothers who were always bad. But I was stubborn from the start. I didn't go to my room. You couldn't see the backyard from my bedroom window, and I just wanted a quick peek.

I stood at the dining room window, hiding behind the long thick curtains, veiled by the white tulle that hung in the centre. I would often play there, gathering the tulle around me and pretending I was a bride on her wedding day. And through the white haze I saw the kittens.

One by one, as Dad found them, he drowned them in a bucket of water. He put them in an old potato sack and put it in the garbage bin.

I wanted to look away, but I couldn't. And with each dunking I felt it inside me. As if I were the mother cat and they were my babies. When he finished and headed back towards the house I came unstuck. My legs somehow got me to my room before anyone noticed.

I hugged Snoopy to my chest and quietly cried into his fluffy white fur. He may have been a stuffed toy dog, but he was my protector. Snoopy and I shared a lot during childhood and he was the only one I could confess all the crimes I'd witnessed to, including the drowning of kittens.

Whenever Dad would mention the bastard cats, I'd run to my room. Mum never had to tell me again.

The problem with puppies on the other hand – which Dad never drowned as far as I know – was they liked to dig in the garden. Dad had no patience for puppies' antics. And their size didn't exempt them from discipline.

Dad's garden was like an urban oasis. I assumed it was his only pleasure as he spent so much time in it. Our yard wasn't big, but every inch held a pot plant of some description. From delicate flowers to staghorn ferns, and fruit trees of every variety. Dad had them all.

A narrow dirt path lined the parameter down one side of the house. A row of bricks held the dirt in its boundary. The rest of the yard was concrete. There wasn't a spare inch in that garden. Any area that seemed sparse had random stalks of parsley or basil. Dad didn't like to waste space. Our yard was like a tiny part of the Amazon, right there in suburbia. Dad's prized veggie garden at the very rear of the yard was the only patch fenced off with chicken wire. Everything else was free range as far as puppies were concerned. They'd learn to stop digging eventually. Their natural instincts didn't stand a chance of flourishing. Their master's mood became their first and only instinct.

Dad grew so much fruit and veg, you'd think he was preparing for another Great Depression. The whole neighbourhood would benefit. No one went hungry in our area. Dad was very generous in that way. It often confused me. I assumed Dad didn't like people very much. He hardly ever spoke to anyone at length, if at all. Idle chit-chat annoyed him, unlike Mum. He didn't like people knowing his business and he'd often scold Mum if she said too much to anyone. Yet he could be so generous to a stranger and so cruel to his own family, and to the poor innocent dogs.

I'd hear them from my room, those gut-wrenching yelps coming from the yard. My stomach would be knotted like a hundred miles of tangled fishing line. My heart hurt with sound as if I, too, could feel each blow. I'd weep and cover my ears to try and muffle the sound, but even Snoopy's long ears didn't work as a buffer.

I did the unthinkable once, when I was about nine years old. I ran out into the yard hoping Dad would stop if he saw me. I'd never been that brave before. Why I thought he'd stop on account of me, I don't know. I must have been out of my mind. When I saw the scene before me I couldn't help the words escaping.

"Dad, please stop. You're hurting him."

I couldn't believe I had actually said it out loud.

Dad's head snapped in my direction. I swear his eyes seemed to glow red as his mouth twisted into a snarl. "Shud up, ya stupid girl, or you be next."

At least he stopped for a second while he yelled at me. Mum came running.

"Gary, for Christ's sake stop it, ya gunna kill that poor bloody animal."

Mum's attempted action only made him worse. He ignored her and continued the beating. She was probably next, a lesson for interfering. I ran back to my room to hug Snoopy. I didn't want to witness another beating that day.

Then one day a new stray arrived. Dad always named the dogs Danny, Max, or Blacky, but they also answered to Dumbo. He would recycle the names as they came and went. For example, there was big Danny, little Danny, stupid Danny, old Danny and so on. That's how we knew which dog was which. But Dad gave the new stray a different name.

He called him Nigga.

"Oh Gary, ya can't call him that for God's sake. What will the neighbours think?"

As if Dad gave a shit about what neighbours thought, or about political correctness. It was the early 70s. The violent human rights uprising in black America had been raging for years. Dad didn't care. If people could still call him a dago and a wog, he could call his dog Nigga.

"I call him what I want. It'sa good name. He look like a Nigga. I bet he be a bus-tard to train."

None of us wanted to think about that.

Nigga was a German Shepard cross. You would think his name implied his colour, but he wasn't totally black. His fur was a swirl of different shades of grey and brindle, an unusual colour and a very handsome dog. We finally worked out what he was crossed with: Nigga was mostly dingo.

'The dingo (*Canis lupus dingo*) is a wild dog found in Australia. Its exact ancestry is debated, but dingoes are generally believed to be descended from semi-domesticated dogs from East or South Asia, which returned to a wild lifestyle when introduced to Australia. The dingo has physical characteristics that are quite different to the domestic dog. It is equipped with strong jaws, a large head, alert, almond-shaped eyes, erect ears, narrow chest and shoulders, a proportionate body and a bottle-shaped tail for balance. It has all the characteristics for a successful hunter. Dingoes have demonstrated great adaptability to the harsh Australian conditions. Typical coat colours are yellow-ginger, but can be tan, black or white, or an occasional brindle; albinos have also been seen. All purebred dingoes have white hair on their feet and tail tip. Unlike most other breeds, dingoes do not have dewclaws. The dingo is a breed that has never been fully domesticated. It is almost never kept as a companion...'

No matter how many beatings Nigga received, he showed no fear or intimidation. He didn't run and hide at the sight of Dad like all the

CHAPTER ELEVEN | DOGSVILLE

other dogs. He'd follow Dad around the yard and would sit near him at the edge of the garden while Dad tended his plants. Dad seemed to have a newfound respect for his companion. Nigga's beatings stopped. It meant something. I'd never seen that before.

I would play with him when Dad wasn't around, even though I wasn't supposed to. Nigga was clever. If he saw Dad he'd ignore me as if suddenly I wasn't there. All his attention was for his real master. Our frivolous relationship was our little secret.

Nigga was fickle when it came to visitors. He'd happily let people in our front gate. His tail would wag, and he'd even let them pat the top of his head as they walked past on their way to the front door.

But when it was time for them to leave, Nigga became a dingo.

The visitors would get halfway between the house and front gate and Nigga would appear from somewhere deep in the plants, blocking their exit. He'd stand tense on all fours as if hunting prey, then bare his teeth and growl, a deep guttural growl that would make all the hairs prickle on your skin.

"Nigga, down boy, down. Stop being silly now. Hush up."

I'd dart in front of the visitor and grab Nigga's collar. I'd hold him close to my body and pat the top of his head. The part that wasn't dingo would kick in. His trance broken by my touch, he'd lick my hand as if none of that had just happened.

Mum didn't like Nigga's unpredictability. She wouldn't hang out the washing unless he was behind the closed gate in the front yard, or tied up. I knew he wouldn't do anything to his family. I wasn't afraid, even though sometimes he'd look at me with the weirdest look on his face.

"Niggaaa, are you being silly? Stop lookin' at me like I'm ya dinner. Good Nigga boy."

My baby voice would reach his eyes and he'd wag his tail, normal again.

Dad thought it was a great joke when the door-knocking Jehovah's came. Every new set of preachers made the same mistake. You'd think they would have reported their findings to their successors. NB: Do not enter 28 Junction Street... Ferocious dog inside and overly aggressive owner. Not worth the conversion.

Then one day everything changed for Nigga and me.

Mum's scream triggered the series of events.

"Gary, hurry, it's Nigga!"

I ran from the back yard to the front gate. Mum was out on the footpath where a crowd had gathered. Nigga had been hit by a car and his lifeless body was in the middle of the road covered in blood.

Dad leaped over the fence like an Olympic high jumper. He scooped Nigga's limp body up into his arms as if it were weightless.

Nigga was barely breathing. Dad carried him inside and laid him down on the concrete under the carport in the front yard. He kneeled beside him and stroked his head with such tenderness I was taken aback by the sight of it. I'd never seen my father be gentle with anything. And when I thought I saw tears in Dad's eyes, an overwhelming feeling to run and hug him almost got the better of me. Instead I did the worse thing I possibly could have.

We were all hovering, watching Nigga's breathing get slower and slower. The sight of my secret pet dying in front of me was more than my brain could process.

"Dad, is he gunna be all right? Can you do something? Can you help him? Dad, you have to help him. Please do something..."

It was the most words I'd ever spoken to my father. They were hysterical and commanding – even Mum shot a look at me as if I'd just slapped him.

And as that abominable last word came out of my mouth I threw myself on top of Nigga, sobbing uncontrollably into his blood-soaked fur.

I was thrown into the air, the force so strong I must have landed 20 feet away. My body came down with a loud thud. Uncovered skin, legs, knees, elbows, scraped along the concrete, blood everywhere. I wasn't sure if it was my blood or Nigga's. I felt no physical pain, not then, but on the inside my body seized up in terror at the realisation that my father had just hit me.

"Shud up, you stupid girl. Can't you see he's dying? How I fix him, you idiot?" Dad roared at me. Everyone in the street would've seen and heard. His eyes burned into me as he spat out the worst of it.

"Did you leave da gate open? Did you do dis?"

I thought my body would self-combust. I wanted to melt into the concrete, disappear out of sight of all the accusing eyes upon me. If only I were invisible.

"Gary, for Christ sake, don't speak to her like that. She's just a kid. Can't ya see she's upset? She loved the damned dog too, ya know."

Mum's bravery in my defence gave me no comfort.

I bolted from the scene like the guilty party of the hit-and-run. I had to get to Snoopy before I was swallowed up into the abyss of that horrific moment. But even Snoopy couldn't help me. He didn't know if I'd left the gate open either. He didn't think so. He was sure I wouldn't do that. We all knew Nigga couldn't be trusted in public.

But what if Dad were right and I had killed Nigga? I was just a stupid girl after all, doing unthinkable things like speaking when I shouldn't and throwing myself onto dying dogs. I probably did leave the gate open.

And I imagined then Dad wished it was me dying in our front yard, not Nigga. Not the only thing he'd ever loved.

I made a pact with Snoopy. One day if I ever had a little girl of my own I'd never speak to her as if she were nothing, and I'd never make her feel she'd be better off dead.

CHAPTER TWELVE

Three's a Crowd

'd almost given up on maternal instincts, convinced I must be missing that chromosome. What I lacked in motherly connection to my daughter, George made up for in his new role as her daddy.

Mum was right. Bottle-feeding was the answer to world peace, but I wasn't prepared for the madness of sleep deprivation. They don't tell you that in the videos.

George took over the night feeds, even when he went back to work. Instead of feeling relieved of the burden I felt a new level of failure. What kind of mother doesn't get up for her baby? What kind of magical father does most of the newborn work?

"Sweetheart, I don't mind. I love it. The nights are my favourite part of the whole day. It's just me and Morgan in the quietness. I stare into her beautiful face while she's drinking her bottle. I don't want her to stop. I just love her so much. Oh darling, don't you just love her so much?"

I knew the right answer, but the truth was I didn't even know if I liked her. I'd smile and say nothing. How could George have more maternal instinct than me?

Those first few weeks were like a plane crash. I was the only survivor, dazed and confused, roaming aimlessly, all sense of direction lost in unfamiliar terrain. Not even home felt real, as if George had moved us into a new house while I'd been in hospital.

Of all the dark times in my life, I've never felt less human than in those early months of motherhood. I was like a ghost in my disassociation – lost between dimensions, not knowing what was real and what wasn't.

My wound wasn't healing quickly enough. It probably took longer with so many layers to bind. The pain lingered as the weight of my belly dragged it down. It was nothing compared to the turmoil in my mind.

I'd spend the days doing what was expected of me. I somehow got things done and Morgan didn't suffer for my shortcomings. It was the strangest thing, like she was someone else's child and I'd been given the enormous responsibility of taking care of her. As if an estranged sister had died unexpectedly and left her baby to me. It was an overwhelming task, but I didn't want to fail my dead sister.

Mum came to help whenever she could. She made good on her promise, taking Morgan on regular weekends to give us a break. It gave George a break. The weekends were his domain when it came to his daughter. He didn't want the break, but he knew Mum loved her time with Morgan. They were both better parents than I could ever be.

Even Dad had a special connection with Morgan. He would hold her and make baby noises like a proper grandfather. The sight of my father smiling and acting ridiculous stunned me each time I witnessed it. Where

CHAPTER TWELVE | THREE'S A CROWD

was that man when I was growing up? Even Dad was maternal, how was that possible? Was I the only failure in this whole bizarre scenario? I expected more from Dad.

"What's with da bottle feeding? Dat's not natural. Give da child some proper food, stupid woman."

That would've been something familiar.

"You'll understand one day, love. It's different being the grandparent. The love ya feel for that child, well, there's nothing on this Earth like it. You don't feel that with your own kids. You still love them, but ya too busy trying to survive and get through all the crap. You appreciate a lot more when ya older. Trust me on that one, love."

Mum might as well have been talking Klingon. I had no idea what she was on about. By the time I understood she was long gone and I wouldn't be able to share with her the depth of that understanding, the recognition of such an unexplainable love.

Morgan was three months old when the unbelievable happened. She was propped up by a mountain of pillows on our bed, intently watching me fold washing. I'd noticed her awareness was changing, as if the world were coming into focus. Everything she looked at seemed like a technicoloured marvellous creation. I envied her wonder. To me, everything was dull and colourless. Each morning I'd wake up with the same heaviness, as if I had to contend with a tedious baby for yet another day. When in reality it wasn't like that at all, looking back.

Morgan was a quiet baby – mellow I'd say now, not then. I wondered if, subliminally, she knew it was best not to aggravate her mother. Maybe she knew I couldn't cope with a problem baby. That might push me over the edge to the real dark side, and who would be her mother then? I spent most of my time wishing her away. If only she were eating solids. If only she were walking. If only she could talk. If only. If only. If. Bloody. Only.

Mum would warn me about that too. It was always the same.

"Careful what ya wish for, love. In a blink she'll be a teenager and, trust me, then you'll be wishing you were back here again."

101

Mum really did have the wisdom of a goldfish sometimes. What sane person would wish to be back in baby land when freedom was just up ahead? I hoped Morgan would leave home as soon as she was old enough. With any luck she'd inherit my wannabe gypsy spirit and travel the world. Any lingering free spirit I'd had was dead inside me by then, long gone to another life.

George exploded into the bedroom. We didn't hear him coming. He dived on the bed and slid along the quilt cover. Washing spilled everywhere. His face stopped inches from Morgan's and he let out a loud "Ahh boo!"

I was about to lose my shit for the mess he'd just made when Morgan started laughing. It was a deep belly laugh, her head thrown back, eyes closed, out of control giggling. She reminded me of a baby buddha. She looked like the caricature from the toothpaste ad on TV, Flip-top head.

George and I looked at each other, startled at her first ever display of humour. We burst out laughing too. My cheeks hurt with the effort. It had been so long since I'd even cracked a proper smile, let alone laughed. We were in hysterics. George kept going. He didn't need much encouragement to act like a clown, and now that he had a new audience, things were about to get very silly. He was in his element with a new playmate to entertain. At last, someone to appreciate his antics. Our Flip-top smiling daughter had come alive.

As I watched each new wave of happiness roll out of her, a switch inside me flicked. It was instant. I scooped her up into my arms and started bouncing her on my hip. Her giggling was infectious as we danced around the room.

I saw her then for the first time. I felt like I'd been sucked out of a dark void into the light. The warm glow of it seeped down into me and she was there then, in my heart.

So this is what maternal feels like.

It was telepathic. And as she looked into my eyes I knew she felt it too.

CHAPTER TWELVE | THREE'S A CROWD

My first hurdle was over. I was finally a real mother. But then heartbreak came when Tara did the unthinkable.

When we'd first arrived home from hospital Tara came to investigate. She took her time sniffing the capsule, and then looked up at me.

Is that it? That's what all the fuss is about? I don't get it, I imagined her saying.

Lost in the chaos of those early months, I became oblivious to Tara's needs. She'd been pushed aside for the new baby. I did the thing I promised her I'd never do. It was the worst thing I could have done.

One day a few months later as I hung out the washing and Morgan was at my feet sleeping in her capsule, I heard a growl unlike anything I'd heard before. The harshness of that sound broke the peacefulness of that sunny autumn day. I felt my skin tingle as goose bumps came up – like a sudden cold breeze brushed past me. I looked down and saw Tara's snout inches from Morgan's sleeping face. She was in attack mode.

"Tara, no!" My reflexes were automatic. In a split second the capsule was high in the air, in my arms, as if it and Morgan weighed nothing. My residual abdominal pain was forgotten.

Tara snapped at the underbelly of the capsule. As I pulled back she realised what she'd done. Her ears drooped down to the side of her head. Her body seemed to shrink as she took a step backwards. As she turned to walk away her eyes lingered on me, waiting for the disapproval. It was too late. Trust was gone. She left me no choice.

When I gave her away to Greg a few days later, I felt a piece of my heart go with her. He lived in the country. His yard was big. I told myself she'd be better off there, where she could run free and play all day. But I mourned her loss as if I'd given away my firstborn child. My only comfort was knowing I could visit.

Greg gave her away without telling me, to a friend of a friend, he said. They had an actual farm, acres of property with cows and sheep. I never saw Tara again or knew what really happened to her. I didn't believe Greg.

Even now when I think of her my soul sighs. I still hold the guilt of what became of her. What fate did I deliver her to? Was I no better than my father? Had Tara become one of the strays, bait for monsters lurking on the streets ready to hand out discipline without remorse. I'd like to think she died old and happy beside an open log fire, surrounded by a loving family. I wonder if she ever thought of me again, and if she hated me for what I'd done. She was the best dog I've ever owned. Only one other would come close to her, but she was years away yet.

We were a new kind of threesome then. I felt solace from Tara's loss only because of my newfound maternal instinct. And although I now felt genuine love towards Morgan, it was still George who was closest to her. Their bond was something I'd never known or thought possible between a father and daughter. I'd seen it on television – *The Brady Bunch, Little House on the Prairie* – but that wasn't reality. I was in awe of their closeness. Morgan was a daddy's girl, and he a proud father. It was the kind of relationship I'd longed for as a child. Still, they annoyed me at times, especially when they'd gang up on me, which usually involved Mum.

Morgan loved her Nanny. They had a profound bond as if Mum were her mother, not me. I didn't mind at all. I treasured their relationship as it allowed me a certain kind of freedom. I didn't worry when Morgan was in Mum's care. Mum didn't drink when she was babysitting. She knew I wouldn't approve. By that time Mum seemed to drink a lot less. Her health problems were becoming more of an issue. Alcohol didn't go well with her medications. Eventually she wouldn't be able to drink at all, and by then she didn't want to.

I'd become accustomed to being the outsider in their *Three Musketeers'* dynamic. Both George and Mum could play with Morgan for hours, having tea parties and teddy bear picnics, hide-and-seek and chasing. I got bored after 10 minutes. Reading to her was usually my best effort. But even George was the storyteller when he was home.

Mum and Dad's house was good for playing chasing. The lounge was the biggest room in the house, with two separate doors connecting

CHAPTER TWELVE | THREE'S A CROWD

to the hallway. It was a perfect circular track for little legs and aging ones to run laps. Morgan would squeal with delight as Nanny closed in on her. She would turn to run in the opposite direction and Daddy would be there to trap her. Their rumbling laughter would penetrate the house. The whole thing looked exhausting. When they played hide-and-seek, Mum and George would pretend they couldn't see her under the dining room table. Morgan would giggle to give herself away when they were taking too long to find her, then she'd shriek in surprise when they did.

"Again, Nanny. Again, Daddy."

Every. Single. Time.

"Mum, if you don't stop you'll have a heart attack. You all need to calm down. You are doing my head in." It was my usual response.

They'd all laugh and sing their little mantra.

"Mummy's a party pooper, stick-in-the-mud, fuddy-duddy."

"Yeah, that's hilarious, very mature." I'd give them my best eye-roll.

Off they'd go again. I'd give up.

Joining Dad in the garden had more appeal than running around the house like a fool. He didn't seem to mind the ruckus and never complained. Who was that man anyway?

I'd go outside and sit with the dogs. They didn't make a noise. I'd think of Tara and all the other dogs of my childhood. Some of those strays were gone as quick as they came. I'd come home from school to an empty yard. Mum told me she took them to the pet shop. I knew Dad probably drove them to the bush and dumped them. Back where they started, only a lot worse off.

I'd wonder if that was what Greg had done with Tara. Did he dump her on the side of a lonely country road to fend for herself? Was she hit by a car? Did a wild animal attack her? Did she starve to death?

The merry-go-round of thoughts would upset me until I was back at the log fire story. I liked it there. That seemed like a much better place to be when karma caught up.

Time passed, and with it came new hurdles. After all my conditioning, Morgan was the least of my problems. The irony – there I was dreading teething, toilet training, terrible twos and a million other shitty things kids do, but there really wasn't that much drama. If there was I can't remember.

No, I couldn't blame Morgan. If only it were that easy. A little shit of a kid would've given me a good excuse for my ever-present dreary discontent.

She'd make up for it later. Mum would be right about the teenage years too. Mum was right about so many things. She wouldn't be around to help me by the time Morgan was 16, when her life changed forever. And by then, neither would George.

CHAPTER THIRTEEN

Signs and Bad Decisions

My sobs would wake me. George would reach for me in the dimness. His touch brought me back into the living, safe from the monsters in my dreams. There were many, but it was my recurring dream that most disturbed me. Details would change, but not the essence or the feeling it gave me: an overwhelming sense of loss and brokenness. A hurt so deep it would stay with me on those days, long after I'd woken.

The monster in my dream was George. But he was also Tony, morphed together like an evil wizard, full of scorn, torturing me with words so cruel and hateful I'd wither at their feet, helpless, pathetic, begging forgiveness, but not knowing what I'd done to be treated so appallingly.

"Oh sweetheart, it's just a nightmare. I would die before I ever hurt you. I don't know why you dream such things."

I'd dreamt it for over 20 years. It started not long after we married, and I would dream it every few months or so. When it finally stopped I'd understand its meaning. In the meantime, it would steal a thousand days from my life. Heavy with dread, I'd try and shake the memory, frustrated with the deciphering.

Mum believed dreams were signs, glimpses into our soul, which was trying to speak to us, guide us, and sometimes warn us. She'd say you just have to learn how to read them – our dreams are never the obvious. Just as well. I was glad about that. If George were anything like the monster in my dream I'd divorce him and run. Or I'd have him killed for being so mean to me. Eventually I'd recover more quickly. I'd push it aside in a few hours. It would gradually fade, forgotten by morning tea until the next time, and the cycle continued.

It seemed every time I conquered things emotionally something shitty would happen, like the dream, or I'd 'accidentally' weigh myself and that would be that, day ruined. God forbid I felt any kind of stability for too long – what a disruption that would be to the dismal flow of my psyche.

To make things worse, we were struggling financially. Mum was right again, although my decision to be a stay-at-home mother until Morgan went to school was non-negotiable. Not that I had anyone to negotiate with except myself.

Having got pregnant against all the odds, and not been able to travel as I had hoped and planned, I had to give motherhood my best shot, and to me that meant being there full-time for the first five years at least. Going back to work was a guilt I couldn't cope with. In those days mothers were less likely to return to the workforce for years, if ever.

CHAPTER THIRTEEN | SIGNS AND BAD DECISIONS

Unless you owned the company, or you were a movie star, why would you? Childcare centres didn't exist as they do today. Child-minding was usually done by suburban ethnic mummas in their cornered-off lounge rooms. A dozen or more babies and toddlers in a confined space wasn't a health and safety issue. I couldn't do that to Morgan. Our mortgage wasn't worth the worry.

We – which really meant I – decided that selling the house and moving away from inner-city living would ease the financial burden and give Morgan space to grow. Our once cosy cottage in Leichhardt became claustrophobic. It seemed to shrink with each passing month as if the walls were closing in on me. I imagined the bricks and mortar held the misery of my post-natal depression. Like rising damp suffocating the surface, its toxicity silently poisoned me with each innocent breath. And besides, the house was never the same without Tara. Her absence was tangible, like a spirit dog unable to leave the place of her human existence.

Yes. A change of pace would do us well. I convinced myself it was the most sensible decision we'd ever made. I was sure Mum and Dad would retire soon. They kept talking about it. That meant they would move to their beach house at Bateman's Bay down on the South Coast of New South Wales – 300 kilometres away. They already spent every second month there. Dad had a business partner by then. After working for 11 years without a night off, not even Christmas Day, Mum had finally convinced him to employ someone to help so he could have a break before he had a heart attack. Dad worked alternate months. He loved his month off.

He eventually had the heart attack during one of those months. Ironic really, 11 years and nothing, not even a cold. As soon as he relaxed, his heart protested. It was probably the two enormous buckets of sea urchins he was carrying up a hill. He and Mum collected them at a secluded beach back in the days when you were allowed to do that without getting fined. They got back to the car and it happened. With no mobile phone and Mum unable to drive, Dad had to drive himself to a hospital while he was having the heart attack. The doctors were amazed he'd survived. He should have died, they said. Clearly, they didn't know whom they were dealing with. It would take more than that to kill The Incredible Hulk.

I was dreading Mum being so far away permanently. Our comfortable routine would change dramatically. I wasn't sure how Morgan would cope without her Nanny. It was bad enough for their month off. It would take a few days for Morgan to settle again, and me. I think it did for Mum too. We missed each other, but it was only a month and it usually passed quickly. We knew she'd be back soon enough. Who knew how often we'd get the chance to visit once they were so far away?

I figured Morgan would adjust better at two than if she were older. It was best to get the trauma of separation over and done with early. That was my rationale. I think subconsciously I resented Mum leaving us, so I thought I'd get in first.

It would've made sense to move south into suburbia, in the general direction of where Mum and Dad would be. Tony lived down south with his family, a few hours before Mum and Dad's beach house. So did Greg. The South Coast seemed the obvious choice. We moved north, to the Central Coast, an hour from the city if there were no problems on the freeway. We didn't know then the F3 – now the M1 – was notorious. Fog in winter, breakdowns and accidents, or simply peak hour could make the one-hour journey three hours or more. I would come to know it as the highway to hell.

Moving north would give us a lot more house and land for a lot less money than moving the same distance south. George worked in the city, so his travelling time had to be considered. If the train commute bothered him he never said, or he hid it well. But George was good at hiding things. I would learn that later.

"It'll be fine, sweetheart. Imagine all the reading I'll get done. It won't be much different really. That 10-minute bus ride takes almost an hour in peak-hour traffic. I'll be glad to have some new scenery to look at."

Visiting Mum and Dad would become a five-hour drive instead of

CHAPTER THIRTEEN | SIGNS AND BAD DECISIONS

four. What was an extra hour? She might as well be on the moon either way.

Mum didn't take the news well.

"Oh love, but why the Central Coast? It's so far away. Why would ya wanna move there of all places on Earth? How will I get to see my munchkin? We're not retiring just yet. I'm not sure you've really thought this through, Marce. It's a big change and I don't know if it's the best thing for you. I don't think you'll cope with country life, darling. You're not like your brothers. You're a city girl."

It was true, but I liked to think I was adaptable. The real truth was that once I got an idea in my head I had tunnel vision, and Mum knew it. The pros far outweighed the cons in my mind, so we simply had no other choice. As always, I wanted it yesterday.

"Love, why don't you wait a few years when the market comes good again? It'll pass quickly, and you'll be better off financially. And I'll have more time with my little chicken. If you move and you hate it, you'll be stuck there. You won't get back into the Sydney market after that kind of financial setback."

Poor Mum was on the verge of tears. She held them back for my sake. I ignored her, convinced I knew what I was doing.

Not once did I consider I might be lonely in my big house on its big block of land. Just Morgan and me all day long with nothing familiar to fill our days, not knowing anyone, far from friends. There wasn't even a local shop. Everything depended on driving. Once I'd been in walking distance of shops, cafés, restaurants and parks – not that I walked anywhere, but at least I had the choice. Not anymore. How I missed the convenience of city living.

George settled easily. As usual he could fit into any surroundings as if he'd been born there. He loved to chat to neighbours. He seemed to know everything that went on in the street. The random bits of information he accumulated about people baffled me. I'm sure he could tell you when Mr Smith in number 86 had his last doctor's appointment, and why.

Or he'd know what little Jimmy in number 42 got for Christmas last year. I couldn't care less about the details of other people's lives, much preferring to mind my own business.

Not so easy when you live in Summer Bay. I was in *Home and Away* soap opera hell. A circus of revolving neighbours borrowing sugar or flour, or just popping in for a chit-chat about the kids and the weather. I thought that only happened on TV. After 12 months of it I was ready to kill myself or the neighbours. Just as well I didn't own a gun.

"Oh, don't be upset, love. If you're that unhappy, then move back to Sydney. So, you'll take a few steps backward. That's life, darling. It's a constant battle. You can move in with us; we're not there half the time anyway. Knuckle down and get saving so you can buy back in the city eventually."

Mum had me at "move back to Sydney". I wanted to jump through the phone and kiss her. A rush of euphoria overwhelmed me with gratitude.

As usual, I wanted it yesterday. We moved back and took our time selling the house. All the work Tony had helped with when we'd moved in paid off. He was good with his hands. Tony could build or fix anything, and like Dad he loved the garden. Unlike Dad, Tony had an eye for landscaping. Where Dad overcompensated, creating a chaos of foliage, Tony was meticulous with the structure and placement of everything in his yard. Plants, flowers, trees, water features – they all had their perfect place. He had created a Japanese garden oasis in the middle of his bush backyard. It was the envy of his neighbourhood, he'd told me. It was clear Tony's creative flair extended well beyond the stage. I guess he'd forgotten all that as he tied his noose with that green bed sheet years later.

It was an advantage not having to rush to sell the house. We received more than expected, but it still wasn't enough. We paid off our mortgage. We were debt-free and had a little left over. We would just have to start saving again to accumulate a worthwhile deposit. I didn't care. We were home in my beloved city, and the carbon monoxide had never smelt so good. Morgan was with her Nanny again. I was with my mum, and it was

CHAPTER THIRTEEN | SIGNS AND BAD DECISIONS

the happiest I'd felt in a very long time.

George flowed in his usual easy-going manner. He had a whole new street full of neighbours to quiz. He was happy too.

We settled into our new routine without too much drama. It was hard living with Dad after all those years. He had mellowed by then, but still, he liked things his way and so did I. I'd look forward to the end of each month when they'd travel back down south. The house would be ours for a whole four weeks and I could clean till my hands were chemically raw. No dirt being trudged in from the garden on Dad's filthy feet. No crap on show when it should be in the back shed or somewhere out of sight. Dad would fix things that most people would throw in the garbage. Cheap plastic containers with odd-fitting lids, tacky ornaments and gadgets from the two-dollar shop that would break within five minutes, but Dad would mend, glue and staple everything. I'm sure he kept Super Glue in business. There were tubes of the stuff all over the house, along with nails, screws and every variety of sticky tape. God forbid if anything wasn't where he'd left it.

"Leave it dere. I know where to find it next dime," he would say in his dry tone, daring me to touch it as I tried to tidy up.

I learned to suck it up. My urge to kill him would dissipate by the time they were due home again. A few weeks later it returned, and I'd count the days until he'd be gone again. And that was the cycle of our lives until they finally did retire four years later.

As usual my psyche didn't cope well with any extended period of contentment. A year after we'd moved back to Sydney something really, really shitty happened. At the time I thought it was just my lousy luck. Years later I'd know it was another sign.

I knew something was wrong before I even opened my eyes. I'd been dreaming. I was Alice in Wonderland. I stepped through the looking glass, falling, falling, down the rabbit hole. Just before I hit the ground my eyes snapped open, jolting me back to life.

My body heaved upright with the force. My lungs expanded like balloons as I gasped to fill them with air. My head pounded as blood pooled in my ears from the sudden movement. I threw the bedcovers back and put my feet on the floor, and when I did it happened.

There I was still falling down the rabbit hole, spinning out of control. But I was awake. How was it possible? Terror seized me. My arms shot out in a desperate attempt to stop myself, to grab on to something solid but there was nothing.

My screams brought George and Mum running to the bedroom.

We were at the little beach house down south, away for the weekend. Morgan was missing her Nanny mid-month so we'd decided to surprise them with a visit.

"It's okay, love, I've got you. Try to calm down now, there, there."

Mum was at my side. Her arms embraced me, holding my head to her torso to keep me steady, as if she knew I was free-falling.

It didn't work. I wasn't sure she was holding me at all. My feet couldn't feel the floor. I couldn't tell if I were up or down. I had no sense of direction. I tried to focus on things, the old beige lamp in the corner of the room, the colourful matador on the wall that Mum had made from a million tiny beads. And dozens of other useless dust collectors in that spare bedroom. It was a kaleidoscope of broken things. My brain was a shattered mess of imagery. I felt trapped inside a spinning top, like a bug in a child's toy.

A wave of nausea overpowered me. Out of control, I vomited right there in Mum's arms, like I'd just eaten a feast. The vomit spun too, all around me like it would if I was an astronaut in space – only it wasn't slow motion, it was warp speed.

The spinning would last six weeks, day and night, relentless in its torture. I would eventually learn it was vertigo.

Vertigo is a sensation of spinning – a specific kind of dizziness... The dizziness that defines vertigo has one of two causes: disturbance in either the balance organs of the inner ear, or parts of the brain or sensory nerve pathways... Vertigo is a symptom rather than a medical condition.

CHAPTER THIRTEEN | SIGNS AND BAD DECISIONS

The day before we'd been at the beach. Little Lilli Pilli was secluded and private, which suited me of course. I was still the size of a small cow. It had been 20 years since I'd been on that beach. Greg and I almost drowned there, caught in a rip when I was about nine. Dad saved us as I took my last breath. I was sure I saw the white light, or it could've been the sun in my eyes. Tony was foraging for crabs amongst the rocks. Just as well. I wasn't sure Dad could've saved all three of us, regardless of his incredible hulkishness. I wondered which one he would have left behind. Probably me.

We had never been back there again. Until now.

George and Morgan were building sandcastles on the shore. She loved her daddy's attention and he adored every moment with his little girl. I loved those moments too, when he took over and I didn't have to pay attention. I craved solitude and cherished my alone time.

I was in the surf, relishing the weightlessness of my burdening body. A freak wave came from nowhere and sucked me down in the undertow. I was tossed and churned like a ragdoll in a washing machine. I fought that wave, but fitness wasn't in my gene pool. The water came down like a king tide and I was a ship's anchor then, held down by the force of it.

A feeling of déjà vu overcame me as I tumbled, arms and legs flapping wildly, unsure of which way was up. I struggled for the surface, gulping mouthfuls of water instead of air. Had that beach been waiting for me all those years? Was it trying to finish what it had started? That bastard wave was trying to kill me!

Eventually it spat me out on the shore. Like a beached carcass – what a sight that must've been. I was grateful for my life, and that there were no witnesses. George and Morgan were still playing, oblivious to my shipwreck. I could've died right there, been washed out to sea and they wouldn't have noticed a thing.

I spluttered and coughed as I got to my knees, and when I stood up it happened.

A loud, piercing, ringing sound deep in my left ear, pain so excruciating it almost brought me back down to my knees. It only lasted seconds. I shook myself like a wet dog. I was traumatised, but at least I'd won. That beach could fuck off for good. I wouldn't get a third chance, I knew that.

The next morning – as I fell down the rabbit hole – I didn't think about my ear. I didn't know then the wave was the culprit. My violent tumbling had dislodged those mysterious crystals in my inner ear, the things that allow us equilibrium. I never even knew I had little magic particles in my ear to keep me upright. And I'd always thought vertigo was a fear of heights. That's called acrophobia incidentally. Equilibrium wasn't a word I cared about. And why would anyone until they don't have it? Then that's all you care about.

Stillness is something people take for granted. Even in sleep, I wasn't still. No matter how hard I tried, I was a cork in an ocean, bobbing in the calm when I wasn't being thrown around like tumbleweed in a sandstorm. After six long weeks I'd made a decision.

"George, you have to kill me. I can't do it myself. I can't stay still long enough to even attempt it. I can't live like this anymore. I'd rather be dead, blissfully still in my coffin."

And I meant it. Not for George to kill me, just to die in my sleep or some other merciful end to my horrendous state of being. I wondered what I'd done to deserve that kind of punishment. Was it karma for all the bad decisions I'd made? Perhaps it was a warning, a premonition of things to come. Or maybe it was a wakeup call, a virtual uppercut to my psyche to snap out of its bullshit.

I had the wisdom of driftwood. At the time it was simply bad luck. Had I been slimmer and fitter I would have challenged that wave like a dolphin, and none of it would've happened.

George found the doctor who saved my life. In one weird, freaky, frightening manoeuvre the world was still again. He threw me around from side to side like a ragdoll as I sat on the edge of his surgery bed in his office. His aim was to get those free-floating crystals back in place. It worked instantly.

CHAPTER THIRTEEN | SIGNS AND BAD DECISIONS

I wanted to kiss that doctor. I'd never been so happy to feel my feet on the ground. Equilibrium was a beautiful, extraordinary thing that I would never again take for granted.

But all pledges sworn in moments of desperation fade into the background of our memory. Like my recurring dream. I could shake that off the minute I opened my eyes after 15 years of it haunting me. By then George wouldn't even turn around when I cried out in my sleep.

"Marce, you're dreaming, go back to sleep."

And I would. It was just my stupid subconscious playing tricks on me again.

Vertigo, too, became a fading memory. I stopped tiptoeing around life. My caution had become a new burden, a tedious drag on the simplest activities. The tilt of my head when I blow-dried my hair, the position of my pillows propped up in bed. Merely bending forward would incite the fear of it happening again. But like the pain of any trauma, physical or otherwise, it too diminishes in time as we get on with things.

And I got on with things. Symmetry didn't concern me then. I had bigger things going on, much bigger signs I'd ignore, as you do, until that incorrigible thing called hindsight slaps you in the face with your own stupidity and all the bad decisions you've made.

CHAPTER FOURTEEN

Miracles in Disguise

We didn't make it to Mum and Dad's for Christmas in 2005. After 10 years in exile, my vertigo had returned. The four-hour road trip was out of the question. If only I'd known it was Mum's last Christmas, I would have forced myself somehow.

The doctor who had saved me that first time was on annual leave and wouldn't be back until February. I tried other doctors, but it didn't work. The six-week wait was torturous. Three separate manoeuvres later, I slowly came good again. It wasn't the miraculous quick fix I was hoping for. I vowed I would never be complacent again, and I never have. No bungy jumping for me. I have a respectful appreciation of equilibrium these days – and a less fanatical fear, which helps.

Looking back, I believe my two vertigo episodes were the mother of all signs. The first one was a prologue to the downward spiral of bad decisions I'd make over the years that followed. The second was blind ignorance in thinking all my bad decisions were behind me.

Before bad decisions were made, however, I would make a good decision – a miracle really that happened one day in August 1995. Mum always said that even good decisions may be disguised as something sinister. Mum's glass was always half-empty after all. When making decisions, she would say, be sure to decide wisely.

"Careful what you wish for, love, ya might just get it. And when you do, ya might realise it's not what you wanted after all."

Mum's cryptic wisdom would annoy me. That statement made no sense. By the time it did it would be too late to tell her.

I was watching TV, eating my way through a box of Snickers. I was still the same weight, 138 kilos. Not a kilo lighter since Morgan was born four years earlier. Snickers were a daily staple back then. It was surprising I didn't weigh more, considering I could eat as much as my father and brothers put together. I'd had that talent since I was a kid. Aged 12, I ate the same amount of pasta as Greg and Dad. At 13, I had a 48-inch waist. Dad had a 48-inch waist. I know because I once had to borrow a pair of his jeans for a school excursion. I didn't own jeans. They didn't make them that big for young teenage girls. The childhood obesity epidemic was decades away. The fat kid was much rarer in those days. Mum had to shorten the jeans, of course. I looked like Elma Fudd. You can imagine what fun my early school years were.

I despised my lack of willpower. I hated my gorging and my inability to be able to vomit afterwards. I would try, but I couldn't do it. I never understood bulimia.

I was no different from the next overeater. I had an obsessive love of food. It gave me the kind of instant gratification that nothing else could. The rush I felt when I ate was exquisite. I would hold onto those few seconds as long as possible as they filled the void inside me, lifting me

CHAPTER FOURTEEN | MIRACLES IN DISGUISE

from the gloom just for a moment. I would feel happy while I was eating, happier than at any other time. And when it was over I'd hate myself again. My internal dialogue would beat me down. I was a scavenger, no better than a pig in a pigpen.

"…You have to stop counting calories and start counting fat," Oprah Winfrey exclaimed.

I stared at the TV, mesmerised by her thinness. I was sure she hadn't looked like that yesterday. Had I missed some episodes, like a hundred kilos worth? I put my Snickers down and paid attention. By the end of the show something in my brain had clicked. I'm not sure exactly what, or how, but Oprah's show had a profound impact on me. As the credits rolled, I felt an overwhelming resolve that I'd never felt before. The very next day I started on a journey that would last 18 months, and I would lose half my body weight.

I know it sounds unbelievable, even impossible for someone like me to convert overnight with the conviction of an Olympic athlete, but I did. I really did.

It was a miracle. A moment – a one-hour show – was all it took to change 30 years of conditioning. My history with food was controversial. In many respects it was my saviour, the root of my happiest memories. But on the flipside, it was a form of punishment, self-inflicted and otherwise.

Like most nine year olds, I didn't like Brussels sprouts, but I really didn't like spinach. As a fat kid I ate most things, but not those. We couldn't leave the dinner table until everything on our plate was gone. Dad didn't tolerate wasting food. He was born in 1933 and survived the poverty of war. I think that had something to do with it.

Mum was a good cook, but she overcooked most vegetables – the way Dad preferred them. One night we were eating dinner, our plates overflowing with food. The green mush was there, taking up way too much space on my plate. I could smell its foulness. I knew it would taste like soiled roots pulled straight from the ground. I couldn't understand how anyone could eat it. Greg and Tony were smart. They ate it first when they were hungriest to get it over and done with. I should've done that.

Dad expected peace and quiet while he was eating. That suited me. The less we spoke the less chance of his losing his temper and throwing his plate at the dining room wall. He once found a long brown hair in his spaghetti and hurled the full plate in the air in a fit of rage. Red sauce and pasta went everywhere. It took Mum hours to clean it off walls, chairs, mirrors, and the stains on the carpet never really came out. Greg and Tony couldn't be blamed for that one, and Mum always had short hair. Dad stormed away from the table like a raging bull, unable to eat, yelling abuse at me as he left the room. He never mentioned it again, but from that day on Mum made me tie my hair back. I was never to wear it loose unless I was in my bedroom.

I still can't walk around the kitchen with my hair down.

"Marce love, eat ya spinach it's good for you."

I froze at Mum's words. I saw Dad's eyes dart to my plate. I felt instant panic, as if I were about to be thrown into a pit of funnel web spiders.

"I can't, Mum, it smells bad. It looks yucky." Those were a lot of words for me to say at the dinner table.

"Eat it," Dad commanded in his threatening voice. That voice could make the hairs on my body stand up straight. The sound invoked goose bumps even on the hottest day.

I stared at my plate and pushed the spinach around with my fork.

"Don' play with it. Eat it," he said louder.

I didn't dare look at him, but I could sense he'd stopped eating to watch me. I willed myself to put the dirt into my mouth, but spat it back out the instant it touched my tongue.

"It's all right, Gary, she doesn't like it. She ate everything else," Mum said gently, trying to avoid any impending disaster. I'll bet she was regretting it then, wishing she'd never opened her mouth. Mum did that a lot – mindless chatter that usually got us into trouble.

CHAPTER FOURTEEN | MIRACLES IN DISGUISE

"She gunna eat every last bit an' she not leavin' da table till she do."

I felt the air being sucked out of the room, as if a big invisible vacuum cleaner was on high speed.

"Oh Gary, for God's sake leave her alone. She doesn't like it. Ya can't force her to eat it."

Mum was so brave – now – in my defence.

"Shud up, woman. She eating it. And she stay dere all night if she have to."

Dad rose from his chair and his fists came down hitting the table with such force everything on it jumped an inch in the air, including us.

I pushed that cold sludge around my plate a hundred times. It got dark. Greg and Tony went to bed. Mum's kitchen was sparkling clean and both she and Dad were watching TV in the lounge. I heard the occasional whispers and then "Have you eat it yet? I'm warnin' you!" Dad yelled, breaking the evening silence like the sound of smashing glass.

I almost wet my pants. I looked at my plate. I pretended it was cake. I blocked my nose ready for the assault.

"Yes, Dad," I answered with a muffled voice. And with lightning speed I shoved that putrid stuff in my mouth and swallowed without chewing.

It was over. The ordeal was over. I was free. My plate was finally empty. Then I let go of my nose.

It hadn't been long enough. The filthy odour filled my head. It was in my mouth, up my nose, the sharpness stinging my senses like toxic fumes. I couldn't control the force of that projectile vomit as my stomach pushed back on the assault, covering the entire table, floor, chairs, and me with the blackened evidence.

Mum rushed out at the noise of it, a look of horror on her face.

"Gary, I bloody told you not to force her, now look what's happened," Mum yelled as she came to my aid.

I started to cry, anticipating Dad's onslaught. I imagined him rushing through the door and dealing with me the same way he'd deal with Greg and Tony. He didn't. I'm not sure why, but I didn't ask questions.

I somehow survived my childhood without any food phobias. I still eat spaghetti (with my hair tied back, of course), and I love spinach. I cook vegetables the way Jamie Oliver prefers, with the right amount of crunch.

I promised myself I'd never force my child to eat something she physically couldn't. I intended to make sure Morgan had a healthy respect for food. I'd worried she'd end up with my DNA, so I did my best to give her a head start. Cake would be for birthdays and special occasions. Chocolate would be for Easter, not as a reward for being a good girl. And she wouldn't know what fast food was until her friends at school told her about it. It worked and thankfully Morgan took after her father, bypassing any fat genes. I was grateful she would never know the cruelty I'd known in the schoolyard.

If only I'd treated my own body with that much respect. I hid my addiction in every nook and cranny in the house. I never ate junk food in front of Morgan. She probably wondered why her Mummy was so fat when all she ate was good food. Looking back, I can't help but notice the comparisons between Mum's behaviour and my own. Was it so different?

Morgan was a big part of the driving force for change after my Oprah moment that day.

She would be starting big school soon. Shit was about to get real. Besides, knowing it wouldn't be long before Morgan had me pegged, discovered my stash, that she would become aware of other people's judgement. The thought filled me with dread. What would her friends say about her big fat mum? Worse still, what would their mothers think?

I imagined I'd have to talk to them at some point. My throat tightened just thinking about it. What would I say? How would I interact? Pretend to be normal like them? They'd have expectations and so would the teachers. They liked mums who helped with tuckshop, school carnivals, volunteered for reading group, and put their hands up for a mountain of other tasks that good mothers do.

CHAPTER FOURTEEN | MIRACLES IN DISGUISE

I'd been practically locked away for four years. I was about to be exposed, thrust out of hiding and there was nothing I could do about it. George couldn't be the mother, not then. I wanted more than anything to swap places with him. I could go off to work and he could stay home, except his salary was more than double what mine could ever be. Unless I could somehow clone him, I had to step up, face reality and make the transition into the next scary stage of motherhood. Something had to give, or I knew my dreary discontent would ruin Morgan's life. Her childhood experiences would be tainted by my own insecurities. I couldn't do that to her.

It was time.

I took Oprah's advice. I changed the way I shopped for groceries, read labels and bought low fat. I changed the way I cooked, using fewer fats, less carbs and sugar. The sugar revolution was a decade away, so it was the obvious sugar and junk I eliminated. I changed my life, our lives. It wasn't drastic for George or Morgan, or even for me to be honest. I was so determined, so desperate for change that it really wasn't hard. I'd never felt that kind of strength in my mind, focused on a goal that actually seemed possible. I wondered if Oprah had subliminally brainwashed me. I didn't care if she had. I didn't even have to hope it would last, I knew it would.

I started exercising. Me – exercise. That was a miracle in itself. I was too self-conscious to join a gym, but Mum bought me a treadmill and I started doing 10 minutes a day. It was all I could manage before my lungs collapsed and my heart rejected the new activity. I gradually increased the time: 15 minutes, 20, 30, until I could do a solid hour. I did that every day without fail.

When I'd lost 20 kilos, Sam – my Maid of Honour – convinced me to try a gym class with her. It took a lot of convincing. Although I was feeling good, 20 kilos wasn't that noticeable considering where I'd started. Still, I went. By the time we'd finished the high-impact circuit class I wanted to kill her. Everyone in that class was freakishly fit and buffed. I'd only seen that in magazines and on TV. I was the elephant in the room, literally. I knew all of them, including the instructor, were wondering what the hell I was doing there, and how I'd got past security.

My nausea almost won. I held down the vomit out of sheer terror that the embarrassment would kill me. I couldn't understand how anyone would put themselves through that kind of punishment willingly. Sam apologised at least a dozen times. She hadn't realised she'd signed me up for that type of class. I probably didn't speak to her for a week.

But I did go back to the gym, 25 kilos later. I went alone. I didn't trust Sam. She might try and kill me again. I started in a beginners' aerobics class and worked my way up. Pump, step, high-impact cardo – you name it, I did it. And I became a runner, me, a runner. It was my new addiction.

How could I have lived 32 years without knowing all I really had to do to fill the void was run? Why hadn't anyone told me that? It takes time to become a runner, a real runner – for it to seep into you at a cellular level. When you first start, the longing to give up, to give in, is overpowering, but if you persevere, if you learn how to run through the discomfort, there is no longer any pain. When that moment comes, your legs, breath, heart, mind and body are all in sync and it becomes an effortless flow. Like a swan gliding across a lake, seamless and beautiful. It took me three months before my ugly duckling became the swan. I'm so glad I didn't give up. Running would fill the deepest voids in the years to come.

A bona fide gym junkie, I'd morphed into one of those buffed freaky people from the torture chamber class that day. At 64 kilos my body was a toned, athletic, super-healthy machine. I was unrecognisable. Anyone new I met had no idea who I once was. No one I'd known for years could believe my transformation. I could have been one of the first ever 'biggest losers' before reality TV. I saw myself as something worthy and, dare I say, someone beautiful perhaps.

It was the strangest thing. In those early days, and for a long time, I'd catch a glimpse of myself in a window or mirror and think someone was next to me. I'd get such a shock when I realised it was me. Never in

CHAPTER FOURTEEN | MIRACLES IN DISGUISE

all my imaginings would I have believed I could look so different – like somebody else.

George was proud of me, but I was the same person to him. Fat or thin, I don't think it mattered. He loved me either way, desired me no more or less, admired me as he'd always done, and showed me the same devotion.

"Sweetheart, you are as beautiful now as the day I met you and you always will be," he'd say a thousand times. He knew it reassured me.

Mum was proud too. Everyone was, even my brothers. Tony was so impressed he started running himself. He was clean then, an AA (Alcoholics Anonymous) sponsor, a respected leader and mentor to those who had unfortunately followed in his footsteps. I was as proud of him as he was of me. Our relationship had grown in strength as the years passed. He stopped drinking and drugging soon after he became a father. I knew he wanted to be a good dad, a better man, and he was… at least for 11 years.

Extreme exercise had worked in my favour when it came to my skin. I was lucky. The only place I had loose skin was on my stomach. I decided to have a tummy tuck. The operation made my stomach flat as a chopping board. I had abs, serious abs. What the hell, who am I?

When I decided to go one step further and have breast implants, it was a game changer. Those saline sacks had hypnotic powers. I never knew boobs were so important to the world at large, certainly to men. I'd heard stories, but they didn't apply to me. The attention my chest drew was mind-blowing. I quickly learned what all the fuss was about. My boobs had a life of their own. They could jump queues, avoid parking fines, get free coffees, and a multitude of other perks. Who knew two mounds of fatty tissue could control a destiny. It was ridiculous – and dangerous, for reasons not obvious to me then.

George and I seemed to flourish in our new social standing. My once agoraphobic persona became the opposite. My transformation was also internal. George, once the life of the party while I stood in his shadow, now had competition. I was the party. Neither of us was used to that. We were the fun couple in the room and people would gravitate to us. We made them laugh, and they seemed to relish in our company.

I was having the best time of my life. Not even in those blissful early years of marriage when it was just me, George and Tara, when sex was loud and carefree in our long honeymoon period before I fell pregnant, had I felt so happy. I had a new connection to life that I didn't know could exist, and I felt an even stronger connection to George. He was my best friend, my soulmate long before anyone used that word. I loved him. The thought of his deceiving me or cheating on me never crossed my mind. I knew he wouldn't. He loved me too much.

And I had no reason to cheat on him. But I did.

Christmas 1966

Mum & Tony - 1963

Me - 1965

Tony, Greg & Me - 1965

Mum & Dad - 1961

Mum & Dad's Wedding Day - 1957

Mum - circa 1955

Dad - circa 1952

Tony, Greg, Dad & Me at Bateman's Bay - circa 1974

Me & Mum - circa 1968

Mum, Me, Tony, Greg, & a cousin - circa 1969   Circa 1971

Me, Dad & Danny - circa 1973

First Holy Communion - circa 1972

Me & Danny - circa 1973

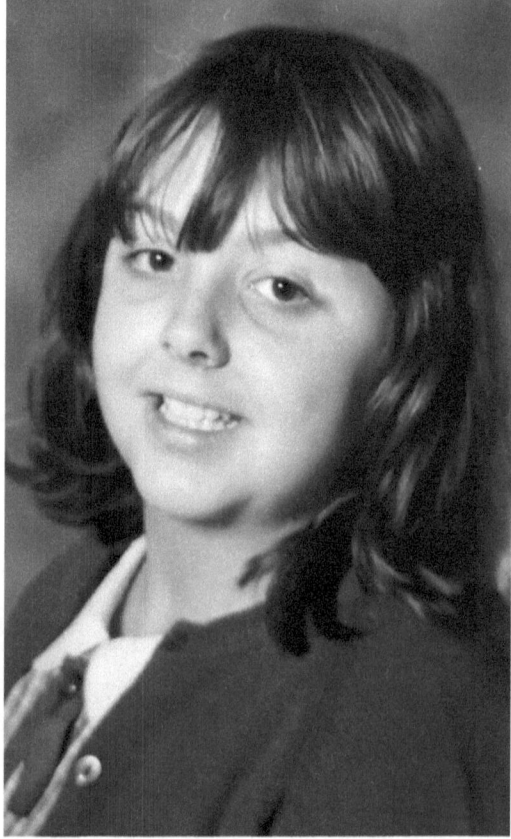
Me Year 6 - 1976

My first day of high school - 1977

Mum & Me - circa 1977

Me & Danny - circa 1978

Circa 1978

Me at 17 – 1981

Tony & Me - circa 1982

Tony & Me, Disco ready - circa 1979

Tony, Me, Greg - circa 1982

Mum, Morgan & Grandfather - 1991

Me & Morgan 1991

Me & Morgan – 1991

My Wedding Day 1988

TONY'S LIFE...

Tony's resting place, in the garden Bateman's Bay

MUM, DAD, MORGAN AND ME – THE 90s

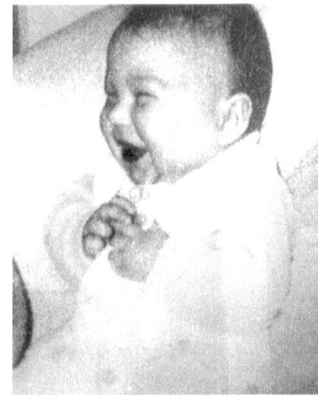

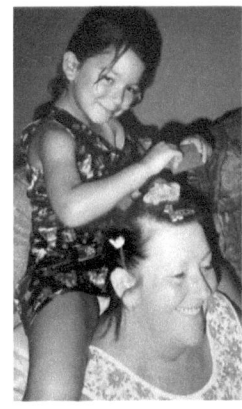

Dad's 60th Birthday - 1993

Mum, Dad & Morgan 2003

2003

In the garden at Bateman's Bay - 2004

Me & Angel – 2002

At Bateman's Bay - circa 2003

Angel - circa 2004

Morgan & Angel - 2002

Tara 1989

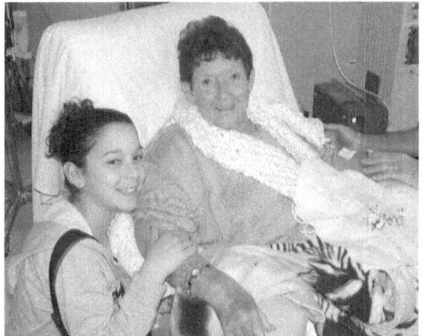
Mum & Morgan at Dialysis - circa 2005

Dad & Morgan - Christmas 2004

Mum & Morgan - circa 2003

Mum & Dad, Sunroom Bateman's Bay - 2006

Dad in his garden at Bateman's Bay - circa 2004

Dad at Malua Beach - 2016

Dad with my granddaughter Mia, her great grandfather – Christmas 2015

Dad & Mia – Christmas 2014

MY WEDDING DAY #2 – 2012 – SEMINYAK BALI

Ramzi & Me - 2015

Mia, Me & Morgan – 2015

Me & My Girls 2016

Morgan's Wedding Day – Fiji, 2017

Mia & Me on Morgan's Wedding Day – Fiji, 2017 – My favourite photo of that day

CHAPTER FIFTEEN

The Ring

George sat on his towel and looked solemnly out to sea. His chin started quivering. I'd never seen him look so sad.

"Did you find it?" I asked.

"No. I must have lost it in the surf."

Not once in 11 years had I seen George's wedding ring off his finger. I wasn't wearing my rings – I only wore them on nights out, never during the day and never at the beach. My rings would annoy me when I exercised, and I was always exercising. I got used to not wearing them. If my ringless finger ever bothered George, he'd never mentioned it.

We were at Tamarama Beach, the next beach south of Bondi. Gone were the days that I hid from crowds. The old me seemed like another life, my memories of it someone else's.

I got up from my towel and sat on his. I put my arm around his back.

"Don't worry, darling, we'll get you another ring. I know it's not the same, but it'll be nice and new."

As if material things like that mattered to George. They didn't. He was sentimental. His ring signified our happy marriage. At least that's what I liked to believe.

And now it was gone. I felt uneasy as a thought popped into my head. It must be a sign. Mum would've said, "You bet it's a bloody sign." My unease turned into a full-blown assault as snippets of recent memories danced in my head, daring me to speak out loud. I tried to keep my breathing under control. I needed to slow my rising heart rate down before it became visible.

I should've taken the opportunity to tell George about the bad decision I'd made months earlier. But I couldn't do it. Not there on the beach. Not in public. Not in what I assumed must be the worst moment of his life.

I squeezed my eyes shut, trying to expel the images, terrified that George might suddenly be a mind reader. My thoughts went into overdrive as I imagined the worst.

What if George's ring was the one thing that kept us together? The thread that bound us and subliminally made us who we were. My absent rings couldn't do the job. Unaware, they had failed miserably. Perhaps that was the real reason I no longer wore them. Subconsciously I knew I didn't deserve the privilege anymore.

The rumbling sound of crashing waves masked my internal noise. It was temporary.

As if on cue with the external noise the actual words came out of my mouth before I could stop them. I could've slapped myself. "Oh my God, what if it's an omen?"

"There's no such thing as omens, darling, that's silly. It was just a freak accident."

CHAPTER FIFTEEN | THE RING

It wasn't what I expected. I thought he'd say the obvious "Why would you say that, darling?" That's what I would've said to him.

George, sensing what he must have thought was my sadness at his loss, hugged me and kissed my forehead. It was typical of him. He always put my feelings before his, as if mine were more important. It was what he'd always done since the beginning of our relationship. I assumed he liked it that way. He'd never said any different. He was easy-going. I was hard work. It was inevitable my needs would come first. I'm sure everyone thought he only wanted to make me happy.

I'd always assumed George's devotion to me was genuine love. He was the kind of husband women wanted: agreeable, never confrontational, and always considerate. Every Friday after work he would bring me flowers. I'd get weekly foot rubs whether my feet were sore or not. He'd buy gifts and cards for no particular reason, beautiful cards filled with the most heartfelt words, and he'd write his own words of gratitude and love. He had the soul of a poet and the heart of a hopeless romantic. His love letters and post-it notes filled dozens of shoeboxes over the years. He was perfect as far as men go, and I was sure everyone who crossed his path must think so too.

"Marce, you are so lucky. Does George have a single brother at home?"

I must have heard that a hundred times from friends and acquaintances. I would be cocky, to the point of rude, depending on who was asking.

"No. Sorry, he's one of a kind and he only has eyes for me."

Guilt hammered at my psyche. How could I be doing this to him? What kind of disgusting monster was I? I knew if I didn't confess it would eat me alive. In a sudden surge of release, I opened my mouth to speak, but George continued instead.

"Don't worry, sweetheart, I'll buy another ring, and no, it won't be the same, it'll be better, so much better."

He looked deep into my eyes, gave me a sorrowful smile and kissed me again. My words dissolved. I couldn't speak. The moment of confession was gone. Soon, I silently promised myself. Next time the moment presented itself I would seize it and tell George everything.

We lay back down on our towels, each lost in our own thoughts. I closed my eyes and pretended to snooze so I didn't have to speak. If I spoke I might blurt it out right there amid the crowd of Tamarama. I visualised his reaction, the look on his face. I couldn't bear it, the unimaginable heartbreak I'd see there. I was sure it would crush him. He might die on the spot and I would be the cause, and then I would have to die too. The shame alone would surely kill me.

For months my mind played tug-of-war as loyalty pulled me one way and desire pushed me another. My internal badgering was relentless, my thoughts in constant battle like a state of perpetual vertigo. I would spin from one spectrum to the other, debating pros and cons as if the act of cheating were a fair argument. What once felt solid now felt broken as my wedding vows echoed from afar, as if Father David himself were condemning me from the heavens.

I could hear the waves lapping at the shore, and seagulls squawking overhead. The sounds of the beach always gave me a sense of peace, but not that day. I wished I could go back in time, make the right decision and change what could never be changed now.

I never thought it possible I'd be the kind of person who'd cheat. I'd spent a lifetime judging those people. I had strong opinions on home wreckers. They destroyed families, wounded souls, all in the name of sex. They'd call it a stupid mistake that didn't mean anything. That would incite a certain rage in me. I categorised cheating with any other unforgivable crime. Criminals who committed crimes should be punished.

And there I was, a criminal now. The betrayed had become the betrayer. How was that possible?

I wondered if my weight loss had given me a lobotomy. Clearly the part of my brain that vowed to honour, respect and cherish had been lost along with the kilos of fat and skin I'd shed, the unwanted parts of me.

So, as cheaters do – as I did – my judgement conveniently changed direction. I decided there were three types of cheaters. The obvious ones who embarked on random sex with strangers because they just couldn't help themselves for reasons only they knew, usually some kind of fetish, an ego trip, a way of validating they still had 'it'. Then the ones looking for something deeper because they weren't getting what they needed at home. The last type of cheater was me. I was neither of the above.

Looking back, of course I couldn't see through my own delusions.

It was desire, no question, but it wasn't intimacy. Intimacy was reserved for my husband, the man I loved. I wasn't in search of something missing, not on a conscious level. I wasn't fulfilling a repressed sexual need or fantasy. It wasn't even really about sex. It was about power. Desire renders anyone weak, especially men. Cheating made me feel alarmingly indestructible. I was in control. I called the shots. It made me feel like a man, and that was the most powerful feeling in the world.

It didn't start that way of course, but that's what it became.

It wasn't a random one-night stand. I didn't get drunk and make an intoxicated mistake, or 'accidentally' sleep with a friend's husband – I'm sure that happens more often than people admit. I didn't plan it. I didn't expect it, but later I'd wonder if that too was simply part of the denial. Did I invite it on a subconscious level? Was there some kind of scent, a vibe I was putting out that I was unaware of? Not questions I would have asked myself then.

I cheated with a guy from the gym. He asked me for a lift home one day. I knew him casually in passing. He was a local. He was at the gym as much as I was, so we'd always smile and say hello. He was obscenely good looking, but it was just an observation. There was nothing sexual about it; there couldn't be, I was a married woman.

We'd never had a conversation, so I'd never stood close enough to him to look him in the eye until that day. When he spoke I felt a twinge in my belly. He was even more handsome at such close proximity. A little knot of fire ignited inside me and I wondered what the hell was going on. I was so unnerved by what I was feeling it caught me off guard and I thought my voice would fail as he waited for my response.

I should have politely refused, made up an appropriate excuse and left the gym, quickly. Instead, "I don't usually give lifts to strangers, but if you promise you're not a serial killer, I might." He laughed.

That was my first mistake.

My second mistake was going into his house and drinking coffee at his kitchen table.

My third mistake, well, that should be obvious by now.

It had been 11 years since I'd slept with another man, or even thought about it. After that day I'd think about it a lot, and make a lot more mistakes.

The shame and shock after that first time was beyond any feeling I could recognise or describe. I had to pick Morgan up from school before I could go home and shower. I imagined every set of eyes upon me as I walked into the playground towards the group of mothers sitting at our usual meeting spot to wait for the kids to run out. I was convinced they could sense what I'd been doing, smell the sweaty deception on my clothes. It was the longest I'd ever waited for that bell to ring.

When I finally got home I scrubbed my skin raw in the shower, convinced George would smell it on me too. I was devastated by what had happened, what I'd done. I couldn't believe it really. The entire act was like an out-of-body experience, looking down at the unfathomable scene below me. Yet I was lost in the eroticism, the undeniable passion like nothing I'd felt before. The taboo somehow made me hungrier for it.

My immediate thought was to tell George about the horrendous mistake I'd made. I knew he would be shattered. I wasn't sure he would even be able to comprehend it. I couldn't comprehend it myself. I imagined it would change everything, and he would never look at me the same way ever again, or speak words of love to me. It would probably end our marriage. The possibility was too much for me to process.

No. What was the point in telling George, breaking his heart, ruining our marriage, destroying our family, everything, for one stupid, idiotic

CHAPTER FIFTEEN | THE RING

mistake that I would never make again. I'd just pretend it never happened. I'd file it away with all the other shitty things I'd filed in the filing cabinet of my mind. I promised myself, swore to God, I would never do it again.

That was a lie of course, but not at the time. I believed it was the first and last time I would ever cheat on George.

It was just the beginning. My life became a matrix of lies, excuses, justifications whenever necessary. I didn't consider consequences. I told myself a hundred stories to give myself permission: no one will know, it'll be my little secret, I'm not hurting anyone, it's only wrong if I start feeling something. And a million other bullshit reasons I'd create to defend my adultery.

A cheater's mind is a fickle thing, a dangerous place to live.

As time passed and I sank deeper into the deception, the power it gave me grew stronger. It was intoxicating, like a kind of drug. Nothing I'd been through in my life had really prepared me for the attention, the lust. I didn't grow up pretty and skinny. I knew nothing of that world. Any popularity I'd attained was for all the wrong reasons.

I can only liken it to a poor person winning lotto, who has no common sense about money. They are unprepared and embark on a frivolous spending spree. They don't stop to consider the future or plan ahead. They see what they want, and they take it. It's a deluded misconception that things last forever, like marriage certificates and tight skin. They are left scratching their heads when their bank balance is back at zero, wondering what the hell just happened.

That's how it felt. I was oblivious to it all. My new body was my lotto win, my jackpot. The more I trained the better my results. Better results attracted more attention. They spurred me on. After a lifetime of self-loathing every time I looked into a mirror, I could finally see someone different looking back at me, and I loved what I saw – on the surface.

I was blinded by the superficial version of myself.

Eventually the 'what ifs' would begin their torture. What if I hadn't watched Oprah that day, and I hadn't lost weight? And if I hadn't lost weight I wouldn't have gone to the gym, and then I wouldn't have had surgery. I wouldn't have met him. I wouldn't have cheated and I'd have a clear conscious. My vows would still be intact. So if all that hadn't happened then maybe George wouldn't have lost his ring in the surf that day. And if he hadn't lost his ring then maybe he'd still be wearing it…

But it did happen, all of it. George's lost ring started a chain reaction of events that would change the course of our lives. My indiscretions didn't end our marriage, not in an obvious way. Not then. But eventually every day that I had lived as an adulteress would demand compensation. It would be a vicious tit-for-tat. I would relive each one of those days in hell, but not any hell I'd imagined. Not the kind of hell I'd known before.

CHAPTER SIXTEEN

Flipping Out

It was eight days before Christmas 2001 as I sat at the dining room table. A sea of white papers covered the stainless-steel surface, the starkness broken by rows of black print and that little green fire-breathing dragon in the top corner of each page. Droplets of sweat trickled down my back as I wiped my top lip with the tassel of my sarong. As if the task weren't daunting enough, I had to contend with the relentless humidity. Why couldn't it be winter when I uncovered such a crime?

Six years had passed since we'd moved back to Sydney from my hellish stint at country life. Mum and Dad retired down south eventually, in the spring of 1999. Around the same time George had lost his ring.

We were still living in Mum and Dad's house. It was just convenient

I suppose. After they left, there was no real urgency for us to move. Their Inner-City home was their retirement plan. I assumed they'd never sell it. It would be my inheritance one day – not that I knew it then, not for sure. We continued to pay minimal rent. It was more like cheap boarding really. It played on my mind, knowing they could get four times that amount for a prestigious suburb like Annandale – 10 minutes from Sydney's CBD.

I loved that house. We'd moved there when I was 16. It held a different set of memories from the house I grew up in. Greg and Tony never lived in Annandale. They were long gone by then, and even I would come and go until I was 18, when I'd leave for good. The house was cosy and homely, and Annandale was relatively peaceful for a suburb so close to the city. It was under the flight path, but that becomes white noise to inner-city dwellers. The house would've been snapped up quickly on the rental market.

I'd push my guilt aside. I assumed if Mum and Dad had a problem with us overstaying they'd say so. We'd be forced to make the move then, back into the scary buyers' market. Then we'd really have to start over. I did wonder if Mum and Dad were disappointed with us. We probably seemed irresponsible to them, not taking any real initiative to stand on our own feet, get our own place again. They'd had a lifetime of disappointment with my brothers and I'm sure they expected more from me. I took comfort in the thought of our bank balance. Mum and Dad would be proud when they saw that kind of progress. So would I.

Extra marital activities stole much of my headspace. I had mastered a routine that worked perfectly in hiding my secret double life – at least that's what I believed. I was in so deep by then, beyond any redemption or forgiveness. I kept on telling myself it'll end soon, just deal with it then. Like a bewildered Scarlett O'Hara in *Gone with the Wind* – I'll think about that tomorrow.

I was distracted in other ways too. Domestically I'd always excelled, so there was never a problem there. Besides Morgan's school life, there were dancing lessons, swimming lessons, sleepovers, parties, and a diary

CHAPTER SIXTEEN | FLIPPING OUT

full of other needs. I wondered how an eight year old could have a better social life than me. I didn't want to imagine how exhausting it would become in her teens.

The only notable thing that had really changed while I was distracted was my responsibility for our financial life. By that I mean paying bills, updating policies, keeping tabs on automatic deductions, and the general comings and goings of our bank account. In the past I'd taken care of those things. George would help if I delegated, or we'd handled things together. He was technical and good with numbers, and a lot smarter than me. I was good at time management, organising just about anything, and remembering details, like when the next phone bill was due. George remembered other kinds of detail. He had an analytical mind, and of course he knew what the neighbours were eating for breakfast and other mindless detail. I guess our different skills complemented each other, not that I considered that at the time. At the time I wondered how someone so smart could be so hopeless. How could George have the talent for intricate computer coding when he couldn't even remember to take the garbage out? I would complain to Mum.

"Oh love, he's like a mad professor – very good at what he does, but not so good in the real world. No one person can be all things, darling, especially men. God forbid they have to multitask – bloody useless. Try to be a bit more patient, love, and thank ya lucky stars he's not like ya brothers."

My once military-style need to control things had clearly been lost with the lobotomy. I had inadvertently surrendered my duty as financial controller to George, who had somehow taken on this role. I must have been very distracted.

As I stared at the blinding white sprawled out in front of me, my focus waned. When had I become so blasé that I, Mrs Anal Retentive, hadn't noticed all those bank statements?

How had I missed all that mail?

My irritation was rising with the room temperature. Frustrated with the rows of information and numbers I just couldn't make sense of.

I was lost in the repetitiveness. My headed pounded with the effort as my brain tried to calculate what couldn't be calculated. As the hours passed I cursed George even more for the chaos of his 'filing system', the disorganised mess before me, and the fact that I had to deal with it. Numbers were his domain, not mine. I resented being in that position, and I resented him for putting me there.

A few months earlier, friends had suggested we should start flipping properties with them. They were amateur entrepreneurs, would-be property moguls, buying apartments cheap off the plan and selling them on completion for more than double what they'd paid. It was a great way to make big profits, serious money, they said, if you had the patience.

They were about to embark on a new venture, a trendy apartment block in Newtown. It was a grungy part of Sydney's Inner West – vibrant, colourful and very sought-after. A large cross section of the gay community lived in Newtown, along with arty types, bohemians and backpacking drifters. Professional power couples favoured the evolving suburb too, and the diversity was appealing. It was a place to be seen in those days. A property in Newtown might be very profitable. I liked the idea of that.

"George, we should do this. Let's use our savings and make it happen. It's a good opportunity for us to finally get ahead, make real progress. I don't want Mum and Dad thinking we're leeches. They've had enough to deal with. We should be on our own by now. It's not fair on them."

He agreed of course, and told me he would get it sorted. Our savings were apparently tied up in a term deposit of some kind, but he would speak to the bank and have the money released. There'd be a penalty, but I didn't care, not with all the money we were due to make in the near future. I assumed George knew what he was talking about. I had no reason to think otherwise. George always did what I asked him, and I trusted him wholeheartedly.

My distractions kept me occupied, until my mogul friends couldn't hold off on the deal any longer.

CHAPTER SIXTEEN | FLIPPING OUT

"Marce, if we don't move quickly now we're going to miss out. With Christmas almost here, that'll be the end of business until February. What's the hold-up anyway?"

I apologised, embarrassed that I had put them in an awkward position. They knew that I was the taskmaster of the family and they probably wondered what the hell had gotten into me lately. I wondered if my distractions were causing me to slip up. Was I losing my grip and becoming careless? Were people starting to notice? The thought made me panic. If my friends noticed a change in me, then maybe George had noticed too. I doubted it. I thought he was more distracted than me most of the time, off with the pixies or wherever mad professors go. I assumed all that code messed with his head – how could it not? I was sure he dreamed in code. Still, perhaps it was finally time to end my indiscretions and start behaving like a proper wife and mother, a good woman again. What a joke!

Yes. It was time. Things had changed. I didn't feel the way I used to in the beginning. I was riddled with indignity and felt out of control. I was over it long ago. What was the point of adultery? It served me no purpose. It was habit then, another burden to overcome and another addiction to rid myself of.

When I followed up with George, he told me he was still dealing with the bank and trying to sort things out. I was really annoyed at that point. I decided to take matters into my own hands, which I should've done in the first place. Until then I hadn't really paid proper attention as I would have a few years back, before any distractions. I couldn't believe I'd allowed George to have full rein on our finances, and to take full responsibility for such an important matter, the outcome of which might determine our future. I was angry with myself more than anything. I should have known George might struggle with the task, given his demanding workload and his lack of entrepreneurial drive. It was not that he wasn't capable of juggling a hundred things if he had to; he just didn't have much faith in himself. I didn't know that then. I just thought he was lazy. Years later I'd wonder if that were my fault. I'd wonder about a lot of things.

When I told George I was taking over, taking back control of our finances, he seemed to recoil.

"You don't have to do that, darling. It's fine. I told you I'm organising things…"

It wasn't in George's nature to defy me. I was taken aback by his continued attempts at excuses. I had a brain snap. I wasn't listening to his bullshit any longer. I demanded the bank statements and every other detail concerning our finances over the past however many years I hadn't seen them. I gave him no choice, and he had left the mountain of files on the dining room table early that morning. He'd gone to work while I was still sleeping. He'd never left for work that early before.

I couldn't wait to see our savings account. I had no idea what the amount was, but after six years of saving I knew it would be impressive. Together with the little profit we'd made on selling our Central Coast home all those years ago, it would have accumulated well into six figures I was sure.

And there I was sitting at the table, piles of evidence before me, but I still had no answers. Like a detective staring at a storyboard of suspects pinned to a wall, knowing the killer was amongst them, scratching their head in frustration, wishing they was psychic. I was doing the same.

After hours of foraging through the mess, I could only conclude the bank had made a massive balls-up. That much was clear – or these were someone else's bank statements. I couldn't identify with any of it. The words, the amounts, might as well have been written in Hebrew. I hadn't been in the corporate world for 10 years, but surely my brain couldn't be that dead.

I called George. He didn't answer, and he didn't return my calls. He always answered, and always returned my calls usually within minutes, or within the hour.

My blood was boiling, and it wasn't from the stifling late afternoon heat.

I called my mogul friend. He had a head for numbers too. Maybe

CHAPTER SIXTEEN | FLIPPING OUT

he'd have some insight into my dilemma. I knew he'd put me at ease and calm me down at least, and I had to be calm before I made the abusive call to the bank.

After telling him the story, giving him the details and answering all his questions, he spoke in a voice I'd never heard before. He sounded distracted, elusive, like he wasn't paying attention at all.

"Marce, the bank hasn't made a mistake. You need to talk to George when he gets home. I can't… I'm not sure what to say…"

"What do you mean you're not sure? How can you not be sure?" I was about to get hysterical.

"Just talk to George. It'll be fine. Keep me posted, and good luck."

Then he was gone. I stared at my mobile phone as if it had just bitten me. What the hell? Instead of calm reassurance I got a pencil straight through the eye. Was the humidity sending everyone mad? My blood pressure went up another notch. I was mortified at my friend's reaction. It only confused me more.

George was late. The latest he'd ever come home from work. By then I'd collated some order into the piles of rubbish he'd left me.

I lashed out the minute he walked through the front door.

"Why haven't you answered my calls all day? What the fuck is going on, George? Do you know about the debacle at the bank? Those statements are wrong. It says we have $200 in our account and there is no evidence of a term deposit. I think someone has stolen our identity."

That was the only sensible conclusion, and it had taken me all day to get there. I had conjured up all kinds of scenarios in my mind: possible reasons, probable outcomes. I was convinced it must be a sinister bank employee milking the system – our bank account – for their own personal gain. It was the only thing that made sense.

I took a deep breath to continue my barrage of questioning. He had a lot to answer and I hadn't even started yet. I was about to speak again, but then I noticed the look on his face.

Like a scene from *The Stepford Wives*, George looked at me as if I were some kind of robotic relic from an era long-gone. I think it was pity I saw. He had sad, puppy dog eyes, as if I were the dog and he was about to put me down. I hadn't a clue that I was about to die.

"Why are you looking at me like that? Fuck, George, what is wrong with you!"

And then it happened. A rambling mass of verbal diarrhoea like floodgates exploding. Never had I seen him so emotionally distraught. Not once in 15 years had he displayed such dramatic storytelling. I didn't even know he was capable of it. Maybe he was more like Tony than I'd imagined. In less than a minute he'd confirm it.

He confessed that he had gambled all our money away on poker machines in dingy clubs and pubs across the city and outer suburbs of Sydney. For almost two years he had been squandering our life's savings. Our future was gone.

I didn't know it then, but it appeared our deceptions had started around the same time. How coincidental. I'd wonder who went first. Was it a subliminal reaction on my part or his? We'd never really know for sure. We'd never really talk about it. Any revelations were years away. In the meantime, George was to blame.

I was right. Someone sinister had robbed us, stolen our identity. I just never imagined George could be the culprit.

It's strange the thoughts that enter your mind when it's trying to cope with information it couldn't possibly be equipped or programmed to deal with.

For a second, I wondered who had cloned my husband and swapped him for the imposter standing in front of me. I wasn't and had never been married to a gambler. I would never marry an addict no matter what the addiction. I couldn't have been married to someone for 15 years and not seen something, anything, that would indicate he was hiding a big, big secret. It just wasn't possible. None of this was possible.

My brain cleared from the mush for a nanosecond, rejecting what it couldn't decipher.

CHAPTER SIXTEEN | FLIPPING OUT

"George, this isn't funny. Of all times to be joking with me… are you fucking serious right now?"

I would have said more, but the anguish on his face confirmed the truth. The realisation stirred inside me as it tried to find a place to rest and fit where there was no space, no room. He kept babbling, and with each unbelievable word I felt a scorching heat inside me, a ripping of flesh, like a grizzly bear had hold of me and was eating me alive, just like in the movie *The Revenant*.

It was incoherent. I heard random words.

"I'm so sorry… please forgive me, darling… wanted to tell you for so long… we'll get through this… please don't tell Morgan…"

With the mention of her name, I was sucked back into my body and I lunged at him. I punched at his chest like a wild animal, my fists so powerful he fell backwards against the wall. I was the grizzly then. I became the attacker. All the while he let me do it. He took his punishment as if he'd longed for it, as if he'd been waiting for it his whole life.

My own verbal diarrhoea spilt forth like Tourette's on steroids. There was no stopping it.

"You fucking bastard… you selfish prick… how could you do this to us… what about Morgan… what about her future… I hate you… I hate you…"

I'm not sure how long it lasted or what really happened next. Morgan was having a sleepover at a friend's house. I was grateful she wasn't witnessing the crimes of her parents.

I lay awake all night. It was the longest of my life. I wanted to kill George for what he'd done. I couldn't get my head around it, unable to accept it was true. I didn't want to believe it. I wanted him to come to my bedside, hold me in his arms, tell me it was all a silly joke and it hadn't really happened, that I was just dreaming.

I visualised telling him my own secret. Finally, the time was right, and he wouldn't dare object. He'd have to forgive me now, because what he'd done was so much worse. That's what I believed. There was no hiding what he'd done. We'd all suffer for his deceit. I could hide my secret forever and no one would have to suffer, not even me. Yes, now we were even.

Of all the betrayals I'd endured, none was more incomprehensible than my husband's deception. I was powerless in the face of destitution, stripped of all control. I'd always imagined the worst of shitty things were behind me, but what unravelled next was a new level of darkness, even for someone like me.

CHAPTER SEVENTEEN

Once an Addict

If George were hoping for a mental breakdown, now that his secret had been revealed, it would have to wait. So would mine. The total sum of our assets was a few hundred dollars. During my audit I'd also discovered maxed-out credit cards, a pile of bills due yesterday, another pile with big bold red letters warning us of legal action, unpaid rent, and it was Christmas in one week. Payday was a month away. Deep shit didn't begin to describe our predicament.

The only other money I found was in a Commonwealth Bank Dollarmite account in Morgan's name. We'd opened it when she started school, planning on giving it to her on her 18th birthday, and set up an automatic deduction. Luckily, I was the signing authority on the account and George couldn't touch it without my knowing. I could've used that money so many times then and in the future, but I didn't touch it. On Morgan's 17th birthday I used that money to buy her first car, cash. It was a bright red second-hand Honda Civic, which I painstakingly wrapped in gold ribbon with a big gold bow on the top. It was a complete surprise! The look on her face was my reward, worth every sacrifice.

I went into damage control, my brain on autopilot. I had to be practical and not let emotions take over. That could come later. I had to keep it together for Morgan. She was 10 years old. We didn't want to ruin her Christmas. I wasn't sure I'd be able to pull it off, act as if nothing had happened. On the inside I was screaming. I was on the edge of an abyss, walking an invisible tightrope, a delicate balancing act between sanity and insanity. My body seemed to vibrate with the pressure. One wrong step and I'd fall in, and then who would I be? I couldn't give in to the blackness that was calling me, not yet. George could pull off normal. He'd had a lifetime of practice, so it seemed. He was a lot like Tony after all. Imagine that.

I had to think, plan, do something about the mess we were in, and I had to do it alone. I couldn't depend on George any more. I couldn't even look at him without wanting to rip him apart. My desire to kill him would give way to absolute brokenness. I'd leap from one to the other. One minute I'd be weeping uncontrollably, the next pacing like an enraged bull, ready to ram whatever got in my way.

My mind was a never-ending dialogue as I searched for clues in the remnants of my memories. Trying to pinpoint specifics: when did it all start? How did I miss the signs? What made him do such a thing? A million questions kept ricocheting in my head.

I waited for the answers to materialise, as if by magic they would. Like one of those 3D picture books from the '90s that appeared to be nothing but splashes of colour across the pages. You had to stare into the centre and focus on nothing at all. Suddenly a glorious image popped out and would take your breath away. Not everyone can see the magic.

CHAPTER SEVENTEEN | ONCE AN ADDICT

George could never see it, no matter how long he stared, and I used to wonder about people who could not see the brilliance of those images. I'd feel sorry for them. How dull their minds must be – clearly left-brain operators.

Yet here I was, blind to my own surroundings, oblivious to what was right in front of me. Had I really been that distracted? I couldn't fathom it. My husband, my George, had a secret double-life all his own and I hadn't a clue. I'd thought I'd been so clever hiding my own double-life. My acting skills could've matched Tony's by then. George wasn't supposed to be the actor, but he was better than both Tony and me. If he were that good, that smart at being one step ahead of me, did he know my secret? Was he more clued up than I ever imagined?

If he could gamble our life away, what else was he capable of? Did he have a lover too? Was there a partner in crime, someone he shared his secrets with? Someone not like me, a wife clearly too clueless to confide in. I could only guess at the answers. I couldn't ask him, and if I had I wouldn't have believed him. After his outpouring that night, he offered very little. My sudden lack of engagement worked in his favour, lucky George.

He kept his distance while I contemplated our future. Everything depended on my verdict and he knew it.

Each day seemed like a week in the lead up to Christmas. It was the school holidays and I wasn't sure if that made it better or worse. Holding it together in front of Morgan was like trying to audition for the acting role of my life, except I had no idea what my lines were. Tony would have pulled it off perfectly with his flawless improvising.

I thought about my brothers. Wouldn't they be pleased their perfect sister was no better than they were? Wouldn't that be the laugh of the century, that I had ended up with someone just like them, only worse? At least you knew what you were getting with my brothers.

My veil was slipping, the mask cracking under the pressure. I could feel a kind of madness growing inside me. All that repressed turmoil, not being able to speak to anyone about it, was wreaking havoc with my psyche. I couldn't call Mum and tell her over the phone, not something like this. She would be horrified. I couldn't begin to imagine what Dad would say. Oh my God, I would have to tell my father my husband was a gambler. How the fuck was I supposed to do that? I wanted to climb the highest bridge and jump so I didn't have to face anyone or admit anything. It would be so much easier if I somehow slipped away, gone before my time. The thought gave me comfort. The feeling unnerved me. Is that how it is, how it begins, the road to actual suicide?

I wasn't sure how long I'd be able to keep it up. I just had to get through the week, make it to Boxing Day when we'd take the usual pilgrimage to Mum and Dad's. I had to take it minute by minute – that was all I was capable of.

January was always Morgan's month with Mum, their favourite time of the year. It was mine too. A whole month of no routine, no drop offs or pickups, free to do as I pleased. I guess the timing of our downfall was good. I was grateful I didn't have to face the mothers at school. We seemed like the perfect family to them, to everyone who knew us.

George sensed my inner war and knew I needed space. He took Morgan to the movies and to visit friends. They made themselves scarce.

When I was alone I'd fall into a broken heap. I didn't have to stand up straight or hold it together. I could rant and scream out loud, and I did. The relief was immense, just for a moment. The neighbours would have heard it all, the mad woman who had clearly lost the plot in number 24.

My face was a swollen mess every time they returned. No amount of cold tea bags could help my bulging eyes.

"Mum, are you sick? You look like a ghost."

How insightful of Morgan, using that word. I felt like a ghost, something that used to be solid, but now just a shadow. I'd give her excuses – new sudden allergies that I'd never had before. She probably wondered what the hell was going on with her mother, and why she was so quiet and strange when she was usually so full of opinions.

CHAPTER SEVENTEEN | ONCE AN ADDICT

George couldn't confess his secret to his parents. He couldn't ask for their help. And we needed help. A small loan at least in the interim to pay the debt collectors would give us a bit of leeway. I refused to ask Mum and Dad, not after everything they'd done for us. I assumed George's shame was too much for him to deal with when it came to his parents. He was their golden boy. He asked me to do it.

"Sorry, Marce, I can't. I can't face them. You'll have to do it without me."

I couldn't believe what a coward he was. It shouldn't have surprised me. His inability to own his shit and then make me do his dirty work took me to new levels of resentment. I did it for Morgan. I needn't have bothered.

They took the news in their usual detached manner, devoid of any real empathy. As if I were telling the story of someone else's life, someone far removed from their world. Maybe George knew all along that his parents would never help him financially — especially to clear a gambling debt, not that we were asking for that. Maybe it was my reaction to their rejection that he was so afraid of. He must have known what the outcome would be. I surely didn't.

The exposition was excruciating. Each word I spoke seemed to tear at my facade, dangerously teetering on the verge of breakdown. If I weren't careful I'd start to cry, and if that happened it would be over. They would see me for who I really was, the same pathetic girl who stood at the church altar all those years ago, still unable to control herself.

They hardly said a word or showed any real emotion. If George's father said anything at all I don't recall. But I'll never forget what his mother said, very calmly, before they stood and walked out the door;

"Well, I can't believe it really. That's terrible news, Marce. What are you going to do? Don't worry, you're a strong woman. You'll cope. It'll be okay. You need to support him and be there for him and you'll both get through this."

With a pat on my back, a kiss on the cheek, they were gone.

My stunned fury imploded as I tried to stand but couldn't. I wanted to smash their empty coffee cups, but I couldn't even bring myself to do that. I knew I'd have to clean it up and I didn't have the energy. I had the overwhelming feeling they thought I was lying, or at the very least exaggerating. I imagined they thought if it were actually true, I probably drove George to it. I was overpowering and too demanding for their meek, gentle son, imposing impossible demands on him like taking care of bills and taking the garbage out. He was such a hard worker, surely his wife should be responsible for all other duties, including cash flow. I was certain they didn't approve of my new lifestyle. I should be at home like a proper wife and mother, instead of parading my scantily clad body at the gym. Better still, I should be back in an office doing a real job, earning real money, not spending it on personal training and massage therapy. Yes, if there was a problem in my marriage it had to be all my fault. Their son couldn't possibly gamble lives away. Their son would know better than that.

Our parents were like day and night. Our mothers were different species; there were no comparisons. How my own brothers would've longed for George's upbringing. Pampered and protected so fiercely. How peaceful to have such reserved parents, all that emotion hidden and so quietly unavailable. What a blissful childhood that would've been for them, for all of us. Yet there George was, no better off in the end – just like my brothers.

I never saw George's parents again. Any contact they had with Morgan would be through George. Morgan was their only grandchild, and would remain their only one – as long as I was his wife. As much as I loathed my in-laws at the time, I would've never deprived Morgan of a relationship with her grandparents. And besides, the last thing I wanted was to appear angry and bitter, the crazy mother. God forbid they should see through my exterior.

Christmas Day finally came. George took Morgan to his parents for the usual Christmas Day lunch. I didn't care that they'd all be there together without me. I was confident nothing would be said behind my back. The three of them would rejoice in the code of silence, nothing unusual there. I was glad to be alone. If by some miracle Morgan believed my lies of feeling unwell, she'd know after that day something was very wrong.

I was exhausted. Not a minute passed without a dozen emotions choking me. From hate to sorrow, anger to sadness, acceptance to denial, disgust to pity, and some other ones I can't describe.

I went out into the backyard hoping the fresh air would give me some reprieve. It was only then I noticed a strange orange glow in the air. It cast eerie shadows over everything. At first I thought I was delirious from lack of sleep and food. Perhaps I had gone mad. Maybe the bowels of Hell had finally opened up and the Grim Reaper was coming for me. What a relief that would've been. Then I realised what it was.

December 2001 had been a record-breaking month of heat. Out-of-control bushfires were raging on the Central and South Coasts. With hardly any wind, the smoke filled the air for a 200-kilometre radius, covering the city in a blanket of dense orange haze.

I lay down on my sunlounge and closed my eyes. It was hard to breathe, but I didn't care. I welcomed the suffocating embrace. I could feel the rays of sun on my clammy skin as if the haze was no match for the ozone layer.

As usual my tears flowed even through closed eyes. They stung so badly.

I felt something touch my leg. Thinking it was a bug my eyes snapped open. Through my blurry vision I saw tiny snowflakes falling all around me. For a split second I thought it had finally happened. I had gone insane or was hallucinating. I blinked furiously and wiped the wetness off my face with the back of my hand. When I looked down there were black smudges all over my body.

"What the fuck?" I thought I must be dreaming.

In one swift movement I sat up and tilted my head skyward, trying to find the source of my mirage. My raw eyes squinted against the cloudless sunny sky. The snowflakes were falling from nowhere.

In my delirium I reached out to touch one, and then I realised it was ash. Like a scene from Pompeii: raining ash. The bushfires were putting on a show all right. It was such a surreal sight I couldn't help but see the irony. How unexpected of the heavens, I thought, as if they too were crying for me – dirty, guilty tears, not pristine white ones. I didn't deserve those.

I was covered in sooty blackness. I thought about the chimney sweep on my wedding day. Of all things to think, it was the worst. That chimney sweep would have a good old laugh – pretentious bitch, that'll teach you to refuse my kisses, he'd say.

If raining ash wasn't a sign, I'm not sure what else I needed.

The next day I drove the four hours to Mum and Dad's alone. I couldn't deliver a blow like that knowing Morgan might hear. I didn't trust my emotions, or Dad's reaction. It was strange being alone on that long drive. Was it a glimpse of how things would be? I hadn't driven solo for long distances since my late teens, when I would take off for the weekends in my shiny white HR Holden with its red interior and loud cassette stereo. I loved that car. We shared a lot. It was my home away from home. I'd sleep in it on the side of the road or on lonely beaches along the way to nowhere in particular. Was I really that brave? Not anymore.

Morgan knew that morning something was bad. Her mum didn't drive to Nanny's alone. I promised I would tell her everything when I returned the next day. She could go to Nanny's as soon as I got home. I hoped by then I'd know what to do. I prayed Mum would be the one to tell me.

I cried on and off the entire drive, my vision dangerously blurred. As I drove through the sharp bends on the highway at Kiama, I looked out at the vast ocean and inhaled that perfect view as I always do. I was mindful that the speed limit drops dramatically on those treacherous corners – one lapse in concentration and you'd end up with the dairy cows far

CHAPTER SEVENTEEN | ONCE AN ADDICT

below, dead of course. I wanted to put my foot down on the accelerator and fly over the edge just like Thelma and Louise. It would be so easy to stop the pain. I'd never have to make another decision. So, so enticing...

The look of horror on Mum's face said it all. The minute she saw me she knew something was very wrong. I assured them both Morgan was fine, but George wasn't.

I sat opposite them in the lounge. Mum was in her armchair, Dad in his. I could hear the waves in the distance through the open balcony doors. How peaceful and calm it seemed before I ruined it.

I hesitated. All that practicing on the drive down useless then, every line forgotten, just like when I was a kid. Some things never change.

"Oh love, for God's sake, what is it?"

It spilled forth, every unbelievable ugly detail. They listened intently, too shocked to speak at first, but their eyes showed their pain.

I focused my attention on Mum, trying not to look at Dad's face. I knew his eyes bore into me with each blubbering word I spoke. I had promised myself I wouldn't cry, but that didn't happen. I thought I would melt with the shame of it. I wondered when his rage would kick in and he'd start with the ranting. Not since my wedding day had I displayed such rampant emotion in front of my father, and compared to my current outburst my wedding day was a tea party. I found it hard to breathe, let alone talk. It should have been an overwhelming release to finally be able to speak about it, but it gave me no comfort, in fact it just made me worse.

I was in Mum's arms then. She was talking, trying to calm me, and I held tight for comfort. I'd craved it for a week. When I finally released her and sat back down, I realised Dad hadn't said a word. He had a look on his face I'd never seen before. It was sadness, not anger.

"Love, you need to separate from George. Trust me. If he's gambled everything away he'll do it again, they always do. Once an addict always an addict. It won't be the end of it, you mark my words. He'll hurt ya both again. What a bloody fool. What the hell is wrong with that boy?'

I didn't expect Mum to be the angry one. It caught me off guard, left me speechless. She just couldn't believe what George had done. She was devastated for me and Morgan.

What I really didn't expect was what Dad said next.

"Don't say dat to her."

"Why not, it's true, isn't it? How will she ever trust him again? It'll never work, not after that kind of deception," Mum fired at Dad, but he kept his calm as he continued.

"People make mistakes, no one's perfect. You don't just trow away a marriage if dey love each other. You try again, start over. Do you still love him?"

Dad looked directly at me as he asked the question. Our eyes locked. There was no escaping it. The shock of his words felt like I'd just been branded with a hot poker. Never in all my life had he asked such a personal question. Out of all the hundreds of thoughts I'd had since finding out George's secret, not once had I thought about love. Now I had to think about it and I didn't know what to say. I was too hurt and angry to think about love; there was no room in my heart for that. Mum made it easy.

"Love's got nothing to do with it. It never does when it comes to addiction. Leave him, darling, you can do it. You're stronger than you think."

I was gobsmacked at Mum's words. They were just so unexpected. Not that I disagreed. Deep down I'd assumed we'd probably separate. I think I was just hoping, by some miracle, there'd be some other way. It was hard to imagine life without George, single again, alone in the world. It just didn't make sense. Separation was something other people did, not us, not our *Three Musketeers* family. But what of Morgan? Would she want to live with me or her dad? She was still a daddy's girl. How does shared custody work? Would she even want to be shared? It was all too much for my small brain to ponder, but I had to be honest. I knew myself well enough to know I'd never get over it. I couldn't cope, forever suspicious of his every move. All trust was gone, so didn't that mean love was gone too?

CHAPTER SEVENTEEN | ONCE AN ADDICT

The enormity of the response broke me. I burst into tears again, I couldn't answer Dad's question.

"See, you made her cry," Mum shot Dad a death stare. "Don't, love. Shit happens to the best of us. It'll all be okay. We'll work this out together and we'll help you. And whatever you decide about George we'll support your decision."

Thank God for Mum. Someone I could finally depend on.

I had a lot to think about, and now I had to consider love on top of it all. My heart was hollow. It fought against any feelings of love. My mind took control instead. I didn't dare confess my own betrayal to my parents. If only they knew it was probably all my fault.

Maybe George's actions were his long-awaited rebellion. He'd probably known of my affair all along. He would never confront me. His inability to do so was probably torture. I assumed his gambling was some kind of cry for help. Did a broken heart make him do it? I wondered if Mum would be so harsh knowing her daughter was no better. I didn't want to think about that. I didn't want to face my own betrayal; it was too much for one person. It was all too much for me. I'd have to protect myself now, more than ever before. And so by the time I got home, I'd made my decision.

CHAPTER EIGHTEEN

Back to the Future

We separated as 2002 began. I still wasn't sure about our future, but I made him leave anyway. He felt like a stranger to me. I couldn't stand the sight of him and my brain didn't work properly when he was around. I couldn't make rational decisions in anger. Any inclination that I might be capable of forgiveness turned to resentment whenever he entered the room.

"I understand, darling. I'm so, so sorry. I promise I'll never hurt you both again if you just give me a second chance. I love you so much…" George whimpered.

Fucking liar.

I'd lost count of the sorrys, and every time he spoke of love I wanted to throw something. It felt like a punch to the gut, not an apology.

"Just leave, George, go... "

I'm not sure where he went exactly. I knew he was with friends. I didn't really care. Morgan was with Mum and Dad, so she wouldn't know about the separation until she got back from school holidays. I had no idea how I'd tell her. I played it over and over in my mind, but I couldn't picture the ending. Her world was about to change catastrophically. My beautiful, happy, fun-loving daughter was about to experience her first broken heart, and by the man she trusted most in the world.

History repeated after all. A broken heart is a broken heart. Does it really matter how it breaks?

My mind played tit-for-tat in the battle to find meaning. The outcome was always the same. My unfaithfulness had subliminally permeated every space of our marriage. I might as well have gambled away the money myself. But I hadn't. The ramifications of my betrayal had nothing to do with our bank balance, or Morgan's future. I still hadn't confessed my secret. If George knew, he still said nothing.

No, I wouldn't take the blame for his actions. No matter how many times my mind went around in circles. My offenses were merely misdemeanours compared to his. That's what I'd tell myself at the end of each exhausting round.

Still, my guilt was always there in the background, like a song you can't get out of your head. The thought of it, of what I'd done, would make my stomach turn and my heart sink. Was that really me? Had I really done something so despicable to my poor, innocent husband, the only man I'd ever loved?

When the truth of it hit me like that, it would take me to the brink of despair. In the house all alone, long empty days turned into weeks. I was scared of my own mind.

I longed to tell George, to rid myself of the burden, to feel whole again. And once I did I'd have to tell Morgan. How could I let her believe

CHAPTER EIGHTEEN | BACK TO THE FUTURE

it was all her father's fault? Her heart would break for the second time, and she'd be the daughter of two deceiving parents. I couldn't do it. It would destroy her faith in me and that might never be reparable.

I started drinking heavily. I didn't even like drinking, but it numbed everything and that was so much better. I wasn't eating, so the effects were much worse. I would vomit most days at some point, and then I'd drink more. It tasted like shit, but I kept drinking. I wondered how alcoholics could keep up the pace without dying. How they functioned at all was a mystery. Unlike Mum and Tony, I'd clearly missed the alcoholic gene.

I'd listen to George Michael CDs and bawl as I swigged my bottle of vodka, gulping the toxic poison as if it were water. Just like in the movies. What a pathetic cliché. But I didn't know what else to do. When I tried to plot my next move my head went to mush, all rationale severed as my nervous system failed me. I'd lost all control. I couldn't even make a simple decision: should I get a glass or just keep drinking from the bottle?

Weeks passed in this state of absolute binge. If I did have to venture out to the shops before I got drunk, I'd start sweating at the mere thought of it. Bumping into someone I knew wasn't an option. What would I say? I looked like a bag lady. Maybe no one would recognise me. I didn't.

The world outside was scary. Everything had changed again. I was back where I'd started all those years ago, afraid to be in public, scared to look anyone in the eye in case they saw right through me. I couldn't fake happy or normal then, not for a million dollars.

I started to ignore my friends' calls and refuse their offers of help. If there were a knock at the door I'd hide and pretend not to hear it. I couldn't stand telling the story any longer, repeating the same words. The more I spoke the more ridiculous I sounded. Paranoia convinced me they were all laughing behind my back – foolish, stupid woman. How could anyone not know their financial position in life? It was the new millennium, not the 1950s. How ignorant to proclaim you had no idea of your husband's gambling habits. What a fucking moron she must be. If it wasn't judgement, it was pity. In my mind that was the story. Eventually friends stopped calling and knocking at my door. I was glad.

One day I ended up at Burwood Shopping Centre. Most of my so-called friends would never go there. Burwood is borderline Western Suburbs of Sydney, undesirable working class, gangster territory to them. With my new status I fitted right in. As I walked aimlessly past shop windows I wondered what the hell I'd been thinking. The fluorescent lighting was brighter than the sun. I caught a glimpse of my reflection and pulled my cap down lower onto my eyes. I looked like a bag lady's handbag. I wasn't fit for the public, yet there I was roaming aimlessly.

I've never felt more alone than in that overcrowded Westfield. The last time I'd been there was with George. We did everything together: grocery shopping, clothes shopping, movies. Friday night was family night – dinner, movie and choc-tops for three. We were inseparable outside work hours.

My eyes started to water at the thought of it. Great. All I had to do was start mumbling and I'd look like a scene from *One Flew Over the Cuckoo's Nest*.

Then I saw what I didn't know I'd been looking for, a pet shop.

Looking straight at me through a mass of black cuteness was the most adorable Rottweiler puppy. The smile in my soul reached my face and the sensation felt strange as my cheeks and lips curved upwards. I couldn't remember the last time I'd smiled.

When I held her tiny furry body against my chest, my heart filled with warmth and love. I knew she was the one. She was the runt of the litter, so she'd been left behind. I couldn't let that happen. God knows what fate awaited her. I would buy her for Morgan and for me, a distraction for both of us. I thought of Tara. I wondered, would this new addition fill the space she'd left behind all those years ago? I couldn't believe it had taken so long to replace her. Maybe if we'd had a dog, things would've turned out differently. Maybe all my attention would've been on the dog, not other distractions. Happy tears fell, right there in the shop. They landed on her fur, but she didn't notice. Her tiny six-week-old body snuggled

CHAPTER EIGHTEEN | BACK TO THE FUTURE

against me. I had a feeling she needed me as much as I needed her.

I named her Angel. I knew she'd save me. She felt like a gift from heaven – finally something normal. I had a new purpose then, and Morgan would be home soon. I had to be responsible for both of them. I stopped drinking, thank God.

Morgan came home. She was excited about Angel, but Mum had prepped her for the bad news and she was heartbroken. Her world had turned upside-down while she'd been away. Her daddy wasn't there any more to tuck her into bed at night and read to her as she drifted off to sleep, still a little girl. I was no substitute. I didn't know how to read properly.

I hadn't seen George at all while Morgan was away. I'd heard – from the few people I was still in contact with – he was getting on with life. In fact, he'd been going out a lot, partying with the wrong crowd. My temperature would rise at the stories. There I was on the verge of a mental breakdown and he was out living it up, not a care in the world. What the fuck? He had caused total destruction and he didn't give a shit, it appeared. Who the hell had I been married to anyway?

By February a new routine was established. George would pick Morgan up and spend the weekend with her. She couldn't wait for his visits. Her face would light up when she heard him at the front door and she'd run into his arms, happy again.

On the inside I would seethe at the unfairness of it all. I looked like the bad guy with my rules and routine, and he looked like Saint Bloody George riding in on his white horse, stomping to the sound of triumph. I'd remove myself from his presence in case my façade cracked and I blurted out everything I was feeling. Then I'd really look like a lunatic. I couldn't allow that to happen. I had to stand tall, no matter how small and angry I felt.

George would take Morgan to his parents. The thought of it gave me lockjaw with all the clenching. I didn't trust how they might influence her. I had good reason. She would come home on those days laden with gifts and a bad attitude. It took all my willpower to control my temper and not ask the hundred questions I wanted to ask. I acted blasé, kept it casual. I wasn't about to become Morgan's psychotic mother. She'd tell George and then he'd know what a mess I really was. His parents might try to convince him Morgan should be with him full time. Better off without her lying mother.

It was a new kind of mind torture.

I was in a perpetual state of alarm, all the while pretending I was coping. Every scattered thought that popped into my head morphed into fact within seconds as if the very idea of the thought would bring it into reality. Morgan had always loved George more, favoured him above me. They were closer than I could ever be to her. Would she choose him? Blame me for his downfall? Will she hate me when she one day learns the truth of my own betrayal? Would George tell her lies? I could just imagine it – darling, you know what your mother is like, impossible, demanding, short-tempered, impatient. She needs things a certain way. She's very materialistic. I couldn't let her down. I did it for her, darling.

Would he manipulate her into thinking he'd had no choice? I was convinced I'd be cast out, that I'd lose her in the end. These thoughts would come and go at random, lasting seconds or minutes or hours. I was on the brink of madness as my mind conspired against me and I couldn't tell anyone. I had a new empathy for the institutionalised insane.

One day Morgan and I were eating dinner. Even the simple act of dinner was strange, surreal. George's vacant place at the table was like a big black X on a treasure map. The empty void seemed palpable in those moments, like we'd stepped into someone else's lives. Nothing was familiar in our single-mother family.

I noticed Morgan wasn't really eating, just pushing the food around her plate with her fork.

"Darling, why aren't you eating?"

"I'm not hungry, Mum." Morgan's voice was a whisper.

I looked at her then. Her face was gaunt and pale; she looked tired,

CHAPTER EIGHTEEN | BACK TO THE FUTURE

frail. The light had gone from her. My once bubbly girl wasn't there. My eyes scanned her as if seeing her for the first time in months. Her little hands, tiny wrists and birdlike arms made me silently gasp. When had she become so skinny? It was so unnerving.

"Darling, you have to eat or you'll get sick. Look how skinny you are. When was the last time you ate?"

Adrenaline surged into my belly as a new guilt took over. How could I have missed my emaciated daughter? What kind of mother was I? What the hell was happening to our lives?

"I don't know, Mum. I can't eat anymore. My tummy feels funny all the time."

My heart seemed to expand in my chest. I bit down hard, teeth upon teeth as I tried to stop my anger erupting. Not for her, for George. I took a deep breath, exhaled long and slow, and spoke as calmly as I could.

"Darling, it's very dangerous if you don't eat. I'll have to take you to a special doctor and you won't like that. Maybe you'd like to talk to someone about all this? Someone who could help you understand?"

I went to her then. I hugged her, and she put her arms around my waist and started to cry.

And there we were the two of us, broken in different ways. Going through things we didn't deserve – well, Morgan didn't, that's for sure. I could only imagine her feelings of abandonment and rejection. The father she was so close to, so connected with, suddenly gone. As the daughter it would be far worse. If my own pain were any indication, then her suffering must be immense. She was only 10. How could her sweet, innocent mind comprehend what had happened? She was the real victim; my poor, beautiful Morgan. And George was free, not having to witness the carnage he'd left behind, the destruction he'd created. But I was the co-creator. I knew it deep down. I couldn't lie to my soul. I couldn't disregard my part in the downfall of my marriage. But on the surface, I had to. For the sake of my daughter, and my sanity.

As each day passed, my thoughts chipped away at my spirit. I stopped faking it. I felt removed from life, like an apparition, helpless, hopeless – what to do, how to fix my daughter? I assumed I'd go completely mad soon enough, and then what, my poor Morgan? But no amount of cuddles from Angel could lift me from the bleakness.

Mum was the only one I could talk to.

"Marce, love, I know how hard this is, but you have to pull yourself together for Morgan. She needs you now more than ever. God knows the damage that's been done; that's blatantly obvious. Don't you abandon her, too. It will destroy what's left of her. My poor little chicken."

Mum was right. Something in her tone snapped me to attention. I had to take action and that required a new decision.

Morgan needed her father. She wasn't whole without him and neither was I. I had to be honest with myself. I still loved George despite it all. Despite everything, he was part of my soul and I couldn't deny it any longer. I had nothing left to fuel the anger. It was gone. I'd finally answered Dad's question. I knew George needed us too. If he didn't rid himself of the friends he was keeping, Morgan wouldn't have a daddy for much longer, I was sure. All that partying would kill him. They were imposters – he just couldn't see it.

I stripped back all my layers metaphorically: pride, ego, and all the delusions that accompany them. If our marriage were to succeed, things had to change. I wanted that. I longed to feel the happiness of an equal marriage. No more boss figure. No more opinions, judgements or dominance. I really didn't have the energy or the will anymore. I don't think I ever wanted it. Being the head of the family was just something I felt I had to do. Someone had to take charge, be in control. Well, not anymore, not like that.

To start again meant taking risks. My first would be to tell George my secret. It was the only way our marriage had a chance. We had to be open and honest – no more secrets, no more lies. If he chose to stay away, then I'd have to accept his decision and find a way to move on. I would tell Morgan eventually, when she was older, when she might understand, and

CHAPTER EIGHTEEN | BACK TO THE FUTURE

hope she wouldn't hate me for it. Only the future could bring the outcome.

I played out the confession in my mind. Each scenario dissolved before it got to the end. Rejection wasn't something I could contemplate. Subconsciously I was sure I wouldn't have to. Sure that George would never reject me no matter what I'd done.

George had maintained his love through it all, sent me text messages regularly. I never answered. When he came to the house, I'd stay in the yard with Angel. Her ears would stand up to attention at the strange voice inside the house. I presumed my absence must be killing him, not knowing how I was really feeling. My ego had the confidence of testosterone.

It was my turn to text – George, we need to talk as soon as possible, if you can, please. I imagined his shock when he received it. After six weeks of silence he'd probably given up on me. He arrived soon after. When he looked at my face I saw a glimmer of hope in his. It was fleeting as he realised it wasn't good news I was about to tell him.

Oh God here I go. Please, please let this end well. I repeated my silent mantra over and over.

He followed me into our bedroom and I sat on the edge of the bed. It was the closest room to the front door. I was afraid my legs wouldn't make it to the dining room table.

"Oh darling, what is it, what's wrong?"

As he said the words, he kneeled on the floor in front of me. It felt strange to be so close to him after all those weeks apart. I could feel the heat from his body. I wanted so much to hug him, to feel that comfort again. But I couldn't, not yet. It might all change in an instant and maybe then I would see the George in my dream. The George I knew hated me.

I covered my face with my hands, but when I felt the familiar touch of his hand on my knee it ruined me. There was no stopping the flood then.

"Don't cry, darling, everything is going to be all right."

No it wasn't. I could feel the sound rising, the syllables taking shape in my throat. My mouth was about to speak words that once spoken I could never take back. I felt as if a hangman were about to push the chair away, out from under me.

"Any last words for the doomed... the abominable adulteress?"

My hands dropped to my sides. I filled my lungs, opened my eyes and looked directly into his eyes. I tried to hold his stare, but couldn't. I looked down. I couldn't bear to see his face when I spoke the words.

"George... I don't know how to say this any other way so I'm just going to say it... I... I have been unfaithful. I had an affair. It ended ages ago. I've wanted to tell you so many times for so long, but I didn't know how to... and then your secret... what you did... and well... now I'm telling you... will you forgive me...?"

As his hands left my knee, I looked at him.

Out of the dozens of scenarios I'd envisioned, none had prepared me for the look on his face. The pain as clear as if it were painted on, etched in every feature. It hadn't been there a moment ago. He looked so old. I saw his soul then. I swear I could feel its sorrow, and the heartbreak.

His chin quivered, and his eyes filled with tears. He shrank backwards and sat on his calves, his knees no longer able to hold him. He covered his face with his hands just as I had done moments before, and sobbed like nothing I'd ever heard before.

If George already knew, he was doing a good job of pretending he didn't.

Oh my God, what have I done?

My heart broke all over again and my words came fast, muddled, hardly audible even to me.

"I'm so, so sorry, darling. Please forgive me. Please say you'll come home. We can put all this behind us, start over and be a proper family again."

He looked at me then, his hands on the floor to balance himself, his face a mess, his nose running.

"But when...? Who...? Why... why would you do that, Marce?"

CHAPTER EIGHTEEN | BACK TO THE FUTURE

Oh. My. God. I hadn't thought about the questions. Not really, not the details. I realised in an instant I'd misjudged things cataclysmically. I imagined he'd forgive me on the spot, no details necessary, no need to speak of it again. That's what George did. That's how he operated.

I was paralysed. It was temporary.

I'm not sure exactly what I said or in what order, but I said a lot. I said it all. We had switched places. I hated the irony.

He listened in silence to my rambling.

"So you'll forgive me? You'll come home?" I asked with hopeful girlishness.

He reached for me then and hugged me tight. A rush of relief overwhelmed me. I was glad he was holding me. The emotional build-up and release left me weak and incapable. I could've slid right off the bed. But then he let go, looked into my eyes and spoke with calm conviction.

"Marce, I do forgive you, but I don't think I can come home."

Those words were so unexpected, so not the words I thought I'd hear, I was stunned.

"I just don't know… I'm not sure… I don't think… I don't think we can be together any more, darling." His voice was shaky, unsure. It was as if even he couldn't believe what he was saying.

At the realisation it could be over, I felt a surge, like I'd just been injected with insulin. I'm not a diabetic. A colossus of emotion roared through me as defeat sank in. I couldn't hold it. Like a rogue spirit had jumped into my body, it took what was left of any dignity or pride. All control was gone.

"What are you saying? Don't you love me anymore?" My voice was desperate, pleading. I didn't recognise it.

He searched my face. He saw something he hadn't seen before. He looked like he'd just accidently killed his best friend.

"Of course I still love you, darling."

A lifetime of habit, and he scooped me into his arms, still on his knees, and I reciprocated with the force of a tiger. I didn't want to let go, imagining it was the last hug.

It wasn't.

A few days later George came home with an enormous bunch of flowers. I'd missed his flowers, his post-it love notes all over the house and his foot rubs. I'd missed it all so much.

I didn't need any of that. I had him, and Morgan had her Daddy back. I'd been such a fool, taking my marriage for granted. I knew I'd never do it again. I vowed to be the best wife possible, and the best mother. I would be a better person, the best I'd ever been. George and I made a promise. From that day forward the past was behind us. We'd both made mistakes, there was no need to talk about it. George got rid of the wrong crowd, which left room for the right people in our lives. We had each other. We were a foursome family again. Angel loved her new second master.

I took my new vows very seriously. I'd sometimes think about all that wasted money, but it would depress me so I'd push it aside. What was the point? The first thing I did was change banks. I hated that little green dragon with a passion. Financially, we'd rebuild. We shared the responsibility. The old me would have garnished his wages and given him a weekly allowance. The new me had to trust, and I did it wholeheartedly. It was my only option. That was the way I saw it. I'd hit rock bottom. I didn't want to see that view ever again. I had a second chance and I wasn't about to blow it, and Morgan, my beautiful funny Morgan, was back to her old self and that was what mattered most.

I went back to work in the corporate world, part-time at first until I found my way around all the new technology. It was daunting. I'd had more confidence at 18 than I did at 36. How was that possible? But I survived, and it helped both financially and mentally.

For the first time in a long time I had hope. I could think about the future and smile. Everything really had changed for the better.

Mum and Dad were true to their word, supportive as always. We paid no rent for the next 12 months until we got back on our feet. Thank God for my parents. I'm not sure how Mum really felt about it all. She never said, and I never asked. I was afraid of what cliché she'd throw at me.

"Oh, what a tangled web we weave…"

Looking back, I recall what a counsellor said to me years later. She reminded me a lot of Mum

"Marce, even if we had a crystal ball and could see into our future, all our wrong decisions, all the pain and heartbreak, everything, we'd still choose that person because we'd tell ourselves, 'It's okay… we'll get through it… we love each other. Love is blind like that…'"

And it is.

I thought my separation was rock bottom. I was wrong about that. By the time I knew it for sure, Mum was gone. But even in death she'd take care of me.

CHAPTER NINETEEN

Twenty Days to Freedom

In the winter of 2006, two years after Tony's death, Mum decided she didn't want to live any longer. She was going to end her life.

We stood on the balcony of the dream house Dad had built for her six years before. He'd demolished the old white fibro home to make way for her 'mansion by the sea'. She'd talked about it her whole life. Dad would rebuild when they retired. After that, he'd fish the days away while Mum pottered, making jams and preserves with the abundance from Dad's garden. The rest of the time she'd read books, hundreds of books.

It wasn't quite the retirement they'd imagined. By the time the house was complete, Mum's health was worse, and soon she went into full-blown kidney failure. A new miracle drug was prescribed to treat her rheumatoid arthritis. She had a severe allergic reaction. The miracle was she didn't die. In fact, she became a case study in some medical journal. Mum was the first case in Australia to survive the worst recorded reaction to the drug. She contracted leukaemia and her white blood cells took over. Her body ulcerated from the inside out, eventually perforating her bowel. She drifted in and out, on the brink of death for weeks. Months later she was home again, but the damage caused by the drug sealed her fate. Dialysis wasn't a choice; it was a life sentence. She regretted it from the start, I'm sure, and would have preferred to let nature take its course. That didn't happen.

The next four years were a busy schedule of hospital trips and recovery days. Three times a week Dad would drive the two hours from Bateman's Bay to Canberra Hospital. Mum would sit while a machine cleaned her blood and made her feel human again. Dad would stay with her, not wanting to leave her side. He never complained. He cared for her as if he'd been doing it his whole life. The violent man of my youth was gone. Mum had always told me he was a good man on the inside, when no one was watching. I never believed her. I thought they were the excuses of a woman in an abusive relationship. But years later I saw that man, which only made it more confusing. Dad's love for Mum was undeniable. It was sad. All too late, I thought.

As we leaned on the balcony railing looking out at the ocean, I wondered if her decision had anything to do with Tony. Did she miss him so much she had to see him again? Was the guilt so overwhelming that she couldn't stand another day of breathing when her son no longer breathed? I tried to imagine that kind of loss. I pray I'll never know it.

If it was guilt, shouldn't Dad be dying too? Shouldn't he die first? At 73, Dad was still strong and fit. If not for his grey hair he could pass for a well-preserved 60. Mum, at 66, looked older than Dad. She'd aged a lot in two years. Dad had never been better.

CHAPTER NINETEEN | TWENTY DAYS TO FREEDOM

The waves crashed against the rocks under the cliff face in the distance. The winter sun was doing its best to warm us, but the chill was winning.

Mum spoke and I listened. There was no real drama in her words. She'd lost the energy for drama long before. I knew how that felt. She sounded as if she were planning an extended trip overseas and wasn't sure when she'd return. She was calm and relaxed. I wondered how that was possible.

"I'm throwing in the towel, love – can't do it anymore. I know it'll be hard on everyone, but they'll just have to accept it."

Her plan was to stop dialysis. Once you stop there's only one outcome, and there's no going back. She would be in hospital, not at home. Dad couldn't cope with that.

"It'll only take a few days, they tell me, so it shouldn't be too much fuss."

As easy as that – not too much fuss. Let's get this wretched business of dying over with, so I can get on with living in the afterlife. That's what I'd think if I were Mum.

I didn't feel anger or regret. I felt a kind of envy. Imagine that, having the choice to pick your own date and slotting it into your calendar, the last entry, ever. Would it be liberating or terrifying? I'd always known Mum was brave, but I never knew how brave until then. She had a guilt-free ticket to the other side, not like suicide at all. She didn't have to worry.

I thought of Monopoly. Go to Heaven. Go directly to heaven. You may pass purgatory (we'll make an exception). You can collect your abundance for all eternity when you get there. Hurry along now.

"This isn't living. It's not the life I want, being a burden on everyone. I know you understand, love, you're the strong one. That's why I'm telling you first, before ya father."

There it was again, the strong one. For a woman who supposedly knew me so well, how could she be so wrong about that?

We both knew giving up would be unforgiveable to Dad. I wasn't sure forgiveness was something he could do. I assumed it came with conditions. I doubt he ever forgave Tony for what he'd done. Not that he voiced his disapproval; not in front of me anyway, that would require a certain level of emotion and some things never change. Mum would need support for that conversation all right – an ally, someone to soften the impact.

"Bloody old fool thinks he's gunna live forever. He probably will. Well stuff that, not me." Mum rolled her eyes for the millionth time at her fool husband.

She reached out with her frail hand and placed it on top of mine. Her fingers were bent and twisted. Her frame had shrunk. She seemed so little. She must be less than five foot tall by now. The robust mother of my youth was gone. I placed my hand on hers as gently as I could, not wanting to bruise her. It didn't take much. Mum would bruise if you hugged her too hard. Dad once broke some of her ribs helping her out of a chair. She had brittle bone disease after the miracle drug cast its spell. Poor Dad, he still didn't know his own strength. He was horrified at what he'd done. With her other hand she patted me, the gesture so nostalgically familiar I almost burst into tears.

I couldn't allow myself to break down, not when she was using words like strong. I had to be the rock she needed.

Don't leave me, Mum. Please, please, don't leave me. I need you. Morgan needs you. I can't live in a world without you.

And a hundred other protests. Instead I spoke gently. "I love you, Mum. I understand. You need to do what you need to do. I'd do the same if I were you. I get it. I don't want you to suffer any more. It's so horrible seeing you in pain all the time, the misery you go through."

And I meant it. I looked down at the garden below. If I looked at her face I was afraid I'd crumble.

Finally, I turned and hugged her. I wrapped my arms around her shoulders and rested my chin against her hair. I closed my eyes and took a deep breath of the sweet concoction, the unmistakable smell of my mother. I wanted those smells tattooed in my mind forever. To recall them at a moment's notice should I need to. If only I'd known then just how much I'd need them.

Dad took the news as we expected.

"You can't. Dat's bullshit. You can't just give up like dat. We don't decide when it's time."

His words cut through the air like a bad smell and hung there like smoke. His face was a contorted mask.

Mum argued her case, and it was a good one. Not even Dad could deny she was fading away in front of us. He tried to convince her to hold out for that long-ago promise of a kidney transplant. It would never happen. Kidneys were rarely available. They wouldn't waste one on Mum. They couldn't even repair her bowel. Too frail. No more operations. She would have to live with it. I think that was her deal breaker. She stopped wanting to eat for fear of the outcome.

What she had to live with was faeces oozing from her vagina in a constant flow of putridness. She had to wear special sanitary pads, which she changed at least five times a day. She wanted to shower often, but even showering was a mammoth undertaking. It left her shaky and exhausted. She couldn't do it alone. Dad helped, but if I were there she preferred me to do it. I didn't mind. I did it for love.

"Marce, the last thing you want in the world is to have your husband wipe poo from ya fanny. It's a horrible indignity, love."

No wonder she wanted out.

Dad had no choice in the end. He was powerless.

I wasn't accustomed to seeing my father defeated. There was real fear in his eyes and I'd never seen that before. I wondered what would become of him when Mum was gone. I knew he'd cope domestically. He was very self-sufficient in that way. The problem would be his mind – and other things, without Mum's voice of reason to reel in his nonsense, which she had come to do more often as they'd grown older, he might go nuts.

Dad might have mellowed, but the world was still a corrupt conspiracy and politicians were the enemy. He was convinced Big Brother was always watching.

"Gary, you idiot. Our phone isn't tapped. No one is listening. Listening to what? Me gossiping to Myrna across the road about books we're reading and what's on the menu for dinner. Ridiculous old fool!"

The sicker she got, the braver she became. Funny old Mum. Dad didn't believe her of course. He'd huff and puff until it fizzled out. Who would call him an old fool after she was gone? Neither Greg nor I were that brave.

Mum had always handled the finances, paid bills, kept things in order. Not Dad's forte. He started working when he was 12. The war had ruined his family. As the eldest son he had to contribute, help his father who had suffered greatly. It was going to be a challenge all right. Would it fall on me to take over? Would Dad expect me, as the only daughter, to take care of things as daughters should? The thought made me sick to the stomach. George would lessen the burden in an admin sense, thank God. My life was in the city, four hours away. Physically the responsibility would become Greg's. He lived close by. How would that work? Their love/hate relationship lingered from childhood. At least for Greg, I was sure.

Yes, Mum's passing would cause a whole new way of life for the ones left behind.

On the 6th of October 2006 Mum was admitted into Bateman's Bay Hospital. She wasn't coming home. She'd given herself enough time to get things in order as best she could. Dad would spend that time denying it. Greg would spend it mourning. I think I was more concerned about him than Dad. He still depended on Mum so much, and she was still saving him on some level. He didn't use heroin anymore, but a lifetime of an irrational sense of reality left him always struggling financially. Mum used to say he must have killed a Chinaman in his last life to have such bad luck in this one. I guess that's one way of putting it. Why a Chinese I'm not sure, but clearly it was bad to kill one. I'd spend the time in a state of self-preparation. What a senseless waste that was. As if anything could prepare me for what was ahead.

I worried most for Morgan. She would be broken at the loss of her Nanny. No amount of counselling would help. She was 15, an age susceptible to lasting impressions. Things that happen at 15 seem to magnify in memory. I knew that very well.

There was one advantage for Mum. She had a say in planning her funeral!

"I want to be comfortable, love. Please don't let ya father dress me. God knows what he'll put on me. I'll look a fright. No shoes please. I want my slippers on. That'll do fine for a coffin."

It was like Mum was online shopping, getting ready for that long-extended holiday. I was daunted. She didn't want to look bad in her coffin. Does anyone look good in it? I would have laughed if it hadn't been so sad.

Visitors came and went in those early days. I'd listen as they said their goodbyes, recalling happy memories with Mum. Everyone got closure, tied up loose ends. How liberating for them.

When the visitors left, we'd talk. Mum was so grateful they'd popped in, as if it were a normal hospital visit and she'd see them again soon.

"It's nice isn't it, Mum, hearing your eulogies before you actually die?' I asked as if that were a normal thing to say.

She agreed it was lovely. The saddest visit of all was when George and Morgan arrived. Mum didn't want Morgan there at the end. She wanted her last memory to be a happy one. I sat a short distance away watching my mother and daughter say their last goodbyes. I dabbed at my eyes until my tissue disintegrated into mush.

"But, Nanny, what am I going to do without you? Who will I talk to? What if I have questions?"

Morgan sat next to Mum's bed, holding her frail arm and kissing it randomly with butterfly kisses, like she always did.

"I'm not leaving you, darling. I'll always be with you, I promise. It's just my body that's leaving, thank bloody God. I don't want you to be scared, love, so I'll come to you in your dreams. I'll answer all your questions there. All you have to do is close your eyes and think of me, and I'll be there," Mum said with such conviction even I believed her. As if she already knew the formalities on the other side. Maybe she did. Maybe her own dreams had already given her that insight.

They talked for the longest time. Mum was still trying to make Morgan giggle with her silliness. Still cracking jokes on her deathbed. It worked. Mum would miss Morgan the most, I was sure, more than all of us. She would be the greatest loss to Morgan.

The visitors stopped. Days passed, then weeks. Why was it taking so long? It wasn't supposed to be like that.

Mum slipped in and out of consciousness. Just when I thought she was about to drift away peacefully, her eyes would snap open. For a brief moment I would see absolute clarity in them. She'd look directly at me and speak as if she were perfectly coherent. How was that possible with the amount of morphine she'd had? She would close her eyes, drift off again into muttered ramblings, speaking names I'd never heard before, in conversation, and I'd wonder was she in the past or the future. One day she said something that broke my heart.

"Marce love, I think they've given me the wrong medicine. I think they're trying to kill me."

My stomach did a back flip. I could sense the fear and terror, as if it were all some enormous conspiracy. Liked she'd been tricked into being there. I felt helpless. Logic left me as I questioned everything. Was it the drugs talking? Or, did she regret her decision? What if she did? It was too late, all too late. My throat felt dry and constricted, but I couldn't cry, not in front of her.

I smiled gently, patted her hand like she'd patted mine hundreds of times, and I spoke as soothingly as I could.

"Mum, don't you remember why you're here in hospital?"

"I'm sick, love, but don't you worry, I'll get better. They just need to give me the right medicine. Can you talk to the doctor for me, fix it?"

CHAPTER NINETEEN | TWENTY DAYS TO FREEDOM

She closed her eyes, asleep again.

I let my heart weep as my head dropped to her pillow. I listened to the rhythm of her breathing. Peace again. I almost gave way to exhaustion, but I couldn't. Deep sleep wasn't an option. I couldn't miss it, her passing. I was certain I'd see her soul leave her body, as if somehow, I'd be privy to that.

Dad, Greg and I would take turns. Often the three of us would be there together, not speaking much, just watching. I slept by her side each night in a portable foldout bed the kind nurses wheeled in. If I momentarily drifted off I'd jump at the slightest noise, wide-awake. I'd check Mum's breathing and sigh with relief. I hadn't missed it.

One night as my head was on her pillow she suddenly spoke to me, very softly without opening her eyes. It was as if she knew I was there and we were alone.

"They're whispering, Marce. They're waiting for me."

Her words broke the silence and seemed to illuminate the dimness in her room.

"Who's whispering, Mum? What are they saying?"

My question hung in the air as I held my breath, waiting. Was I about to get a glimpse into the other side? She didn't answer. After the longest time I was about to lay my head back down, but then she spoke again, in the same hushed soothing voice.

"Be strong, love, be so strong. It's gunna be okay. You'll get through it. Just remember…" her words faded, unfinished, drifting away into the night, lost in the ether.

It unnerved me. What should I remember? Why would Mum tell me to be strong when she already knew I was? I had a feeling she wasn't talking about her dying. I pushed it aside, assumed it was delirium. I couldn't do much else with it.

As she slept, I traced my finger over her crooked hand and stopped at her perfectly manicured acrylic pink nails. I smiled to myself and whispered.

"Seriously, Mum, why bother with the nails? No one's going to notice when you're dead."

Trust Mum to have her nails done for her deathbed. It was her only vice by then, those and her hair. Her hair and nail lady would do house calls in the end, knowing Mum was too frail to travel to the salon.

It had been 19 days since Mum was admitted to hospital. It was barbaric to see her withering away. How was it possible? It was supposed to take a few days, not three weeks.

"Why can't they fill the syringe and get it over and done with? I'll fucking do it myself if they won't." I'd vent my frustration on Greg. I couldn't stand the thought of Mum's suffering. She wasn't speaking anymore. Those haunting words to me were her last. Greg assured me she wasn't suffering. She'd had too much morphine to feel anything, he said. I figured he'd know.

On the 20th day I had a feeling it was the day as the dawn filtered through the windows.

By 9am the sun was shining bright through the glass doors of the little balcony adjoining the room. You could enter the room privately if you wanted to avoid curious eyes from the corridors of the ward. Everyone knew room 106 could only mean one thing. Those visitors were relatives of the soon-to-be-dead. Patients who entered that room would come out on a gurney, guaranteed.

I knew every nook and cranny, every imperfection of that hateful room. The beige walls that had once been blue, the colour visible through the cracks. Scuff marks on the floor the cleaners never seemed to notice. The furniture, décor – it all needed updating. That little country hospital was stuck somewhere in the past, its equipment the only indication we were in a new millennium.

We'd tried to make it as homely as possible. The nurses said it was comforting for patients to have familiar things around them. A wind chime hung in the archway between the room and the balcony. Tiny blue dolphins danced in the sunlight as the breeze from the bay blew gently

CHAPTER NINETEEN | TWENTY DAYS TO FREEDOM

through the open doors. It was warm for October.

The glow of that morning seemed different. Like the changing of seasons as summer turns to autumn, then winter. It always makes me melancholic when the sun retreats from our hemisphere, north to Europe and beyond. As if the impending winter will bring tragedies we aren't prepared for. But it was mid-spring on Mum's last day, October 26th. It felt ominous, regardless of the sunlight, the warmth. Maybe Mum's departure had the power to change climates. Would October always feel this way from now on, I wondered?

"I'm just going to change her dressings," the morning nurse said as she came in. We were there together, sitting close to Mum, but we stood and moved to make way for the nurse, watching from the end of the bed.

Mum's arms and legs were bandaged by then. Gaping sores had formed over the weeks as her blood slowly poisoned her.

The nurse hesitated just for a second as she looked at Mum. I was the only one who noticed. She continued, slowly, gently, to unravel the dressing on Mum's arm. As the last layer of cotton bandage peeled away, so too did the skin on Mum's entire forearm. As if it were an extension of the bandage, not two separate things.

An enormous open wound exposed pink bloodied flesh, veins and bones and all the things you might see in an autopsy. Not the things loved ones should see.

A sound like a wounded animal escaped me, and I felt my knees buckle. Out of all the crime shows I'd ever seen, and my fascination for medical documentaries, nothing had prepared me for that moment. My legs couldn't hold me, and Greg must have sensed it. He put his arm around me, held me to his side, and said, "It's okay, Marce, she can't feel it. She can't feel anything now. She's already gone."

I looked at Mum's face and her last breath wheezed out of her mouth. Her chest fell and stayed there. It was true. She was gone. And I didn't see her soul float away like in the movie *Ghost*. It was the strangest thing. She didn't look like Mum anymore, just a resemblance of her. How quick our humanness leaves us. Just like Tony.

I looked at Dad and saw a tear roll down his face. I'd never seen my father cry before. I'd see it again in the months that followed. Greg cried too. I hugged him and wept into his shoulder.

The soft sound of the nurse's voice broke our embrace.

"I'll leave you to say your goodbyes. I'm so sorry."

She'd done her best to put the bandages back in place so Mum wasn't exposed. It didn't matter. The image would be burned in my memory forever.

We stood in silence around Mum's bed. We each touched her as we said our private goodbyes.

Minutes passed, and my mind filled up. I wasn't sure how I'd walk away. To leave Mum there, knowing I'd never see her again. Life outside that room would never be the same.

"Dat's it den, we should go," Dad said as he stood to leave.

He cleared his throat and tried to wipe his eyes without us noticing, his steel guard firmly back in place for the moment as the wall went up once again. Greg and I stole a quick glance at each other. I knew we were thinking the same thing.

What the hell is he going to do now?

The moment was lost as I snapped into recovery mode. I started my mental checklist. Mum was relying on me to keep it together and get things done. There was no time for real grief, not yet. Dad wouldn't know where to begin, and Greg had been lost in his grief for the past 20 days. He'd want to help, but I knew he was too broken. I had a feeling his struggles were just beginning. What would become of him, I wondered? Mum's last words to him came flooding back "Take care of ya father, love, look out for him. He'll need you. He won't say it, but he will. Promise me. Promise me, Greg."

"Of course I will, Mum, I promise," Greg had replied dutifully.

Greg's reliability hadn't improved with age, but a promise to Mum was his law. I was sure he'd keep his word although I wondered how, con-

CHAPTER NINETEEN | TWENTY DAYS TO FREEDOM

sidering his strained relationship with Dad. I wasn't sure how Greg really felt about him by then. Was the past still there just under the surface? Was that why trouble plagued him? Was his bad luck his inability to let go of the past? I think they tolerated each other for Mum. I always imagined Dad wished it was Greg who'd died, not Tony. If he had to lose a son, why couldn't it be his least favourite? Did Greg think the same? Had he always known Tony was Dad's favourite? If he did, how could he possibly keep his promise?

I got on with the business of Mum's passing. George and Morgan arrived, and not a minute too soon. Being alone with Dad in the house was daunting, uncomfortable and bizarre without Mum. How could I make conversation with a father I'd rarely conversed with? Our silence seemed amplified in the quietness. George took over. He knew how to talk to Dad better than any of his children. It always intrigued me, George's easiness around Dad. Thank God for my supportive husband. I'd need him more than ever now that Mum was gone.

CHAPTER TWENTY

Fix You

The haunting words of Coldplay's song 'Fix You' drifted through the silence at Mum's funeral. The crematorium was filled with family and friends paying their respects. Not much had changed in the two and a half years since we'd gathered there for Tony's funeral in April 2004.

Broulee Crematorium was a simple structure built in 2003. Like a sanctuary in the middle of rolling green pastures and open paddocks where black and white dairy cows dotted the landscape in all directions. The building was surrounded by acres of gardens that hadn't yet had a chance to flourish fully for Tony's massive gathering. I didn't realise how many people he had known, or how beloved he was. I don't think Mum and Dad had expected anyone would show up for their criminal son. But over a hundred people came. Some stood. There weren't enough seats for everyone. I guess the sleepy coastal town of Broulee New South Wales didn't usually have enough people to fill a crematorium.

Mum wanted an open casket, like we did for Tony. Dad thought it was morbid, but he didn't have much say by then. She looked peaceful in a Stonehenge kind of way. Our outer shell seems to resemble a statue once the soul is gone. No matter how many times I see a dead body, they never cease to intrigue me. My first was in 1992 when my grandfather died, Mum's dad. He was a chronic alcoholic with emphysema from smoking since he was a boy. I don't know for sure, but I assume his father, my great-grandfather, and his father before him were all alcoholics. I often wondered why Mum was one and not just her brothers? At least that's what I used to think growing up. Two of her brothers were, but why Mum? Her sister wasn't an alcoholic. I never really thought of Mum as an alcoholic. She was happy and jolly when she drank, and we rarely saw her legless, as she would put it. Grandfather was a classic alcoholic. He drank methylated spirits when all his money was gone. He'd roam the streets and sleep wherever he passed out, like the down-and-out drunks in movies like *Pay It Forward*, where Angie Dickinson played the part of the drunken grandmother almost as well as my grandfather.

I must have been five or six years old when Mum told me we were going on an adventure, just the two us – no one else could know. It would be our little secret. I remember it clearly. We caught the bus and got off at the row of old rundown terrace houses on Crystal Street, Petersham. I'd learn the names later. Just metres across the road stood a pub, the Oxford Tavern. It's still there today, looking just as sleazy. Neon lights in the shape of naked, curvaceous women flash in all directions as signage, beckoning lowlifes: 'topless waitresses inside!' I doubt there were flashing neons when I was a child in the '60s – that probably wasn't even allowed!

Those houses were a kind of halfway-house for derelicts. Today we'd call them crack dens. Imagine that, the dealer right across the road.

CHAPTER TWENTY | FIX YOU

Whoever turned those terraces into halfway-houses clearly hadn't put much thought to it. Mum took my hand and we went to one of the middle terraces. She opened the door, and as we walked in the overpowering smell hit me first: urine mixed with vomit – not that I could pinpoint that at the time. Terror seized me as my eyes adjusted to the dimness. I squeezed Mum's hand tight and tried to wrap my other arm around her legs and hide behind her skirt.

"There, there, love, it's all right. Marce, it's just ya grandfather, don't be scared. Now be a good girl and stand still."

Mum pried me away and coaxed me towards a wall as she made a beeline for my grandfather, who was slumped on the floor near the opposite wall. Piles of dirty clothes and rubbish, broken bottles and cigarette butts were everywhere. Grandfather's clothes were filthy, and so was he. I'd never seen him like that before, with stubble on his face and unruly hair clumped together as if he'd been showering in his own vomit. He was unrecognisable. He looked dead.

"Dad… Dad… wake up… wake up…"

Mum's hands were on Grandfather's shoulders trying to shake him awake. She was trying her best to stay calm with me there in the room, but I could feel every cell in her body as if it were mine, heightened with fear, dreading the worst. Maybe he was dead. He wouldn't have been the first to die in those houses, I'd learn later. But then he opened his eyes.

"Ohhh, Lonie, how ya goin', love? Come to fix ya poor old Dad, huh…"

Mum's family often called her Lon or Lonie. Her siblings couldn't pronounce Yvonne when they were little, so her nickname became Lon and it stuck.

Mum let out a sigh of relief. I must have been holding my breath too, because when I breathed it felt as if I'd been under water too long and I'd only just made it to the surface.

Grandfather squinted as he looked in my direction.

"Eyy, there's the chook-a-look, what you doin' 'ere pork chop?" Grandfather's words were slurred, but as always he was happy to see me.

I was still frozen to the spot, unsure of what I was seeing. He opened his arms for a hug, but Mum told me to stay put. I had no intention of moving even if I could.

"Later, Dad, you bloody stink. Let's get you cleaned up and we'll sort something out. When was the last time you ate? You stupid old fool!"

Mum was trying to lift him so she could get him into the shower. I stayed put and was glad I didn't have to help her undress him.

It wasn't the last time I'd see Grandfather like that, but after that first time it got less distressing. Mum would always clean him up, and sometimes he'd come to live with us. He'd stay until he was better – sober until the next time – when he'd leave and eventually do it all again. Back to square one. Mum would get so angry she'd threaten him and refuse to help. That's when Dad would step in and surprise me.

"What you mean, woman, you just leave him on the street to fend for himself? You can't do that, he's your father. He need a feed and a warm bed an' we give it to him."

No matter how many times I saw Dad's *Jekyll and Hyde* personality, it still surprised me. Mum would always fold when her anger wore off. However, many times he needed rescuing, it was clear they adored each other, and that Mum was Grandfather's favourite and he was hers. His other four children didn't have time for a no-good drunken father – well, not like Mum anyway.

Grandfather died on a warm night in March 1992 in Eversleigh Hospital, Petersham. The hospital is gone now, replaced by a block of units. Eversleigh was just down the road from that row of terraces. They still stand, frozen in time. When I stopped for the red light at the intersection on Crystal Street and Canterbury Road – and I must have stopped there a hundred times over the years – I'd look to my left and see it there, the derelicts' den, and I'd always think of Grandfather sprawled out in the putridness on that scary, scary day. I'm not sure why those terraces haven't been replaced with unit blocks. If I were the owner I'd bulldoze them all and I wouldn't replace them with housing. I'd build a park or a shrine – like Ground Zero in memory of those who'd lost their lives and for all the other shit that went on in those hateful terraces.

But when I saw Grandfather take his last breath, despite his condition it was peaceful, gentle. His passing seemed so undramatic – unlike his life, and unlike Mum or Tony.

I'll never forget seeing Tony in his coffin. I couldn't if I tried, Mum made me take photos. A ghoulish thing to do, but I didn't mind. I wanted to. It had been so long since we'd seen him, and Mum wanted a recent photo. Why, I don't know. It's not as if she could frame it for the mantelpiece. God, I hoped not.

We arrived early. I didn't want anyone to see me with a camera – Tony's freaky sister doing a photo shoot with her dead brother. That's fucked up, man.

Mum wanted his body covered, to hide the tattoos. So there he was, just his head on a pillow, his face protruding from a bed of white satin. It looked macabre. It reminded me of trips to the beach when Morgan would bury George in the sand, his entire body underground, both laughing and giggling, and George eating sand. There'd be no more trips to the beach for Tony. His neck still bore the mark of the noose. That was why he was completely covered.

That wasn't the worst of it. His face still had the deep purple patches left from his hanging. Nothing had changed since that hateful night in the morgue a week before. How was that possible? It only added to the disturbing sight. Poor Mum and Dad had to witness the very thing I'd hoped they'd never see, minus the tube, thank God. I couldn't believe an undertaker could be so careless, not masking the disfigurement. I had to be civil, given the circumstances, as I spoke to the funeral director.

"Why does my brother not have any make-up on? You can't leave him like that. His daughters will be here soon. They'll be traumatised enough as it is."

"We are terribly sorry, Ma'am. We haven't employed a trained artiste as yet, having opened so recently. They are hard to find in these parts."

Had I been more like Tony, I probably would have punched him. I wanted to yell at him, or at the very least convey my disgust at his lack of empathy. Clearly, he had no regard for the family of a criminal. Had someone informed me, I would have brought my own makeup and attempted to do the job. There wasn't enough time to do anything about it. I imagined what Tony would say: "Oh mate, you're friggin' kiddin' aren't ya? You incompetent fucks. Stone the crows, Marce, not my most handsome self. Try and get my good side for the photos will ya?"

After Mum and Dad, George and Morgan had said their goodbyes to Tony and then they sat down and left me alone with him. A veiled partition of white chiffon separated the coffin from the rows of seats below. The curtain was still in place, hiding the coffin until the crowd arrived. I put my hand on the cold white satin where his shoulder would be. It felt like solid rock, hard stone, unmovable.

"Sorry about your face, Tone, you know I would've fixed it," I whispered to him. *"No worries, Sis, she'll be right,"* I imagined he answered. I moved my hand to his face and traced the outline of his features with one finger. All rock, nothing human, only a vessel. I touched his eyelashes then, so soft, so delicate. Slowly, gently I moved across each one of his long, brown, gingery lashes, savouring that feeling. It was the only thing that felt alive on his body.

I bent down and kissed his cheek, his forehead, and there it was, what I'd been deprived of in the morgue nursery, the last kiss, the last touch of my brother.

This time, with Mum in his place, it was like *Ground Hog Day*. They'd employed a make-up artist by then. It looked odd to see Mum all made up like that. She never wore makeup except lipstick. Whoever applied it clearly liked the diva look. It was unnerving. I hadn't brought a camera, not for any particular reason other than I forgot. Just as well, Mum would've hated those photos. The only familiar part of her was her feet and those bright pink slippers. She looked so silly, but that was Mum.

I took my seat and stared at the scenery outside. The glass walls gave

CHAPTER TWENTY | FIX YOU

the room a false sense of freedom. I felt trapped, despite the openness. Dozens of rosellas, cockatoos and ibis flew in unison against the backdrop of the clear blue November sky, as if they were related, a blended family.

I looked at the cows in the distance, heads to the ground, munching away, not a care in the world. I wish I were a cow. For once I meant it as a statement, not as a description of myself.

A sudden interruption to the music brought me back to the present. George was fumbling with the projector. He'd spent days creating a CD of images set to music, Mum's life. How she would have loved it. We had planned on starting the funeral that way, but George seemed to be having technical problems – unusual for him.

He looked nervous, jittery. Not himself at all. I assumed he was upset, emotional. Losing Mum was like losing his own mother. In fact, I can definitely say he was closer to my mother. She certainly knew him better. I could see beads of sweat running down his forehead and gathering on his upper lip. He lifted a finger to wipe the wetness away, but he needn't have bothered. He just kept sweating. He needed a towel, not a fingertip. It wasn't at all hot in the air-conditioned room, so I wasn't sure what was wrong with him. He glanced in my direction and I saw total panic in his eyes. Was it just me or did everyone notice?

He was taking way too long getting things started, and I was getting anxious.

What the hell are you doing, George? I said in my mind.

"Marce, tell him not to worry. It's fine," Dad said solemnly, but I knew he was embarrassed about the delay. I assumed Dad was dealing with his own anxiety with such a large crowd.

I joined George at the projector, about to whisper obscenities in his ear when the music started again. Finally, he got it working. Disaster averted.

Images of Mum's life flooded the screen suspended above her coffin. It was difficult to see on such a bright day, but we were all there, laughing, celebrating birthdays, getting married, having babies, and the babies growing up. It was a beautiful montage of life – all the good memories played out in tune to that evocative, heartfelt song.

People were sniffling and blowing their noses, then giggling as the fun, silly parts of Mum's life unfolded with each passing slide. She would have liked the giggling. When the tribute was over, George was the first to speak. He'd regained his composure, thank God, and did Mum proud in his touching speech of love and gratitude. He spoke for me too. I couldn't do it. I was terrified of public speaking in a normal situation. Breaking down in front of all those people wasn't an option. It would be wedding day hell all over again, only worse. I did speak at Tony's funeral though. I'm not sure how I found the courage to do that.

George did well, so did Morgan. How brave she was. She wrote her own speech for her Nanny and stood proud to read it. She didn't lose control. She was nothing like her mother.

The rest of the day I did my best at acting the strong daughter. As always, the warm host, overdoing it with food and drink, making sure everyone was satisfied as we sat around the lounge telling stories about Mum. I didn't cry. Mum would've been proud.

I called Dad every day for the next month. He would weep openly and say things I never thought he was capable of. "It's so senseless… all the pain in the world… why would she want to leave? Was it me? Did she want to be free of me? Is that what everyone thinks?"

Wow. Words like that from Dad could only mean one thing. He was remembering. He hadn't forgotten the past at all. Was the guilt finally catching up with him? It left me bewildered and heartbroken in a new way. I had no idea what to say, or how to react to his emotional outpouring. I'd say stupid, meaningless things, "There, there, Dad, you'll be all right. Give it time. Mum wanted to be free of pain, that's all. She'd had enough of suffering. She is with you, don't worry."

Ridiculous things to say to my father, since he believed once you're dead it's lights out – nothing.

He never spoke of it again. I stopped calling every day. He said it

CHAPTER TWENTY | FIX YOU

wasn't necessary. He was fine now. He seemed to adjust relatively quickly, on the surface anyway. I'd call once a week. It never got easier. I always felt anxious just before I'd dial his number every Sunday. The short conversations were always the same: weather, tides, the lack of rain, the latest world catastrophe, terrorists, the conniving politicians, and plants. Dad could speak easily about what was growing well in the garden and what wasn't. He should have owned a nursery. He probably would have had a happier life. Maybe we all would've.

Dad rarely asked questions beside the occasional formality "How's George and Morgan?" It was I who led our conversations. Imagine that, me the leader. Like extracting teeth, it was so far beyond my comfort zone. So, I took on a different persona when it came to my phone calls with Dad. I never spoke about my life, my feelings or problems like I could with Mum, and he never asked. I became interested in all the things Dad liked to talk about. It was easier to engage if I stuck to the topics of his choice. Not that I knew much about politics. I voted for the opposition. It was something I could never tell my father. I doubt he would have spoken to me ever again. He might have legally disowned me. The shame would be too great.

Our conversations would stay that way for years, except for one long interruption to our routine. It happened five months after Mum died, and it would be Dad's turn to leap from his comfort zone into unchartered territory.

CHAPTER TWENTY-ONE

It's About the Rent...

The third anniversary of Tony's death is a day I'll never forget. I always dread the lead up to March 25. In fact, I would come to hate the month of March entirely, despite my birthday, and Dad's and Greg's — three Pisces with three extremely different traits in one family. I felt no kinship to my fellow fish.

It was a Saturday that year, 2007, and I woke feeling heavy-hearted. In the five months since Mum's death I'd been melancholic and depressed. I missed her. She was constantly in my thoughts. Life wasn't the same. I felt disconnected, ungrounded. Not being able to talk to her daily left a void I hadn't felt in years. My escape was food again. I'd gained weight.

I went for my usual Saturday morning run. It had become more of a walk. Every extra kilo matters when you're a runner. I had a bad feeling. It was beyond grief, more than that. I felt frustrated and annoyed at my discontent. Something was niggling at me. It wasn't my usual internal ramblings. It was my displaced marriage. I was unhappy but trying my best to deny it – on the surface anyway.

As I powered down Lilyfield Road towards Leichhardt Aquatic Centre, I thought about something Sam had said to me three weeks earlier. We hadn't seen each other in years. Life happens, different paths. But our friendship never faltered when we did get together. Like no time had passed at all. Ours was a real friendship. Sam never held back when she had something to say – that never changed.

"Marcy, what's wrong? You seem sad, unhappy. Is it your mum? Or something else?"

I was taken aback by her observation. I thought I was faking so well, too! Ten minutes together and she'd ripped up the carpet and got to the crux of it. I had no choice but to confess when it came to Sam.

"It's George. It's my marriage. You know me too well. I'm so unhappy."

It felt good to say it out loud. I hadn't said the words before, not even to myself, not consciously. That would require digging deep and admitting failure – not in my current repertoire.

"Then end it. Why are you wasting time? Life is too short to be so unhappy, Marcy. I know twenty-two years together is a long time, but if you're that unhappy it may as well be a death sentence."

I was speechless, reeling at her words. Had she gone mad? I didn't understand how she could propose something so drastic so casually. It was impossible of course. George and I made a pact back in early 2002. We were in this marriage forever. We had to make it work. Divorce was something neither of us wanted. I still believed in marriage and aimed to redeem the vows I'd broken for the rest of my life. I owed George more than he owed me. Sam never knew about my infidelity, only his gambling. She might have had a different opinion of me had she known the full truth.

CHAPTER TWENTY-ONE | IT'S ABOUT THE RENT...

I would have to have a tough conversation with George, tell him how I was really feeling so we could fix it. I knew there was something bothering him. I'd wonder if it were me, what I'd done all those years ago. I imagined he probably thought about it a lot. I would if our roles were reversed. He'd become so aloof - a workaholic, and short tempered. I assumed - when I wasn't blaming myself - he was just getting old and tired and moody like his father. The thought of him becoming like his father was too depressing to contemplate. I'd said nothing, fearing the worst - that I'd come across as a nagging wife.

"Look, Marcy, I know what you're thinking, but trust me, you're stronger than you know. You will survive on your own. It's hard, but it's not the end. There is life after separation and divorce. Look at me, I've done it twice and I'm not dead. I'm happy and better off, let me tell you!"

I laughed, but on the inside I was having a panic attack. Sam might as well have been talking Italian. I couldn't understand. Was she really suggesting George and I shouldn't be together anymore? Could she be right? Was she overreacting or was I so deep in denial I couldn't see the truth of it?

I felt a twinge of anger - old habits. The thought of failure was the same as losing control. Neither agreed with my psyche. Bull-headed stubbornness was my coping mechanism.

"Yeah, yeah, just give me a reason. That's all I need, Sam, for George to give me a reason and I'm gone. I'm so outta there."

Tough talking bullshit.

I don't know why I said it, but I spoke with a strong conviction I didn't feel. I guess I didn't want Sam to think I was weak and pathetic. I wanted to be strong like her, but I wasn't. I never had been. I admired her courage, her can't-keep-me-down, don't-fuck-with-me attitude. Her ability to rise above her shit was inspiring. I always felt stronger in her presence. Maybe that's why I said it.

It had been haunting me since that night, and as I ran around the water's edge of Rozelle Bay towards Iron Cove Bridge the words echoed in my head – give me a reason, God, just give me a reason.

I was exhausted by the time I walked back up the hill on Lilyfield Road. It hadn't seemed so steep an hour before. I heard a faint voice call out to me from across the road and saw an old lady, in her late 70s, I guessed, standing at her front gate wearing a red cardigan. She was waving at me and kept repeating "Come girl, I have something to tell you, come…"

It freaked me out. She looked like the witch from *Hansel and Gretel*. I'd never seen her before and I'd run that road a hundred times. I looked around as if she might be talking to someone behind me. There was no one else. It was early in the morning. At first, I thought she might be a mirage. Was I imagining it? I slowed my pace but kept to my side of the road and tilted my cap up to look at her. She said it again, only this time it seemed menacing, urgent. My arms tingled with goose bumps and they crept up to my neck. I pulled my cap back down and ran like hell without saying a word. I can't explain why I did it, except she scared the crap out of me.

It was so disturbing that I didn't stop running until I got home. I looked over my shoulder just in case she was chasing me on her broomstick. I blurted it out to George, borderline hysterical, giving him every creepy detail.

"Can you believe she said that? What do you think she meant? Maybe she's psychic. Oh my God, maybe she had a message from Mum. Shit. I should have stopped and listened. I should go back. Why the hell did I do that?"

George gave me the weirdest look and didn't really respond, except agreeing it was weird.

I sank back into my numbness.

"For fuck's sake, George, is that all you've got? Hello… Anybody home? I'm over here, talking, contributing to life and conversation – you should try it sometime." My internal voice spoke in melody like a song. I said nothing and walked away.

CHAPTER TWENTY-ONE | IT'S ABOUT THE RENT...

The witch lady had been on my mind all day. By early evening I felt so bad for running off like that, poor lady. What if she needed help? What if she were in trouble? I would go back tomorrow and knock on her door and apologise for my awful behaviour. Yes, that's what I'd do. That never happened.

Ten minutes later the phone rang. It was Dad. Dad rarely called. I did the calling. He didn't like to waste money on long distance calls. He had a mobile phone, but mostly he just looked at it. His mobile was for emergencies and incoming calls only. If I mistakenly called the mobile instead of the landline he never answered.

I was mildly concerned when I picked up.

"Hi, Dad. What's wrong? Is something the matter?"

After some awkward, random words he got straight to it.

"It's about da rent, Marce. I just thought you should know. It hasn't gone in the bank since Mum died."

We were paying rent again after the gambling debacle five years before. It took a while and it wasn't full rent, but it was something, and now Dad was telling me it hadn't been paid for five months.

"What do you mean, Dad? It's an automatic payment. Are you sure? Why haven't you mentioned it sooner?"

I assumed Dad was confused. I wasn't sure how he was coping with the bills and everything. He said he was fine, but I had my doubts. I knew he struggled with banking now Mum was gone.

"Didn't want to bring it up. Just sayin', Marce. George might be up to his old tricks. You sure he's not gamblin' again?"

I almost dropped the phone. I couldn't believe Dad had said it, or that he would even think such a thing. It wasn't possible. That was so long ago.

"Don't be silly, Dad, he wouldn't do that. No way. I'll check the online banking and let you know what's happening. I'm sure it's nothing."

I ended the conversation. I was annoyed at Dad for saying something so mean about George, especially since he'd helped him so much with the paperwork and things. Dad was probably just being paranoid as usual. I realised I'd called him silly. I was glad he'd let that one slide. He must have known I was upset.

I waited for George to get home. He'd taken Morgan and a friend to a party. They would be back later for a sleepover. It kept Morgan occupied, so I didn't mind sleepovers.

As each minute passed I got angrier. At Dad, not George. How dare he say such a thing? The man had no filter and didn't care how his insults affected anyone else. Is this how it was going to be from now on? Would I cop the brunt of his nonsense now Mum wasn't around?

I sat at the computer and realised I needed the password. Since when did the password change? I tried calling George. No answer.

By the time he got home I was so frustrated I couldn't think straight. I blurted it all out, hardly taking a breath, complaining about Dad, not for one moment thinking anything was really wrong.

George stood holding onto the back of the chair, not sitting down to logon frantically as I would do under such circumstances. He stared blankly at the computer screen, at me, then back at the screen. All the while I was rambling on about passwords, stupid banks, Dad's insults and his paranoia. I think it was the most I'd spoken in months. Then I noticed George was just standing there, doing nothing.

"George, can you please log on? I need to call Dad. He's waiting for answers."

He didn't budge, just stared at me.

"What the fuck, George? What is your problem? Can't you just take action without being told, without me nagging you for a change? Please, the password."

Nothing. He just looked at me. I noticed his face then, and somewhere in the recesses of my mind something sparked. I knew that face. I'd seen it before. And he saw my recognition.

"Marce, darling, I have something to tell you and I've been trying to—"

CHAPTER TWENTY-ONE | IT'S ABOUT THE RENT...

"Don't fuck with me, George. Don't you dare joke with me right now."

"Darling, I'm not joking…"

The recesses of my mind jumped out from the murky shadows into the fluorescent bright of my present. The spark ignited into a full-blown blaze.

"Oh my God. Oh my God! You're gambling, aren't you? Is Dad right? He can't be right. Tell me you are not gambling again?'

It all happened very fast from there. The adrenaline pushed my heart to its limits. I had never felt it reach such heights. Was I going to have a heart attack?

"I'm not gambling, Marce…"

In a nanosecond the beating reduced to a bearable palpitation in relief. It was temporary.

"It's not gambling, darling… it's worse than that… it's meth, crystal meth… I've been using ice. I have an addiction. It's a very big problem… I don't have to log onto the banking to tell you the money is gone, it's all gone again… I'm so sorry, darling…"

"No… no… noooo!"

My voice drifted into quiet oblivion. I knew my body was falling, but I couldn't stop it. I saw him reach for me and then I saw nothing.

The next thing I remember, we were sitting opposite each other at the dining room table. How did I get from the office at the front of the house to the dining room at the back? George couldn't have carried me. I was too heavy. He would later tell me I walked. I have no memory of that.

Confused, I sat in dazed silence. What had I missed? Was this what Alzheimer's felt like? George was speaking so fast I couldn't grasp his words. Too many words. Too much noise. Details that made no sense, had no logic. All kinds of specifics whooshed past my ears – drug dealers, meeting places, smoking pipes, money spent… Why was he telling me this? I was dreaming. Yes, I must be dreaming, I thought.

"I'm going to get help, darling. I'm very, very sick. I've been wanting to for so long, but I didn't know how. I knew I had to tell you, and now it's going to be all right…"

Sick? He didn't look sick, he looked crazy. He sounded crazy. I wasn't dreaming. It was real, and I was in shock. I mean that in a literal sense. I felt the oddest sense of calm as I stared at the stranger in front of me, the wolf at my table.

"Please don't tell Morgan, darling, she doesn't need to know. We can get through this together, start over again, properly this time, if you'll help me. Please say you'll help me."

Start over properly? I had already started over properly five years before. He'd been deceiving me all along. He'd lied to me. Again. He had never started over. I was in it alone. He was living a secret double-life – probably the entire time I thought we were being open and honest with each other.

How, how could I have missed the signs again? What the hell was wrong with me that I was so blind, so ignorant of what was right in front of me? How could I not know I had been sleeping next to a monster?

And the words came as if I were channelling something higher. As if I'd been practising the speech my whole life.

"Help you? You think I can help you? I can't. I won't. You have to leave, George. You can't be trusted anymore. You won't do this to us a third time. I can promise you that with all my heart. But I'm telling you this, so listen hard. I'm not doing your dirty work. You will tell your daughter what you've done before you go. She has a right to know why her father has ruined her life for the second time."

I have no idea where the words came from. I spoke calmly, with dignity and integrity, as if I were born to it. I continued as I told George how it had to play out until Morgan's friend was gone the next afternoon. Had there been no friend sleeping over it would have turned out differently, I'm sure. I couldn't change plans so late in the evening. Two upset teenage girls wasn't something I could cope with, even on a good day.

"I'm going to bed. You tell Morgan and her friend that I'm suddenly very sick and I don't want to contaminate them. You'll be normal, you're

CHAPTER TWENTY-ONE | IT'S ABOUT THE RENT...

good at that, and you'll have fun with them, make breakfast and take them to Norton Street Fair for the day tomorrow. I won't come out of the room until you've all gone. Then I'll pack your stuff. You can sleep on the lounge tonight. After Morgan's friend has gone home you'll tell Morgan what you've done, so she'll understand why you have to leave. I don't care where you go, but you will be gone by tomorrow night. I don't want you here anymore. Do you understand, George?"

His face was distraught. He was in disbelief. I imagine he wasn't expecting that. He tried to protest, beg forgiveness, plead, and pledge his love for us. I wasn't listening. I wasn't even looking at him really. I was looking through him. I walked to the bedroom and quietly closed the door. There was nothing left to say.

I thought about the old lady in the red cardigan early that morning, convinced now she knew my fate and was trying to warn me. She was psychic. George's reaction when I told him. He knew she was psychic too. I imagined he wanted to seize that moment, but I'd walked away too soon, his moment lost. I thought about Mum's last words "Be strong, love, you'll get through it." Mum had seen the future. I knew it without question. I thought about my words to Sam: "Give me a reason, God." Who knew God actually listened! He gave me a reason all right. I thought about my recurring dream and finally understood, and in time the full extent of its meaning would surface. A million things like pieces of a giant jigsaw puzzle materialised before me on that long, long night.

How was it possible that my father sensed it? Imagine that! What he didn't know was the whole truth, and I somehow had to tell him. I'd have to tell the world. I'd have to be there for Morgan. Dark didn't even begin to describe the months that followed.

CHAPTER TWENTY-TWO

Into the Abyss – Part 2

George left on Sunday night, March 26, 2007 – 24 hours after the phone call from my father. Just like that, we became a statistic. It was two weeks since our 19th wedding anniversary and I was single again. Eventually it would occur to me – although we'd been together for 22 years – we didn't make it to our actual 20th wedding anniversary. Twenty years was a milestone, such a majestic even number to end a marriage, unlike 19, an ugly odd number that lacks effort and screams loser. Who separates in their 19th year of marriage, for fuck's sake? At least keep the secrets for another 12 months. Twenty years would sound way more impressive when I retold the story a hundred times in the future.

My mind concocted an array of irrational thoughts as I slowly went insane. Scenarios infiltrated every nook, every milky surface of my brain.

The virtual jigsaw puzzle grew to epic proportions as more pieces fell into place. Like the car he'd bought in my name last November. Believing it was a gesture of love and that he was finally taking the initiative at the saddest time in my life. I hadn't owned a car since we'd first met. Company cars came with his package. George used public transport, so I always got the car, lucky me.

Was it possible George had anticipated his departure since November? Did he plan it, knowing when he told me his secret he'd be gone regardless of my reaction? Was the car purchase simply made out of guilt? I'd have no car once he left. How would I get Morgan from A to B? Pickups and drop offs without a car would be impossible. He did it for her, not for me at all.

Was he so sure of what I'd do? He used it to his advantage, making it work in his favour so it would appear to be my choice, when all along it was his, the leaving. Was all the begging and pleading rehearsed so he would seem the victim and I the bad guy when he'd retell his version of the story God knows how many times in the future? When family and friends found out, would they condemn me for kicking him out on the street like a bully, a cold-hearted bitch, at the worst time in his life? He needed help, support – he had a disease and I had no soul or empathy. Is that how everyone would see it? Is that what he was hoping? Would Dad see it that way?

He didn't. My father was horrified, disgusted at what George had done after all the sacrifices. He couldn't fathom what George had become.

Poor Dad did his best to console me, as much as he was capable. He wasn't accustomed to seeing his daughter a hopeless, out-of-control mess.

"Don't cry, darlin', no sense in cryin'. You be okay. Give it time."

Dad had never called me darling before. It was the strangest thing to hear him say. He'd say it again many times in the years that followed. Greg went straight to anger in his shock and disbelief.

CHAPTER TWENTY-TWO | INTO THE ABYSS – PART 2

"I'll fucking kill him if I ever see him again. What a fucking idiot!"

Neither Greg nor Dad would ever see George again.

Greg would do his best to comfort me, in a rogue kind of way. He knew the game better than anyone and, surprisingly, his advice did give me a kind of solace at times.

George had kept his word that night. He was the one to tell Morgan. I heard the car door slam and she ran into the house, up the stairs to her room. He packed his car and left soon after. She came to my bedside and I'll never forget her face. It was like witnessing the passing of time, aged before my eyes, a metaphoric change. Something had broken inside and was now etched on her face, a tell-tale sign of heartbreak. Her flawless face now flawed. The evidence of life is in our faces – every loss, every disappointment, every breaking point. I see it now in hers. I know that damage and have seen it many times – in my mother's face, in my brothers', and in my own reflection. Her face was too beautiful for that kind of damage, too young for that kind of heartbreak. We huddled together for the longest time, not speaking, just in each other's arms.

Morgan had turned 16 in January, and had recently started her second-last year of high school. The timing couldn't have been worse. She was broken in ways that would affect her life for years to come. Her grades nosedived and that would impact her final marks. She wouldn't be able to apply to the university she'd hoped for her chosen career. Her path was altered forever. All those years of school and striving for one goal, wasted, ruined, and I was helpless in her turmoil, too lost in my own.

How the world turned on its axis in those early weeks and months! Imagine Dad and Greg supporting me. I wouldn't have believed it possible a year earlier.

Sam was there physically. She led me through hostile terrain like a shepherd and I followed her. I was too raw and broken to put up any kind of façade in her presence. She didn't care. She loved me just the same. Looking back, I doubt I would have survived without her.

The five stages of grief started immediately. The cycle would continue for over a year. I knew George wasn't dead, but his departure was just as permanent as Mum's and Tony's. I hadn't felt that kind of grief for them. Maybe I'd been saving it all and was experiencing it in a triple dose – tripled again because it was me. I was convinced I must be the only human being who had ever felt such agonising pain. The ego can't think beyond that. Surely my kind of pain would kill anyone else? I was certain it would kill me soon enough.

The madness continued, a carbon copy of five years earlier only worse, much worse. I have no solid memory of the six weeks that followed, only snippets here and there. I didn't go to work. I wasn't capable of dealing with the public. They gave me bereavement leave – how appropriate – and generously continued to pay my wages. They knew I needed them. It was the kindest thing an employer had ever done for me, and one less worry in the short term.

Instead of drinking, I started running at all hours of the day and night, through rain and hail – it didn't matter. I didn't feel the elements, just the excruciating, indescribable pain. It tore at every microcell of my body. It never stopped. Even in my dreams I could feel it. My tears penetrated the very walls of the house and echoed even when there was silence.

I started talking to God, on my actual knees like in prayer. Clasped hands, eyes closed, like I did when I was a little girl. I would visualise the heavens, the angels, the saints, and saw them as if I'd been seeing them my whole life.

"Dear God, please help me. I don't know how to make it stop. Please take the pain away. I'm not sure how much more I can take… I promise you, God, with all my heart, if you just give me a second chance at life I will do so much better. Please don't let me go crazy."

But mostly I would talk to Mum.

"Mum, are you there? Can you hear me? Please help me, Mum. Tell me what to do, tell me how to breathe without the pain. I need you, Mum. I can't do this alone. How could you have left me," I would sob into my

CHAPTER TWENTY-TWO | INTO THE ABYSS – PART 2

pillow every night.

Morgan would come to my bed some nights. She'd hold me, stroke my hair and try and comfort me.

"Oh Mumma, it's going to be okay. Nanny will help us. I know she will. She knows everything that's happening."

Our roles had reversed. Morgan became the comforter, the mother, the protector. I became a helpless burden, even to myself. I had nothing to give her, no strength, no words, none of the things I should have given a daughter at the worst time in her life. It would become my greatest regret, but at the time I wasn't able, not capable. I didn't even know who I was anymore.

Then one night I drove to The Gap. I'm not sure of the exact timing, but I think it was in May. I was always worse when I was alone and could cry all night without a witness to consider. I didn't have to try and mask the sound when Morgan wasn't home. My prayers were not being answered. Why wasn't Mum helping me? Why wasn't God? The pain intensified with time, not the opposite. It took me to new levels of hurt. It was physical. I knew only I could make it stop.

I'll never forget how I got out of bed in the middle of the night, didn't dress, went to my car and somehow drove. I knew someone who had taken their life at The Gap many years before. There is no chance of survival. It's not a cry for help. It's a guaranteed checkout.

A driving force to escape the misery, the blackness now anchored to my life, was what got me to that cliff top. I'd always imagined a decision like that would be calm and serene, since it would be the last decision. It was nothing like that of course, until I heard Tony's words: "Sis, don't do it… don't take your life… it's not your time… think of Morgan… don't do what I did to my girls… You are going to make it."

It wasn't the end of course. I didn't hear Tony again, not that I recall, but I heard Mum and saw her in my dreams. She was there. She'd always been there. It just took that night and Tony's words to open the portal. A sliver, the dimmest beam of light, the slightest imagining of hope danced somewhere in the recesses of my mind, waiting, knowing, one faraway day the revelations would come, and I would understand. I would understand it all then.

If it sounds crazy, maybe I was, but Tony's words saved me. I'm sure of it. Imagine that, lessons from the grave.

Years later I'd visit a psychic for the first time. I'll never forget his opening: "Okay, Marcy, your Mum is here. We need to talk about George… Oh my goodness… your pain was extraordinary, wasn't it? You feel on a very deep level… deeper than most, I must say…"

You're shitting me; finally someone who got it!

He knew about The Gap. I'd never told anyone what happened that night. He knew it all, every… single… thing. I was converted, a sceptic no more.

Twenty-two years of stuff can't fit in one carload. George would have to return for the rest. I recall packing his things and putting them in the back yard under the carport, so he could collect them without entering the house. I was meticulous in the packing, making sure everything was neat and in order. Later I'd wonder why I did that. Shouldn't I have thrown it all out on the street like they do in the movies? Or, better still, burnt it all in a bonfire. That would've been more appropriate given the circumstances.

The back shed held the evidence of a lifetime of lies. I'd search it in the hope of finding clues, something that would give me closure. I would never get it from George. I learned the shed was his safe house, where he committed his crimes out of sight, pretending to be busy. I had never questioned his absences or late nights, assuming he was working as always.

"If only these walls could talk, hey Angel girl," I said to her as we stood amongst the piles of boxes and rubble – years of storing what no longer fit in the house.

She looked up at me panting, her rump swaying back and forth as she wagged her invisible tail.

CHAPTER TWENTY-TWO | INTO THE ABYSS – PART 2

"If only you could talk, Angel, I bet you'd have a lot to tell me."

I patted the top of her head and she licked my hand in response. I searched her eyes, but she said nothing.

"Where should I begin, girl? Which pile of crap should I start with?"

George saved his collection of magazines, bits and pieces, apparatus, all kinds of junk I had no use for. George was a hoarder, I realised. He was more like Dad and my brothers than I had ever thought possible.

I picked up a random magazine and as I flicked through it a photograph fell out. I reached for it before Angel had a chance to lick it. It was a group of people, five couples. I didn't recognise anyone except George. They were in a restaurant having dinner, celebrating something. They were all looking at the camera smiling. The chair next to George was vacant. On the table in front of the place setting was a stylish beige handbag with a long gold chain. A red jacket hung on the back of the empty chair. George's arm rested on the chair as if embracing the invisible person sitting there.

"I don't remember taking that photo, Angel, do you?" I knew she was tilting her head towards me, but I was mesmerised as I held the photo inches from my eyes.

I took in every detail. It was an old photo. George was younger, 10 years perhaps, maybe more. The décor, the girls' hairstyles – I guessed mid-90s. Nothing about the photo sparked my memory.

It suddenly occurred to me that I don't buy beige handbags and I didn't own, nor had I ever owned, a red jacket, not that I could remember. I wore black. It was slimming. Colour was not my thing. Only during the fit slim years was I outrageously confident with colour. The photograph was before that. I probably would have been at my heaviest.

It hit me like a freight train. I wasn't taking the photo, someone else was. George's invisible date had captured that moment. My hands started shaking and my heart raced. My head dropped as if it had just become too heavy to hold up.

Angel whimpered and pushed up against me as if to give me a hug.

She could feel my heartbreak again. She knew the drill by now.

I sat down on the dirty concrete floor, my legs unable to hold me. Angel was ecstatic to have me at her level. She licked me like crazy, always licking. I didn't care. I let her. I covered my face as I cried into my hands. It was all I could do; I was too weak to push her away.

New despair came with every piece of the jigsaw puzzle that kept slotting into place. Instead of closure, there were only more questions. Whom had I been married to? The layers and depth of the deception overwhelmed me to the point of total breakdown. I questioned everything. Was any of it real or was it all a lie? Did George ever love me, or was it just the idea of love he was in love with? Could it be possible nothing had changed since I was 15?

I was sucked back into the abyss of the past as the truth materialised in front of me, right there on that cold hard floor. Boys and men lie to get what they want, even husbands. They'll risk wrath and karma to take everything, materially, emotionally and physically, and when they don't need you anymore they toss you aside, irrelevant, forgettable, unlovable.

There I was again, abandoned in the dirt, left for dead with nothing but the searing pain.

CHAPTER TWENTY-THREE

Take Me Away

It was days away from my 15th birthday when it happened.

I followed Tony one night. I knew he'd sneak out his window to play pool with his mates at the pub. He often left the house that way to get up to mischief. He was 16, but he wasn't allowed the same freedom as me.

Dad would leave for work each evening around six and return about 6am, give or take an hour. Those hours were crucial for me. Mum always let me out to visit friends and have semi-sleepovers under one condition. I had to be in my own bed before 5am in case Dad got home early from work and happened to open my bedroom door. In all the years of my life Dad had never opened my bedroom door, so I never understood Mum's curfew. Still, I did the right thing, which was why she trusted me.

Tony on the other hand, rarely did the right thing. No matter how many beatings he got from Dad, nothing stopped him, which was why he couldn't be trusted.

"Fucking idiot sons, what de hell is wrong with yous? You think I joke when I talk… I show you respect."

Dad would show him all right. He'd handcuff Tony to his bed, beat the shit out of him and leave him there until morning. He couldn't sneak out then, not cuffed to the bed.

Looking back, Dad's career choice was a disadvantage. If he'd had a normal day job, maybe home life would have been different. I probably would've spent my teenage years locked away in my room like Rapunzel, and if I had been, that night wouldn't have happened.

"Mum, I'm just going to Vicky's house to hang out. Won't be too late, okay," I called from the front door.

"Okay, love, be good."

I could have told Mum that Tony had snuck out, but that'd be no fun. And anyway, as much as he annoyed the crap out of me, I hated it when he got into trouble. Our sibling rivalry was no match for our comradeship. We were in the war together, brothers-in-arms. Not once did I ever believe they deserved what they got, no matter how stupid they were or what they'd done. I'd cried a million tears for them over the years. It was all I could contribute.

Tony didn't know he'd been followed. I had no trouble getting into the pub. I looked a lot older than I was. Back in those days publicans were more flexible. Checking IDs didn't happen – well, not for me anyway. It wasn't the first time I'd been in a place like that and it wouldn't be the last before turning 18, when it would be legal. By then I'd be burnt out, over the whole scene.

I spotted Tony up the back, playing pool just as I thought. When he saw me, he threw his pool stick on the table and bulldozed his way towards me.

CHAPTER TWENTY-THREE | TAKE ME AWAY

"What the fuck are you doing here? Get home, you brat, before I get you into big trouble."

As if I were ever in big trouble.

"You'll be the one in trouble," I fired back. "I'll tell Mum you snuck out and Dad will kill you, so shut up and mind ya own business."

I turned away, ignoring him, and walked to another part of the pub. Missing out wasn't something that appealed to me. Why should Tony have fun while I was stuck at home? I had to be in the loop at all times. He went back to his game of pool in a huff. I scanned the crowd for a familiar face to see if any of the gang were there, but I couldn't see anyone I knew.

Then I saw him.

I'd had a crush on John for the longest time. He was older; even older than Tony. I thought they knew each other, but they weren't friends or anything. Everyone knew John. He was so good looking, tall, with light brown hair that hung in his eyes. He was a surfer dude, every girl's dream. I was leaning against the bar when his eyes locked on me. His lips moved, and I thought he smiled ever so slightly. I turned around expecting to see some petite blonde surfer chick behind me, someone the opposite of me, but no one was there.

He started walking towards me, and my heart dropped to my stomach. My mouth felt dry and sticky like I'd just eaten an unripe banana. I needed a drink. Oh my God was he really standing beside me? He ordered a drink and turned to face me, then started talking. I couldn't believe what was happening. He was talking to me. How was that possible? I wanted to be cool and sophisticated. I didn't want to blow this opportunity. He bought me a drink. It helped, finally, moisten my mouth. I could talk properly. We spoke for what seemed like ages. I didn't know where the words were coming from, but it was the best conversation of my life. It was like a dream come true. So this was what it felt like to be wanted. He must really like me, I thought. Why else would he be so kind? It was a miracle.

I was glad Tony was out of sight on the other side of the pub. He liked to pretend I was a pain in the arse, but he was my protector, whether I liked it or not. He'd have something to say about me talking to surfer dude. I was drinking too fast. He kept buying more drinks and I didn't want to seem ungrateful. I forgot about Tony then. I forgot about everyone. I was lost in that delicious moment of flirtation and wanting, shell-shocked at my sudden change of luck.

"It's getting really noisy in here, would you like to go for a walk?"

A shot of adrenaline exploded through me like I'd never felt before. Now I knew he really liked me. I was sure he wanted to kiss me, but obviously not in the pub. He knew I had a crazy older brother, everyone knew that. No one messed with Tony and no one would dare mess with his little sister.

We slipped out the back door and the cool night air hit my warm flushed face. It made me dizzy. My head was fuzzy, but I was too excited at the thought of a kiss to care about my wobbly legs. As we walked slowly down the quiet street into the darkness, he gently slipped his hand into mine and I almost died with the touch of his skin.

Oh my God, this is really going to happen. I was oblivious to my surroundings, chatting away like a stupid teenager, and then he let go of my hand. My heart skipped a beat. I knew it was the moment and I turned to face him anticipating the kiss.

He looked at me with the strangest look. Not the kind of look I thought he'd have at the height of desire and want. I didn't recognise the look at all, and then without saying a word he turned and walked away.

A bolt of lightning shot through me, I was instantly sober. The chilly darkness engulfed me as every detail came into focus. The half-moon cast faint shadows over the landscape and I realised I was in a grassy vacant lot. I could see the pub in the distance. I hadn't realised we'd walked so far. The muffled sound of music and voices drifted on the wind, the only sign that I was still in civilisation. Those few seconds seemed like hours as I watched him slowly disappear. John was gone.

I didn't understand what was happening. I was about to call out

CHAPTER TWENTY-THREE | TAKE ME AWAY

to him but a sudden fear gripped me and I was stuck to the ground. I couldn't move or speak.

Six figures appeared from the darkness as if they were apparitions. Where had they come from? I couldn't make out their faces, but I knew he wasn't one of them. None was as tall as he was.

Every cell in my body was telling me to run, to scream, to do something other than just stand there. I'd never felt fear like that before. I was in its grip, bound in an invisible strait-jacket.

Run, you stupid idiot, said the voice inside my head.

It was too late. They pushed me to the ground with such a thud I wondered if something had broken. They sniggered and laughed as I tried to cover my knees with my dress. I tried to stand, but it was hopeless. They kept pushing me down. I was powerless to do anything. I started to cry, begging them, saying that they had the wrong girl, it was all a mistake. "I'm with someone," I tried to protest.

"Shut up, you fat slut. Make one more sound and you're dead, bitch," they laughed.

So I did my best to shut up as they got on with the business of rape.

The ground was cold. I could smell the earth and I imagined I'd soon be in it. I was about to die and no horror movie I'd ever seen had prepared me for this. They would bury me there when they had finished with me, I was sure of it. The putrid smell of rotting leaves would be with me for all eternity.

The first one pushed my face into the dirt. It went into my mouth and I knew it was the taste of death. When he finished, I prayed for a quick end. But it wasn't over. I felt the weight of the second one. He was much heavier. I knew then they would each take their turn. I would not escape. All the while I tried to stop my stifled sobs, but it was hopeless.

"Shut the fuck up, you dumb bitch. If you don't stop that fucking noise we'll really give it to you," one of them kicked my foot for emphasis.

I squeezed my eyes shut not daring to look, not that I would've seen much. If only the moon were full instead of that useless sliver. But on second thoughts maybe not, maybe the sliver.

I went inside my mind, to the place where the inner voice resides. We all have one – some are louder than others. It all comes down to awareness, I suppose. I'd always been aware of my inner voice, mostly in the dark times when it spoke loudest, always reassuring me I'd get through it. But it wasn't until now that I spoke back, as if my desperate plea could make the voice materialise and protect me...

Help me, please help me. Take me away from here. Make me invisible. Please, please make them stop... take me away... please take me away, I chanted over and over in my head.

And she did.

I felt myself being lifted up and I could hear her so clearly. *You don't have to feel it, Marce. Come with me, dear, you'll be safe up here. I'll take you away as you wish.*

And there we were, high above it. We were the stars and the moon and the sky looking down on that pathetic girl with dirt on her face and her underpants around her ankles. They were holding her arms and legs. There was no hope for that girl in the dirt. She refused to open her eyes and squeezed them ever tighter. She was a twisted broken doll, ready for the rubbish tip. We couldn't feel it then and we didn't want to see any more, so we went higher still into the night sky. We saw the blinking lights of our city far below, like a sea of scattered fairy dust in a fairy tale from hell.

And when I thought it was over, the worst was yet to come.

CHAPTER TWENTY-FOUR

In the Aftermath

The details of what happened after my attackers fled are sketchy. I didn't go for help or back to the pub to find Tony. I wanted to, but my clothes were torn and I was filthy. I couldn't let anyone see me like that. I somehow got home to my bedroom unnoticed. Mum must have drunk herself to sleep.

I don't remember showering or cleaning myself up, but I'm sure I did. I don't remember getting into bed, falling asleep, or if I slept at all. If I did I don't recall any dreams or nightmares. I don't remember waking up or having breakfast or any other ordinary activity. My next memory after that night is very clear. As if 38 years hadn't passed at all. Somehow in the filing cabinet of my mind it knows exactly where to find that folder, and in it every explicit detail.

The shock must have worn off, because an overwhelming feeling of hatred consumed me. My tears stopped, replaced by thoughts of revenge. I started plotting how they should die and I knew who would hunt them down and kill them.

When Tony got his hands on the bastards that raped his little sister, God help them.

They would beg for their lives and I would be there watching, sniggering the same way they had. Doomed, they'd feel the terror and probably wet themselves like I did, like the dogs of my past did too, tied to trees, beaten, helpless. They wouldn't stand a chance when Tony's wrath came down on them, and they too would feel like nothing but the dirt on the ground. Then we'd be even.

I would go to Tony and explain the whole disgusting ordeal and what they had done to me. I imagined he wondered why I'd suddenly disappeared from the pub. He might have come looking for me. Knowing Tony, he probably already knew. Nothing got past him easily. I bet he'd already dealt with them. Hopefully they were dead and buried in that vacant lot, sucked in, fuckers. We'd have to keep the secret and we both knew how to do that.

Yes, Tony was the only one I could trust with my revenge. He was the only one who had seen me. I prayed he'd witnessed something.

By the time I got to Tony's bedroom door it was as good as done in my mind. I'd worked myself up into such a state I was having trouble breathing. My heart raced at the anticipation of the news and what he'd done to them. A sense of victory was already mine.

As I was about to open his door it flung open, as if he knew I were coming.

"Oh, thank God you're here," I said, but then I saw the look on his face and I stopped dead still.

"You fucking dumb bitch… you stupid slut… What the hell have you done?" Tony snarled through gritted teeth, trying to keep his voice down.

CHAPTER TWENTY-FOUR | IN THE AFTERMATH

He stood in the doorway of his bedroom, blocking the way so I couldn't go in. His arms folded across his chest, he looked down at me as if I were a cockroach.

"What?" I said in disbelief.

I didn't understand what was happening.

"You heard me, ya cheap slut."

"What? How can you say that to me…?" I could hardly get the words out.

I searched his face and stared into his eyes. Pure hate was what I saw. I started to tremble. I could feel the bile rise from my stomach into my mouth and I could taste the foulness of it.

"Word travels fast, Marce, and you're the local gang-banger from what I heard. How dare you embarrass me in front of my friends? Do ya know how this makes me look?" He pushed his face towards mine for emphasis and practically spat the words at me.

The action made me step backwards. My temporary paralysis was gone.

"Tony, please, listen. Don't say that. It's not true. You don't understand. I swear to God, they raped me…" As I said it I reached for his arm, but he pushed my hand away.

Frustration and anger rose in me as I tried to continue.

"Tony, can ya just fucking listen to me? It was a trick. They tricked me. You were there, didn't you see anything—" He cut me off mid-sentence.

"I saw nothing, you fucking liar. That's not what I heard. You weren't supposed to be there and now everyone knows my sister's a slut. I hate you."

Somehow the quietness of the curse made it seem more powerful than if he'd yelled it at me.

My mind was trying to make sense of something that made no sense.

"But Tony, please, I beg you…" Anger left me as desperation set in. I couldn't hold my tears or finish what I had to say.

"Shut up, an' stop cryin' before Mum hears ya. I swear if you ever tell on me for anything ever again I'll tell Mum you're a gangbanger. Ya won't be so perfect then, will you?" he hissed at me as he closed the door in my face.

He would have slammed it if he could, if Mum weren't somewhere in the house and Dad weren't sleeping. I dropped to my knees, the wind knocked out of me as if he'd punched me.

I wished he had. It would have been kinder than what had just happened.

It took everything I had to swallow my vomit. I leaned my head on the closed door trembling uncontrollably. Silent, deep, heaving, guttural sobs, made worse by their unreleased power, rolled out like waves. I don't know how long I was there – an hour, a minute, a few seconds. Eventually I sat back on my calves and rocked back and forth as if I were autistic.

I felt it before I tasted it. Blood. My head was bleeding. I must have been leaning too hard on the door. I couldn't feel any pain. I was numb to anything physical.

How was it possible my brother, my Tony, believed them and not me? I wanted to die. I wanted to go back in time and go to Vicky's house like I was supposed to.

I waited a minute longer, hoping that any second Tony would open the door, pick me up and hug me. It would be a joke, not real, just another stupid prank. He would hold me tight and tell me not to worry, it would all work out, he'd make things right. He'd make them pay for what they'd done. He'd be so sorry that he'd scared me like that.

The door wasn't going to open, and he wasn't going to say sorry. I was an idiot to think he ever would.

Back in my room I stood in front of my long wardrobe mirror and stared at my fat puffy face. From somewhere deep inside me a loathing I'd never felt before became a part of me. More than ever, stronger than before, I hated what looked back at me.

He's right. It is your fault. You lied to Mum. You weren't supposed to be there. Maybe you did ask for it. Maybe you deserved it. Maybe you are a slut.

CHAPTER TWENTY-FOUR | IN THE AFTERMATH

I wanted to tell Mum so desperately. To feel her arms around me and for her to tell me everything would be okay. I'd always been able to tell Mum anything. She was always on my side. But Tony was right. I'd lied to her about where I was going, and I never used to do that. It would break Mum's heart if she couldn't trust me. I was the only one she could trust. I wasn't sure how she'd feel knowing I'd been to pubs and clubs, already drinking and doing God knows what. Even Mum had her limits, I was sure. I convinced myself that what if, like Tony, she blamed me for what had happened. She would never look at me the same way. I wouldn't be her special girl anymore, her Chicken Licken.

So I never told her. I never told anyone, but I can't speak for Tony. I'm pretty sure he didn't tell Mum. She certainly never said anything, and I doubt she would've let it slide. I never dobbed on him again, I knew he would've made good on his promise. I imagined he was smug to have something over me like that for the rest of his life, if he even remembered.

We never spoke of it again.

Things changed after that. I became reckless, uncaring. I hid my promiscuity from everyone, even girlfriends. I kept my secrets to myself. I was alone then, an only child. I had to protect myself, depend on no one, do my own fending but I wasn't very good at it.

Mum knew something had changed. She must have been at her wits' end trying to figure it out. Bemused at the antics of her teenage daughter, how she'd become so difficult, the one she least expected to disappoint her or give her grief.

Each night I went to bed and prayed I wouldn't wake up. I wanted to feel nothing. No more hurt and emptiness, no more anger or hatred, and the thousand other things I'd feel from then on. But each morning I woke up. The disappointment overwhelmed me.

I tried to kill myself. One day I took every pill in Mum's medicine cabinet, which was a lot. She had pills for every aliment known to man. After I'd done it I got so scared I ran to tell her what I'd done. I was hysterical.

"What? Why would you do that, you silly girl? Oh my God!"

She rushed me to the hospital and they pumped my stomach. It's an experience you don't want to remember. I knew I'd never do that again. Next time, if there were a next time, I'd do something more effective, like jump to my death from a great height. Messy but easier, I imagined.

Mum never got her answer, why I did it. I let her believe my rookie attempt at suicide was my own self-loathing due to my fat issues, and the cruelness of kids' taunts.

I wondered if she ever considered my change of personality might be something else, like maybe my upbringing and all I'd witnessed somehow haunting me. Now that I was getting older, my awareness growing, did she wonder if my rebellion was part of the injustice of it all? If she did think that, she never said.

All the faceless boys of my teenage years meant nothing to me. I made sure they remembered me though. I was special, different from other girls. I was the girl who gave them everything. I would be branded in their memories for the rest of their lives. Sure they would never forget me.

Later, I'd wonder if my rapists would remember me too. When they were on their deathbeds and their lives flashed before them, would they see my face? Would they remember with shame and regret what they had done all those years ago? Did they rape again, or was I just a one-off, a novelty? Did they grow up normal and get married, have children? When they held their first daughter in their arms did they think of me? Would they feel cold-blooded fear for their own daughters, knowing too well that predators wait in the shadows for innocent girls?

Did karma get them, or will it still, I used to wonder.

There were times when I'd think about my own deathbed. When I died, would I know the truth, see the faces of my rapists and finally know who they were?

It doesn't matter now. I stopped wondering long ago.

CHAPTER TWENTY-FOUR | IN THE AFTERMATH

Tony and I eventually mended our relationship, but I don't remember how or when or under what circumstances. There's some kind of gap in my memory. All I know is we became very close as we reached adulthood, and it was as if I had dreamt it all. As if it must have happened to some other girl. I just keep her memories locked inside.

CHAPTER TWENTY-FIVE

The End of Wars

That day in the shed when I found the photograph, a proverbial Pandora's Box opened. Memories would spill forth and accost me at random, day or night, as I tried to piece together long-forgotten details. Things I'd mostly ignored at the time were now insights, clues, cries for help, carrots dangling before my eyes.

If I'd hoped for any kind of accountability from George, I'd never get it. I didn't have a chance after what happened next.

Something George had said at our last goodbye would stay with me for a long time. It would cost me hours of therapy, endless self-analysis as I delved inward, stripping back the layers, questioning the very fabric of who I was. It was as if the carpet that had covered my life for centuries had been ripped up and replaced with concrete, not a rug or hiding spot in sight. It was all there on the surface. There would be no absolution as I searched my soul for reasons why his words were so wrenchingly hurtful and affected me so deeply.

"I just don't like who I am when I'm with you."

A new George stood before me and spoke with the confidence of a gladiator, relaxed, head held high, wearing new clothes. I thought to myself, *when did smart casual become a part of his repertoire?* The old George would've lived in his track pants if he could. He exuded something I'd never seen before. It was power, courage, conviction. I wondered how he could have his shit together so quickly. Only a month had passed since he'd revealed his ICE addiction. I didn't even know what day it was or when I'd last eaten. How was I the mess and he the warrior?

"What... what does that even mean? Are you telling me you don't love me anymore, easy as that?"

The sound of my voice took me by surprise. There I was again, the helpless needy little girl, the pathetic co-dependant woman not coping on her own. I recall thinking just moments before, *I'm going to give in, forgive him, tell him to come home and stop this insanity for all our sakes.*

George looked past me as he stole a glance at his reflection in the full-length mirror. He smoothed a crease in his jumper and removed some invisible lint. Then he looked at me with such pity I could have dissolved right there on the floor.

"Of course I still love you, Marce, I always will. But I think we both know we can't be together anymore. I'm on a new path now..."

I had no idea what a new path meant. The person in front of me was a stranger.

"...and I'll make myself available when Morgan needs help with her maths, I know you can't do it..."

I drifted in and out as he continued to speak. I could smell jasmine outside the open window as if spring were in the air, not mid-autumn. I saw Angel in the yard looking up towards the voice she once knew, sniff-

CHAPTER TWENTY-FIVE | THE END OF WARS

ing the air as if it were telling her the unfolding story. Flashes of memories filled my head, past, present and future, how was that possible? As if I were about to take my last breath and I could see my life in retrospect.

"Careful what you wish for, Marce... Once an addict always an addict... Be strong, love, you'll get through it..." Mum's words always echoing.

Then a dead calm came over me. I cut him off mid-sentence and put a stop to his newfound superiority.

"George, it won't be necessary. I'll get a tutor for Morgan, someone she can depend on. You can go and live your new path, and I'll do the same. Now get the fuck out of my house. You don't live here anymore."

I never knew the word fuck could sound so dignified. I did my best to match his strength as I held my head higher. I crumbled of course the minute he closed the door behind him. Wailed like a newborn baby. He never returned to the house and he stopped all contact with Morgan for reasons that would become clear much later.

"I just don't like who I am when I'm with you..."

Those words, full of accusation, blame and hate, were the catalyst, I suppose, for my next move. It took time. My self-scrutiny was brutal. I wondered how such words could be attached to me. Me? Were they a depiction of who I was? Was I so obnoxious, cruel and loathsome that I had ruined George's life so completely it was I who turned him into a gambling drug addict? I must be an ogre. Had history repeated itself in the worst possible way? Was I the replica of my father after all?

It was then I started to examine myself on a microscopic level. I had to if there was any hope I might find a new path. I found Joy, a counsellor. I figured I couldn't go wrong with her. A name like that must be a good omen.

Joy led me back, deep into the past, not just mine but Dad's, as she asked questions about my childhood. At the time, in my stout denial and previous scepticism of counsellors, I wondered what my childhood had to do with my husband's ICE addiction. But I trusted Joy more than I thought I could, and I had to be honest if I were going to survive.

The letting go and opening up felt violating. I recalled things, stories Mum had told me about Dad's life. They would start to make sense eventually.

Dad was ten years old when Germany invaded Italy during WWII. The peaceful farm in the village where he lived with his parents, his aunty, his younger brother and two younger sisters was taken over by German soldiers. Dad's father became a prisoner of war, locked up until Italy surrendered. Dad's mother and aunty would cook and wash clothes for the soldiers who had occupied their home. The soldiers would get drunk and do horrible things, and Dad witnessed his mother and aunty being raped and beaten. At least that's what Mum said.

One day, Dad was working in the fields when a bomb dropped. His aunty was blown to pieces and he saw her leg hanging from a tree. How does an ten year old un-see that? I can only imagine the horrors he must have witnessed. I've seen all the movies.

Dad being the eldest had to become the man of the house, doing men's chores and obeying the Germans. He didn't go to school after that.

When the war was over his father came home. He was one of the lucky ones. He survived. I think my Nonno took his anger out on his eldest son. By then Dad would have been 12. I'm not sure why a father would do that after everything his son had been through. I can't say for sure what Dad endured until he ran away at 17.

Migrant ships sailed from Naples taking people to the promised lands of Australia and Canada. Dad flipped a coin, or won a bet, I can't remember which. Not unlike Jack Dawson when he sailed on the Titanic, except with a better outcome. Australia won. Dad was hoping for Canada, I'm not sure why. The fishing perhaps, or the climate.

"I could be in Alaska right now instead of dis godforsaken heat."

I must have heard Dad say that a hundred times during the long humid summers of my childhood. Mum hated the cold, which is why he could never convince her to emigrate to Alaska. Lucky us, I can't imagine

CHAPTER TWENTY-FIVE | THE END OF WARS

growing up in the snow and ice.

The ship *Hellenic Prince* left Naples in March 1952 and arrived in Melbourne in August. I'm pretty sure Dad was supposed to get off at Fremantle in Western Australia, but he probably took one look at the barrenness and changed his mind. I would have stowed away too – not an iceberg in sight in that sunburnt landscape.

Dad was detained somewhere in country Victoria. He had little money and spoke no English. He'd heard from his fellow immigrants about work up in far North Queensland. Good money could be made cutting sugar cane.

He escaped somehow and travelled alone, heading north, jumping freight trains, hitching rides, begging for food along the way. He made it to the sugar cane fields and worked for the six-month cutting season. He learned some English and made friends. During the other six months of the year they would head south to Sydney, where there was plenty of work for bricklayers, builders, and riggers. Dad studied for his rigger licence and became a rigger. Looking back, I see what an achievement that was for someone with practically no education and unfamiliar with the English language.

Dad worked on the Harbour Bridge alongside Paul Hogan in the mid-1950s.

When Paul Hogan became famous for stand-up comedy, Dad used to shake his head and roll his eyes.

"Bloody idiot, always was a larrikin on da job."

Secretly I think Dad liked him. He'd try not to laugh when Mum turned on the TV to watch the *Paul Hogan Show*. Mum loved Paul Hogan. So did Tony. In fact, Tony could do a good Paul Hogan *Crocodile Dundee* impersonation: "that's not a knife… That's a knife!" Tony even looked like him a bit, funny how he could take on the aesthetics of his characters.

Dad worked this routine until he met Mum in a pub in Sydney in 1956. He was 23. Mum was 16, and three months pregnant. Uncle Jacko was born in October. He would have been three months old when Mum and Dad married on Australia Day in January 1957.

Dad never returned to Italy. He never saw his parents again. I never understood how he could do that, or why he didn't want to go back to his homeland. He would never reveal what he was thinking, of course. Dad did love his parents, I'm sure. He sent money to them for years, right up until they died in the late-'70s I think. I never met my grandparents or knew anything about them. If Mum told me, I don't remember. Dad did mention his hometown, his mother's maiden name and a few other details in later years after Mum died. I wish I'd been a better communicator, asked more questions, seized those moments. I didn't.

One of Dad's sisters came to visit when I was very young. I don't remember her at all. Other than that, he never saw his siblings again either. They stayed in touch with letters and photographs. Mum would write long letters for Dad, as he didn't write very well. He would dictate as she wrote, and eventually she would write her own letters to his family. Dad's siblings couldn't speak or read English, so Mum went to night school to learn Italian. She could understand a conversation and write, but she was never very good at actually speaking Italian. Her Australian accent murdered every beautiful syllable of that romantic-sounding language. She just couldn't get her tongue around the melody of the words. I tried to learn with her, but I lost interest. European languages are hard with all that feminine and masculine jargon. I had enough trouble with English grammar.

Apparently, Dad did teach us to speak Italian before we went to school, but it was lost after that. I don't remember. It wasn't spoken at home, so why would we bother? Dad didn't insist, and he always spoke English except on the rare occasions he was on the phone to family in Italy. I sensed that Dad didn't care much for his heritage and spent most of his life trying to forget it. Even though he could at times be traditional, boast of the old Italy, reminisce about trees, plants and food from his homeland, Dad wasn't like other Italians I knew. I used to put it down to the fact he'd married an Aussie so he had no choice but to let go of any

CHAPTER TWENTY-FIVE | THE END OF WARS

Italian way of life, but I wonder now if his past made him want nothing to do with it. Perhaps it was the reason he chose Mum. She and her family were so far on the opposite end of the spectrum, Dad might as well have married into a family of kangaroos. He'd often taunt her about being part Aboriginal. Not that there's anything wrong with that, but she wasn't of course. Any evidence of Mum's Scottish ancestry had been lost in translation long before. She couldn't have been more Australian.

I can only guess how it might have been for Dad, what demons he carried to make him the man he was. I could never bring myself to ask him. I wanted to so much, but I just couldn't find the right words, or the courage.

Dad died on a warm, sunny day in December 2016. He was 83. In a serendipitous act, he breathed his last in much the same way as Mum, in the same room – 106 – possibly in the same bed, in Bateman's Bay Hospital, exactly 10 years and six weeks later.

I couldn't have imagined it if I'd tried, nor could Dad I'm sure. I always thought he'd die in his sleep, peacefully without incident. That didn't happen. A massive stroke two weeks earlier sealed his fate. I don't think he thought his time was up for even a minute. He wasn't even close to his hundredth birthday so there was no way he was going to check out. Even though he was 95 per cent paralysed and couldn't speak much, he would never willingly stop fighting. Seeing Dad so helpless was heartbreaking. Watching him lose the fight was pitiful.

When he did speak he demanded whisky and water. He was constantly thirsty when he wasn't asleep. Greg and I gave it to him. There was no point in saying no. The doctors knew how it would end; they didn't protest. Dad didn't wither away like Mum. He was still a hulk of a man. It took four or five nurses to move him with Greg's and my help. Eventually all that liquid worked against him. Dad's lungs filled with fluid until it was impossible for him to breathe. He drowned slowly until a last big shot of morphine put him out of his misery.

I was alone with him when the end came. He fought it with everything he had left. I held his hand and whispered gently, the last words I would ever say to him: "It's okay, Dad, it's not giving up. It's just letting go for now. I know Mum's waiting for you. Don't be scared. I love you, Dad, until I see you again… please just let go."

I kissed his cheek and when I did his eyes squeezed tight as if a bright light were blinding him. His jaws and teeth clenched as he pushed that breath out like it was the hardest thing he'd ever done. And I saw the release as the chains of his existence fell away. Dad's war was finally over.

I did then what I could never do in life. I threw my arms around him and hugged him, just like I'd done with Nigga all those years ago.

CHAPTER TWENTY-SIX

50 Shades

I filed for divorce in May 2008. It was the only real closure I'd get. I went alone. George didn't go. There was nothing to settle, easy really, no assets or money to divide or fight over. I had imagined walking out of Sydney's Downing Centre, the biggest courthouse in Australia, a new woman, but instead of feeling free, I felt isolated and alone. That was that. I was really on my own then, single again for the first time in 23 years.

My war ended eventually, on the front line at least. I'd find my way to a new normal. I struggled for those first few years, but life would settle. I lost the weight I'd gained, which was good for me psychologically. Not that I was trying. Who knew divorce was an appetite suppressant…

I remember the first time I went out on my own to an event as a single person. And not just any event – it was a ball, a gala dinner at Sydney's Town Hall to raise money for some foundation. Not that I could contribute; I needed a ball of my own, someone to raise funds for me! But wealthy friends had invited me and purchased my pricey ticket, and they wouldn't take no for an answer. I'd been locked away, unable to face the world. I couldn't imagine going out socially – dressing up, sitting with couples at dinner, being the third wheel, the solo person in the room. How was it possible? I was once the life of any party or gathering, but now just the thought made me hyperventilate. I was back where I'd started all those years ago. All my fears were back. It was too much to contemplate. It took everything I had just to get up and go to work each day. Trying to apply make-up while you're crying is near impossible. My face seemed permanently puffy. I'd dab and pray, take a deep breath and brace myself as I walked through the office doors. When the workday was over I'd get in my car, start the ignition and burst into tears again, the relief of surviving another day overwhelming.

I did my chores, cooked dinner, showered, and got into bed on auto-pilot and then, exhausted, I would drift off to sleep on my wet pillow. That was my routine for over a year. I honestly thought it would never end. Looking back, I have no idea how I did it without actually killing myself. Imagine my terror when my friends insisted I must dress for a ball and prepare to have fun back in the land of the living. I'm not sure how I pulled it off. I can't remember the prep work, but I do remember being there, the glamour, the decadence – conversations, stringing words together somehow. I'd anticipated questions. It wasn't so much the small talk with strangers I was dreading – although I was – it was running into people who knew me, and having to face their questions. They would be curious to hear the gossip, once my forte and now my enemy. To see me alone without George would seem bizarre, I imagined. We were Marcy & George, the perfect couple – from the outside. Nothing else would make sense. At least that was how I saw it.

But what I remember most was the feeling of being there, the indescribable loneliness I felt during every minute of that torturous event. My gut was in a perpetual state of anxiety, twisted in knots that weren't translating to my face, thank God. I couldn't eat – all that delicious food, what a waste. I couldn't even bring myself to drink so I pretended, and when my friends were good and drunk I made my escape. Like Cinderella running for the pumpkin carriage, before the stroke of midnight I ran down those Town Hall steps and jumped into the first cab I saw. I sat in silence, unable to speak another word. Poor cabbie, what a pretentious rich bitch he must have thought – how ironic. As we left the city fringes and approached the Anzac Bridge, I looked towards Blackwattle Bay. Down there in the darkness was the spot where George had asked me to marry him while we were parked in my old HR Holden, and we'd made love right there on the back seat, a million years ago…

    I suppose the night of the ball was a kind of icebreaker, a turning point, though of course I didn't know it then. Eventually I started to think about sex. Those last five years with George, our clean slate, our starting over, hadn't really translated to the bedroom. Some people say sex can never be the same after one of you has cheated. I just couldn't get past the guilt. I'd imagine what George might be thinking. I knew what I'd be thinking had our roles been reversed: is he thinking of her or me? Our sex life was doomed…

    By the time it was over I couldn't even remember the last time we'd had sex. Add my lost year to the equation and, when the opportunity did present itself, it must have been over three years since I'd had sex. How the hell was that possible!

    I realised that my sexual prime would soon be over, and the thought depressed me beyond words. I might have been 44, but I wasn't ready for that. Now 44 might seem old to some, but given my ability to defy the aging process I was really 34. It wouldn't last. In the meantime, I would conquer my newfound virginity and milk every opportunity thereafter. But, before my new sexual freedom was cemented, I had to conquer that first time.

An innocent dinner with girlfriends – another event I was dragged along to – turned into an unexpected encounter with an acquaintance. Well, he wasn't really an acquaintance of mine, he was an old touch-footy buddy of George's. When he walked through the restaurant doors I remembered him and cringed on the inside. I hadn't anticipated running into any of George's friends, and the last thing I wanted was to be recognised as George's ex. I hated my new marital status; divorced wasn't ever supposed to be me. I used to tick that box on forms and it would mock me every time – loser. To my horror, the guy had a few friends at my table and he somehow ended up sitting with us. I wanted to leave, but instead I had to pretend I was as normal as the others. The small talk was excruciating to begin with. A few drinks later and I realised he was flirting with me. And then it turned out he wasn't really a friend of George's after all.

"Marce, George must have rocks in his head to let you go. If you were mine that wouldn't happen. He's a dickhead. You are looking seriously hot by the way."

It had been so long since anyone had flirted with me that I wasn't entirely sure if he was generalising, being polite, or just trying to make me feel better. I assumed he must be under 30. He clearly had no filters – I was an old woman compared to him. I was still in a perpetual state of disarray and didn't know whether I was coming or going, or who I really was without a husband. I also wasn't sure what George's friends knew – not much if this guy thought George had let me go. The idea that George could still be living a lie, not owning his shit and telling people God knows what, grated on me and gave me an injection of confidence to reciprocate the flirt like a pro, like I was a natural, as if I weren't a clueless divorcee at all. It was temporary.

By this time I was in his embrace, in the heat of the moment, I froze. My head swirled with visions of past sexual encounters, marital and otherwise. I couldn't expel them no matter how much wine I drank or how loud the music was. It wasn't supposed to be like that. I was a single, mature woman in my prime. I should be devouring the Adonis before me with sexual abandon – uninhibited, raw, a lioness conquering her prey. Instead I behaved like a silly schoolgirl. I needed an invisible cloak all over again. I wanted to die at my display of emotional dysfunction.

He was wonderful, gentle, caring, and he put me at ease with kind, loving words, held me in his arms as if we were old lovers, the best of friends. It was quite extraordinary really, looking back. How differently that situation could've panned out, considering my history and the patterns of my life. I wanted to have sex then, eager and willing, but when we did, it was as if he were my teacher and I his student, a virgin, touched for the first time. Ridiculous really! It was the strangest thing, having a man inside me after so long, feeling him penetrate me in ways that felt so foreign, surreal, because I knew so completely it wasn't my husband's penis. How did I even remember what that felt like?

That night was an important night in my evolution, although I didn't know it then of course. Something he said to me the next day as I drove him back to his car flabbergasted me for months and months and became one of my greatest insights – a catalyst for change that would alter how I approached men from then on. Our conversation on the drive was easy banter all things considered, given the previous night's catastrophe. I imagined it would be awkward and silent, but it wasn't. We joked and laughed, and he even put his hand on my leg at one point. I had no delusions. I was a one-night stand, and we both knew it. I said something funny and we laughed, and on his face was a look I couldn't describe. Had I known him better I might have recognised it.

"What?" I asked coyly as my eyes darted back and forth.

"Marcy, you're just a girl, aren't you? A sweet little girl, broken and beautiful, with a big heart. I can tell. But you are different, aren't you? Where have you really come from? You sure are the hottest milf I've ever nailed."

And therein lays the 20/30 psyche of the single male. I'd never felt so old. Still, I was glad he ended on that note. It distracted from the enormity of his words in the lead-up. If he'd left that hanging I might have driven into the nearest pole. I focused on the milf part.

He kissed me goodbye and wished me luck and then he was gone. I knew I'd never see him again and I was glad about that. How could a complete stranger see into my soul like that? I felt violated, betrayed, demoralised – not by him, by me. I was mortified, disgusted at myself that I had somehow allowed vulnerability to wrap its hateful arms around me and worn it like a straightjacket for the entire world to see, for my first lover in years to see! What did that say about me? Was I so pathetic, such a damsel in distress? Was that the vibe I was giving off? How could I bare my soul so easily, give it away freely to just anyone who paid me a compliment or showed me the slightest kindness? If that were so, I was destined to fail again and again, attracting the wrong kind of men. I knew what to do – what I did do after that. I knew the game of emotionless sex better than most women, or men for that matter. I had forgotten it that night, but I'd remember again. I was a cheater from way back; random sex I could do, as empty as it was. But this baring of soul wasn't something I could deal with and from then on I would close my heart to every lover who crossed my path.

Years later I would think of him, my drought-breaker, the guy who led me back into the world of sex. Then I would wish I could have my time over with him. I would've given him something to remember me by so that when he thought of me words like 'broken little girl' would not come to mind. I would've let my dominatrix alter ego take the reins – or whips rather – handcuffs, neckties, whatever his heart desired, and whatever mine did. I would be living *50 Shades of Grey* while EL James was writing it! But there would be no Round 2 with drought-breaker. He was married by then. I had one golden rule during my years of sexual freedom: no married men, no exceptions. Homewrecker was not a title I would ever wear again. I'd done enough wrecking in my own home. I couldn't risk wrecking someone else's. So my lovers were young, usually a lot younger than me. It was safer that way; less chance of their being married.

CHAPTER TWENTY-SIX | 50 SHADES

A closed heart is a lonely existence. I was a mystery to my lovers, I'm sure. Some wanted more, and when I sensed it I would miraculously get a promotion and need to relocate interstate or overseas. Or something would happen, some disaster, and I'd be off the grid permanently. They must have thought I was CIA or in witness protection – not that I ever said that. A time would come, however, when I couldn't stand another minute of the emptiness, the hollowness of casual sex. That feeling far outweighed my 50 shades of fun, and I would want more.

CHAPTER TWENTY-SEVEN

Sundays

I had no desire to marry again. After more than two decades I'd had my quota. If someone asked me if I thought I'd marry again, I'd assume they didn't know me very well. Only a state of drug-fuelled euphoria could make me say 'I do' again. I came to the conclusion I wasn't the marrying kind, and probably never had been. That would explain a lot.

Still, I knew I didn't want to grow old alone. The thought saddened me. After years of sexual freedom, I started to wonder what it might be like to wake up next to someone again, especially on Sunday mornings.

Sunday was the loneliest day of the week as a single person. I'd often be melancholy. I would reminisce about the past, play mind games with the 'should haves' and the 'what ifs', think about goodbyes never spoken and questions unanswered. They all seemed like fresh wounds on Sundays, no matter how many years rolled by.

But by Monday morning as I got ready for work I'd shake my head at my silliness, convinced the Sunday persona wasn't me at all. It was just my old shadow rising, giving voice, trying to exist where it didn't belong anymore.

I started online dating and created a profile with the help of Kelly, a girlfriend from work who had been doing it for years. She taught me the ropes, and she was very clear about sex and dating. Kelly believed you shouldn't have sex for at least the first three dates, not if you were serious about finding a partner.

"Marce, if a guy is into you he'll wait. Remember why you're doing this. Your 50-Shade days are over." I'm sure she was right, but what were we, 12?

The dating game was tricky. I came to the conclusion that all the good men were married, unavailable, or gay. The rest were still teething – I'd had enough of that – or harbouring a hidden agenda. My resilience to deception didn't improve after my walls came down. The first guy I actually let into my life – by now it was 2010 – turned out to be living another kind of secret double-life. He had a wife and young daughter he had forgotten to tell me about. We'd only been dating three months, so the parting wasn't too painful, for my heart at least. My mind was another thing. Clearly, I still had no sixth sense, no skill to detect imposters lurking behind their masks. I assumed I had some kind of invisible radar projecting, luring them in: manipulators this way – come get me.

I did improve after that. At least I like to think so. A year later I met another man and he didn't have a secret double-life. I asked him straight out on our first date, as if a predator would tell me the truth anyway, but I had nothing to lose by then.

"Okay, mister, I want upfront, genuine honesty. Let's cut to the chase and hopefully save time and misery. Are you a drug addict? Married with children? A gambler? A rapist? A serial killer? A con artist? Do you have

CHAPTER TWENTY-SEVEN | SUNDAYS

a criminal record of any kind? Trust me, anything you tell me from this point on will not shock or faze me."

He laughed.

"I'm not kidding," was my poker-faced response.

None of the above, thank God. He didn't run in the other direction after his interrogation. I secretly gave him brownie points for that. It did become clear, though, that he was still in love with his ex-wife. I knew it was too good to be true. She'd run off with another man. He hadn't seen it coming. He had the saddest eyes, poor guy. She would call him unexpectedly, whenever she got bored with her current toy boy, and he would always take her calls. I'm not the competitive type. I knew I deserved more than that. It wasn't worth the shit.

Six months later I was ready to date again, at least I thought I was.

"Hi, Ramzi, I'm really sorry, but I have to cancel our date tonight. I hope you don't hate me."

I probably should have said no to the needle full of dermal filler that had been injected into my face earlier that day, knowing I had a date later that night. I was 47 and even though I could pass for 37, Botox could only do so much. My timing could have been better. My date with Ramzi was a first date, and first impressions matter.

I wondered if my decision to go had been a subliminal one. I'd been single for five years, except for the two boyfriends – I use the term loosely, of course. I'd been doing the online dating thing for a year. My urge to dust was far greater and seemed way more exciting than another disastrous date. I was over it. In fact, earlier that week I had told myself that after the two dates I had planned for the upcoming weekend I was taking a break from dating. If, or when, I could be with someone again, it would surely happen naturally.

I hadn't given up on love. Despite everything I'd been through, I still believed someone must be out there who would be worthy of taking a second chance with me, someone who could be trusted – after the break that was.

"Oh no, that's too bad. I was really looking forward to it too. Why, did you get a better offer?" Ramzi asked.

He made me laugh, which hurt my face but I didn't care. I was grateful he didn't hang up on me.

"No, of course not, and I feel terrible. I wouldn't usually cancel last minute. How rude of me. I'm really sorry."

"You've been thinking about the kids, haven't you? *The Brady Bunch* not your style?"

Ramzi was joking, but I could tell he was genuinely disappointed.

The Brady Bunch hadn't crossed my mind. Ramzi told me in our very first phone conversation that he had five kids, all boys under the age of 14, with two ex-wives. Any other intelligent woman would have hung up politely and crossed that one off her list. Morgan was 21, an adult. Most memories of young motherhood were vague by then. I never had to consider children while I was dating. The men I'd dated didn't have kids, or had grown adult children like me. Boyfriend number one doesn't count, seeing as I didn't know his kid existed.

I had been shocked when Ramzi first told me about his five sons. My first thought was how unlucky to end up with five boys. Hopefully at least one will be gay. My second was how on Earth he had the energy in his forties for young children. Why would anyone want that many children in the first place? I could only assume he was a devout Catholic or very wealthy. It didn't matter, because he was divorced. He didn't need energy. His ex-wives needed it.

My experience of divorced men had taught me they move on quickly. Many go on to have new families and see less and less of their old families. Some men, like George, totally disregard their children altogether as they find new paths to pursue. In George's case it was another woman. He had met her at a Narcotics Anonymous meeting two weeks after leaving the house, in April 2007. Imagine that. No wonder he had the confidence of a gladiator. He was clean and sober, and all sexed up in the honeymoon phase of his new relationship, while I was freefalling into the abyss of

CHAPTER TWENTY-SEVEN | SUNDAYS

hell and his daughter was in therapy and failing Year 11. His honeymoon must have been over around the 18-month mark when he wanted to reconnect with Morgan. Fathers like that don't think about the impact of their abandonment on the children they leave behind, nor how it may affect their future. It's not unique sadly. I know mothers abandon children too, but it's rare. What mother doesn't feel like running away most days of the week? But they don't actually do it.

Ramzi's kids lived in Perth. I lived in Sydney and so did he. He was there for work, but he travelled to Perth every second weekend to see his kids. He never missed a fortnightly visit.

Ramzi was a once-a-fortnight Dad. That was way better than most, and theoretically I could live with that. Not that it had anything to do with me. I'd probably only ever see him once like all my other online dates, and that would be the end of it. I didn't really care how many kids he had or where they lived.

"I haven't been thinking about kids at all. It's not that…" I hesitated.

"Don't tell me you have to wash your hair." He was still joking.

I wanted to be honest, but some men are weird about cosmetic procedures and some are totally turned off by them. I wasn't sure I could lie. My days of lying were behind me.

"Okay, I'm going to be honest. I had some fillers today and I've had a bit of a reaction. It's not pretty. Trust me, if you saw my face right now you'd want to cancel!"

"Fillers, what do you mean?"

Shit. Ramzi didn't know what fillers were and if he didn't know that he probably couldn't handle the B word either. I had a feeling his ex-wives were low maintenance vanity-wise. I should have lied.

My commitment to defying the aging process would catch up with me one day, I was sure, but it hadn't earlier that morning. The Polish beauty holding the syringe to my face won. As I stared into Ashka's sultry blue eyes through the frozen fingers of the latex glove she held to my cheek, she could have told me the syringe was full of liquid Draino which would work miracles on my face and I would've believed her.

She was far from the clutches of time. Her face was perfectly symmetrical, her lips full and pink and luscious. Possibly the most kissable lips I'd ever seen on a girl. I imagined men would get lost in those bedroom eyes and daydream about what those lips could do. I had a feeling she didn't know how beautiful she was.

"Marcia, you won't be swollen. You'll look fabulous for your date tonight, I promise. We all need a bit of a lift now and then, don't we?"

Ashka's warm smile reached her gorgeous eyes with a look of knowing and empathy as if we were near in age, on par in our sisterhood, except I was probably her mother's age and she was not much older than Morgan.

"Okay, if you say so. I just hope I don't look like the Cat Lady by tonight."

She laughed. "Not at all. Maybe some slight bruising, but nothing that a little concealer won't fix."

By 5pm I knew Miss Poland had lied. There wasn't enough concealer in the world to fix the mountains that had appeared where my cheeks once were. There was no way I could go out in public like this. I felt bad about cancelling just hours before the date, but I also felt a sense of relief. I'd actually been looking forward to it, but by then I held no expectations of success in the online dating scene.

Ramzi had seemed very down to earth. We'd had a few long phone conversations and they were easy and comfortable. He was a good talker, and that would help when having dinner with a stranger. My rule was not to go for dinner on a first date, but when he asked I had a feeling it would be okay with Ramzi.

But, thanks to Ashka the smiling assassin, I wouldn't be meeting him that night.

"Dermal filler," I said. "It's cosmetic, used to plump up lips and things like that. My beauty therapist put some in my cheeks today. I've never done it before and my face looks like I've gone a few rounds with

CHAPTER TWENTY-SEVEN | SUNDAYS

Mike Tyson. It's really not a good look. Do you mind if we rain-check?"

He laughed, and then he got serious and said something I wasn't expecting. It changed everything.

"Listen, Marcy, I've really liked getting to know you over the phone. I have to be honest, I'm disappointed. I was really looking forward to our date. Now, I don't know about fillers, but what you need to know about me is I'm the least superficial guy you'll ever meet. I don't care what your face looks like, I know you're a nice person and what's on the inside is what matters most to me. But I totally understand if you still want to cancel. I know women and I'm sure you want to feel and look your best. Of course we can rain-check, but I really, really wish you would reconsider."

I don't know what it was exactly – the kindness in his voice or the genuineness of his words – but something spoke to me from somewhere deep, and I knew I had to go. A warm feeling came over me and I couldn't remember ever feeling that, not from someone I'd never met before.

I was still silent, analysing what I was feeling and why I was feeling it.

"And she's hung up on me…"

He made me laugh again. I couldn't believe I was actually contemplating going out in public looking that scary. I had to take the chance. I just felt if I didn't I might not get another one.

"Okay, but you've been warned. People will stare at you thinking I'm your battered girlfriend so brace yourself, mister!"

He laughed and told me I was funny. Me. Funny. I didn't feel funny. I felt nervous.

I gave him my address. He wanted to pick me up. I'd never done that before either. Who gives a total stranger their address? I panicked at my stupidity. It was temporary. When I walked outside to greet him he pretended not to notice my face, and I pretended I'd forgotten too. He looked exactly like his profile photo, tall, handsome, bald and a smile that would outdo even the Polish beauty. He had better lips too.

The hours flew by as we shared our stories of life and dreams and everything else easily. He had such warmth and honesty about him. We laughed all night and I didn't feel my face at all. I really did forget about it.

When he drove me home we kissed. A lot, and they were the most erotic kisses of my life. I couldn't remember the last time I'd been kissed like that, if ever. And even though it would be Sunday in a few hours, I knew it would be the best Sunday I'd had in years. I had a feeling Sundays would never be the same again.

Incidentally, we both had dates organised for the next day, which we both cancelled. We didn't know it at the time, but later we would talk about our first date and how we both knew we'd found a keeper.

CHAPTER TWENTY-EIGHT

Second Chance

Ramzi was unlike anyone I'd ever met before. We were inseparable from the start. The speed at which our relationship developed was like we were living in dog years. Five years of being single and dozens of failed dates had given me lots of experience. I knew what I didn't want in a man. Ramzi was the opposite of all that.

Ramzi slept over in week two. I didn't take the sleepover lightly. That was commitment. Before Ramzi, my nocturnal habits were my business.

I gave him the key to my front door in week three, and by week four we were planning our old age together. It was one night over dinner near the end of our first month of dating that I, *me*, said the unthinkable.

"We should get married."

The words fell easily, naturally, from my lips as if I were ordering another drink. Words like that usually scared the shit out of me. The M word had always been my deal breaker. Not even George Clooney would get a second date if he mentioned the M word. If anyone got nuptial on me I was out of there. And there I was, breaking all the rules as if I were a crazy person and we were drunk in Vegas. It wouldn't have surprised me if Ramzi had run from the restaurant. Hell, I would have.

But I wasn't drunk. I hadn't been daydreaming about knights on white horses coming to save me. I'd given up that notion long before. I just had an overwhelming feeling that we'd waited a lifetime, maybe several, to be together. I'd never felt so connected to another human being.

Ramzi reached for my hand. He smiled warmly and chuckled. I imagined he assumed I was joking. But then he saw something as he searched my face, and he got serious.

"Would you want to get married again?"

"Well, I didn't think so. Not in a million years. If anyone asked me a year ago it would've been a resounding no. But here I am proposing, and I wouldn't joke about that. I'd definitely marry you."

I meant it. It was weird, as if someone were speaking on my behalf. Someone traditional and way too starry-eyed, surely not me. But I loved him. How was that possible after mere weeks? I could feel his love as if it were tangible. I had no doubt he loved me. It was honest and raw. Nothing hidden. Ramzi was so completely without guard, not a wall in sight, no secrets. He seemed the oldest soul I'd ever met, as if he knew life was short and precious, not to be wasted on bullshit or being fake.

I'd never felt grown-up mature love before. But here it was.

"So you're not joking, you're serious? If I asked you to marry me you'd say yes?" Ramzi looked deep into my eyes as his words flowed like warm chocolate syrup.

I had a sense he'd been thinking the same thing and was perhaps a little disappointed I'd asked first. He was the traditional one after all.

"Yes, I would." Not even Botox could stop my foolish grin.

CHAPTER TWENTY-EIGHT | SECOND CHANCE

"In that case, Marcy, will you marry me? I love you so much already it's mind-blowing. I would be so proud to be your husband."

There it was. The real proposal as it should be, minus kneeling on one knee and the ring. Those would come soon after.

"Yes, I will. I'd be proud to be your wife too. I love you more than I thought possible. It's ridiculous just how much I do. I feel like I've known you for years."

I didn't care how the speed at which we were travelling seemed to anyone else. Marriage might not have been in our original plans, but there it was. We both wanted the same things. Doesn't everyone? To be loved unconditionally, have open communication, and no secrets. Faithfulness, trust, respect for each other. It's simple really.

When I believed I deserved it, the right love came to me. I went through every shitty thing imaginable, but look where it brought me.

I had a feeling marriage would be very different the second time around.

Epilogue

Ramzi and I eloped. We were married beside the pool in a private villa in Seminyak, Bali. It was August 2012, exactly three months, two weeks and six days after our first date. Seriously, who actually does that unless they are drunk in Vegas?

I told Dad when we got back that it was a spur of the moment decision. As far as he knew, Ramzi and I were going on a holiday. Dad also didn't know we'd met three months earlier. I told him we had met through work a year or so before and our friendship eventually became a relationship. It sounded way better and more acceptable for Dad. I didn't like lying, but this was Dad. I couldn't tell him we'd met online. He would've assumed I'd been preyed upon by some sinister cult member, or the government must be onto us. Why? Only Dad would know the answer to that.

Dad actually warmed to Ramzi quickly, to my surprise. I think he must have known Ramzi wasn't intimidated by him. Ramzi looked him in the eye when he spoke, and never refused whisky when Dad offered some. Greg was more dubious, but he came around eventually. I can only imagine it was some sort of big brother protective thing. As if I needed it by then. The irony wasn't lost on me. The only opinion that really mattered was Morgan's.

"Married? Wow Mum, really? I never thought you'd marry again. What's the hurry? Is someone dying of cancer?"

No one was, thank God.

"Well, Mum, I guess at your age no sense in wasting time. You need to settle down again. I'm just glad you won't be dating any more losers. I really like Ramzi."

Ramzi loves Morgan as much as he loves his sons. She is the daughter he never had. It's weird that he never had a little girl amongst all those boys. He is such a daughter kind of dad, affectionate, loving, sensitive, always wanting hugs and kisses, and he loves to chat. Ramzi is the kind of dad teenage boys are embarrassed by, all that touchy-feely stuff. Boys are weird like that.

Children and younger ex-wives aside, the first year of our marriage wasn't easy. It was around this time my body started the long arduous trip into menopause. Hot flushes, weight gain and feeling anxious weren't the kind of newlywed life I'd hoped for. Worst of all, no one tells you about the vagina dramas that slowly unfold. As oestrogen leaves the building, so do all traces of natural lubricant. Penetration becomes a minefield of razor-sharp edges, an obstacle course that requires prep work and caution. So even if the mind is still willing, your vagina calls the shots. My days of spontaneous *Fifty Shades of Grey* kind of sex were becoming a distant memory. There's nothing like strategic planning to kill all aphrodisiacs. It was a head fuck I wasn't prepared for. It's not like Ramzi and I had history, clearly. A husband of 20 or 30 years would presumably be more aligned with his wife's needs, or lack thereof, given his own declining testosterone levels. He'd definitely know his wife well, and although he might not be prepared or equipped to handle her change of life – and even if she wasn't either – at least their years together might give him some advantage.

It concerned me greatly, especially since Ramzi is seven years younger than I am. I imagined he knew little about the workings of mature women. His first wife is 13 years my junior, his second is 17 years younger than I am. Seventeen years! When she was born I was heading towards sexual burnout. It was a mind game I couldn't win. I would've much preferred to bypass that kind of baggage. No amount of Botox or fillers could take me back that far. I doubt even surgery could do that. Ramzi didn't care about age differences, lucky me. Together we'd navigate new sexual territory. Eventually I found the solution in the form of bio-chemical hormone replacement. Who knew a tiny peppermint troche dissolved in my mouth each morning could take me back to *Fifty Shades* – lucky Ramzi. He kept his word regardless. A woman's heart and soul, my heart and soul, are the only aphrodisiac he needs – lucky us.

In February 2013, Angel died. Like Tara, it was like a child dying. I still haven't replaced her. Six years on, I think it's time. Life just isn't the same without a dog by my side.

Morgan fell pregnant unexpectedly to her childhood sweetheart, Daniel. They would be parents at 22. The shock of it almost sent me back to the dark side. Being a grandmother wasn't something I'd ever thought about. Grandmothers were old, knitted booties, and smelled like rosewater. Out of all Morgan's school friends, she would have been voted most likely to succeed without marriage or children, given her experiences. At least that was how I would've voted.

My granddaughter was born one week after my first wedding anniversary. I heard the news from a friend. I wasn't there. Morgan and I had fallen out after an argument on Mother's Day of all days, when she was four months pregnant. She had moved in with Daniel's parents. I became the estranged parent then. How was that possible? It was heartbreaking. I missed it all – Morgan's pregnancy, helping with the nursery, the birth, those terrible first few months. Unbelievably, I wasn't there for her the way Mum was for me. I imagined Mum watching. How she would have cried.

I met my granddaughter when she was three months old, a week before I left Sydney. I'd come to the conclusion after six months of silence and no responses to my text messages that Morgan and I might never reconnect, or if we did it would probably be turbulent like her relationship with her father. I was sad and miserable. Not how I had dreamed my second-chance life would be.

Ramzi was sad too, for me, for Morgan and for his boys. He felt he was missing out. I would come to learn that being a part-time father really messed with his head. His contract work in Sydney was temporary. Perth was really where he wanted to be, sooner or later. I just always imagined it would be later – much, much later.

I contemplated my losses – Morgan, my granddaughter, Angel – and considered my circumstances. I was bored at work. I'd lost my motivation and drive. I hated being in the same house that I'd shared with George. The *feng shui* was all screwed up. I decided it was time for a new beginning. I needed a new start if my marriage were going to make it. If we moved to Perth, at least Ramzi might have a chance at good parenting. It was a tough decision, but I felt it was my only option. Dad took the news like any other news – not a big deal. It was not like I'd see him any less. Five trips a year, plus a phone call every Sunday. That was our routine, and nothing would change.

I emailed Morgan the news of my move to Perth. It changed everything. She invited me to visit and meet her daughter. I never expected to fall so in love the instant I laid eyes on my beautiful granddaughter Mia. I was so proud then of my new name, Nanna Moo, or just Moo Moo as it became.

Leaving then was heartbreaking, a cruel twist of fate. Morgan and I became very close. Our relationship blossomed in ways I couldn't have imagined. Who knew distance could bring us so close together? My bond with Mia is like nothing I've ever known. The love I feel is deep in my soul. We are connected in ways that defy time and distance.

In the beginning I wondered how my heart would cope with not seeing Mia regularly. Each time I return to Sydney the part of my heart she owns comes alive again. When I leave her it aches for days, but I know it's temporary. It fades until next time. Such a bittersweet journey.

My love/hate relationship with Perth softened gently as the years went by. Still, it will never wholly own my heart the way Sydney does. No matter how many ocean sunsets dazzle me, they will never shine brighter than the sunrises over Sydney Harbour. A home in both cities is our plan, now that we've created a balanced dream.

I find myself in Perth – the most isolated city in the world they say – surrounded by the energy of six male figures. I can't help but see some kind of irony in that. Universe, you are seriously twisted. I guess I've still got a lot to learn. With all these boys it is bound to be tricky. There'll be plenty of shitty days ahead I'm sure, God help me.

The thing about clean slates is that they can't erase all the shitty things from the past, but somehow, miraculously, as time passes it all starts to make sense. My life is where it is because that's where it's supposed to be. Ramzi has taught me about the power of faith. I am who I am because of all the shit I've been through. I can't change it and, if I could, would I really want to?

Fuck yes, this is me after all.

But, then what story could I tell?

Not this one. The alternative would be way too boring.

Acknowledgements

I want to thank my collective writing sisterhood. We have collaborated, encouraged, supported, travelled, laughed and cried together. Lisa, Judy, Xanti, Jan, Louise, Kylie, Athina, Claire, Pip, Kerry, Mylee, Michele, Dalit, Cheryne, Hilary, Lorraine, Shana, Marion, Brigid, Ginny and Katrina, who knew the writing journey – and our dysfunction – would connect us so profoundly, and release so many great stories into the ether. I can't wait to read every single book.

I want to thank my social media tribes for the support, likes, and comments I receive, and for your Facebook polling input when I needed it. An author's life can be isolating. Knowing there is a cyber-hood reminds me daily that I am not alone.

Joanne Fedler, without your mentoring and guidance this book wouldn't be what it is today, and for that I'll be forever grateful. You are the Queen of blurbs and taglines. Thank you for your contributions.

To my talented editors, Clare Wadsworth and Amanda Spedding, you have individually polished this book to perfection. I couldn't tell where my voice ended and yours began. Above and beyond my expectations, what a gift you both are. The timing, as they say, meant to be.

Julie Postance, self-publishing consultant extraordinaire. I'm so glad my gut feeling didn't let me down. When it fits, it fits. Thank you for sharing so freely your wisdom and knowledge.

Thanks to all the wonderful women (and men) who took the time to read my manuscript and give praise to my story. I'm humbled by your testimonials and hope that every woman (and man) who reads this book feels the same way.

For the friends – old and new – who have stuck by me, believed in me, and always supported me unconditionally. Sean, John, Mark and Carlee, Matt, Santina (Sam), Vicky, Jill, Cathy, Kelly, Gidge (Monica), Sharman, Carolyn, Maria, and Marina, I'm not sure I would have made it without you. My gratitude and love for you are always present.

A very special bear hug to Sean Ashby, John Scott, and Mark Sandilands who have helped me navigate the fickle paths of my existence both personally and professionally. Your business prowess, expertise, and connections have been invaluable. Thank you for your endless advice, support and love, for spoiling me over the years and for your unwavering faith in me. I am nothing without you. Well, life would've been duller for sure.

For my daughter Morgan, her very existence saved me more than once. She was unaware. I am humbled by the lessons of motherhood, which I'm sure she'll keep dishing out. If only I could have lived in the moment during her young life, instead of inside my head for most of it. I'm so grateful I can make it up to her by being present with my granddaughter Mia, or 'Boopy' as I call her. She is the light and joy of my life. Mum was right about a grandchild's love, there is nothing on earth like it.

And for my husband Ramzi, who continues to prove me wrong about boys and men. Some can actually be trusted, imagine that. Your honesty and love transcends every myth I've ever believed and every hope I've longed for. Thank you for being the man that you are. With the faith and patience of a saint, and a soul as old as time itself, I believe you are the positive to my negative. It helps even when I think it's annoying. I love you more than I thought possible. In the end love really is all that matters.

About the author

Marcia Abboud and her husband are living in Melbourne, Australia. Born and raised in Sydney, where her heart belongs, she travels there often to be with her daughter and granddaughter. She is working on her second book Every Fabulous Thing. She hopes it won't take long, but given her history shit is bound to happen…

For people who don't know her, Marcia is pronounced Mar-C-a, not Marsha, as in *The Brady Bunch*. Her friends call her Marce, or Marcy. She'll answer to most names except Marsha.

For more photos that accompany the book, visit her website.

www.marciaabboud.com/gallery

You can follow Marcia at:

⦿ www.facebook.com/marciaabboudauthor/

⦿ www.instagram.com/marciaabboudauthor/

www.ingramcontent.com/pod-product-compliance
Lightning Source LLC
Chambersburg PA
CBHW032029290426
44110CB00012B/731